JOHN WOO'S

7 BROTHERS™

CREATED BY
JOHN WOO

SCRIPT
BENJAMIN RAAB
DERIC A. HUGHES

COLOR CONSULTANT
LAURA MARTIN

ART
EDISON GEORGE

PROJECT MANAGERS
REUBEN THOMAS
S. P. KARTHIKEYAN

COVER ART
DAVID MACK

PROJECT MANAGER
- COLLECTED EDITIONS
SANDEEP NAIR

ORIGINAL SERIES COVERS
CELIA CALLE
JEFFREY SPOKES
MICHAEL GAYDOS
(WITH R. C. PRAKASH)
DAVID MACK

EDITOR - COLLECTED EDITIONS
MAHESH KAMATH

ASSISTANT EDITOR
NEHA BAJAJ

COLORS
R. C. PRAKASH

EDITORS
CHARLIE BECKERMAN
MARIAH HUEHNER

LETTERS
SUDHIR B. PISAL
NILESH P. KUDALE
NILESH S. MAHADIK
RAKESH B. MAHADIK

CONSULTING EDITOR
LORI TILKIN

JOHN WOO'S 7 BROTHERS

VOLUME 2

7 BROTHERS™

VIRGIN COMICS

Chief Executive Officer and Publisher
SHARAD DEVARAJAN

Chief Creative Officer and Editor-in-Chief
GOTHAM CHOPRA

President and Studio Chief
SURESH SEETHARAMAN

Chief Marketing Officer
LARRY LIEBERMAN

SRVP - Studio
JEEVAN KANG

VP - Operations
ALAGAPPAN KANNAN

Director of Development
MACKENZIE CADENHEAD

Chief Visionaries
DEEPAK CHOPRA, SHEKHAR KAPUR,
SIR RICHARD BRANSON

Special Thanks to
Frances Farrow, Dan Porter,
Christopher Linen, Peter Feldman,
Raju Puthukarai, Mallika Chopra
and Jonathan Peachey

TIGER HILL

Partner
JOHN WOO

Partner
TERENCE CHANG

Senior Vice President
LORI TILKIN

SEVEN BROTHERS TPB Vol. 2 - The Blood That Runs, February 2008 published by VIRGIN COMICS L.L.C. OFFICE OF PUBLICATION: 594 Broadway, New York, NY 10012. Printed in Canada.

"Govern a family as you would cook a small fish—very gently."
—*Chinese Proverb*

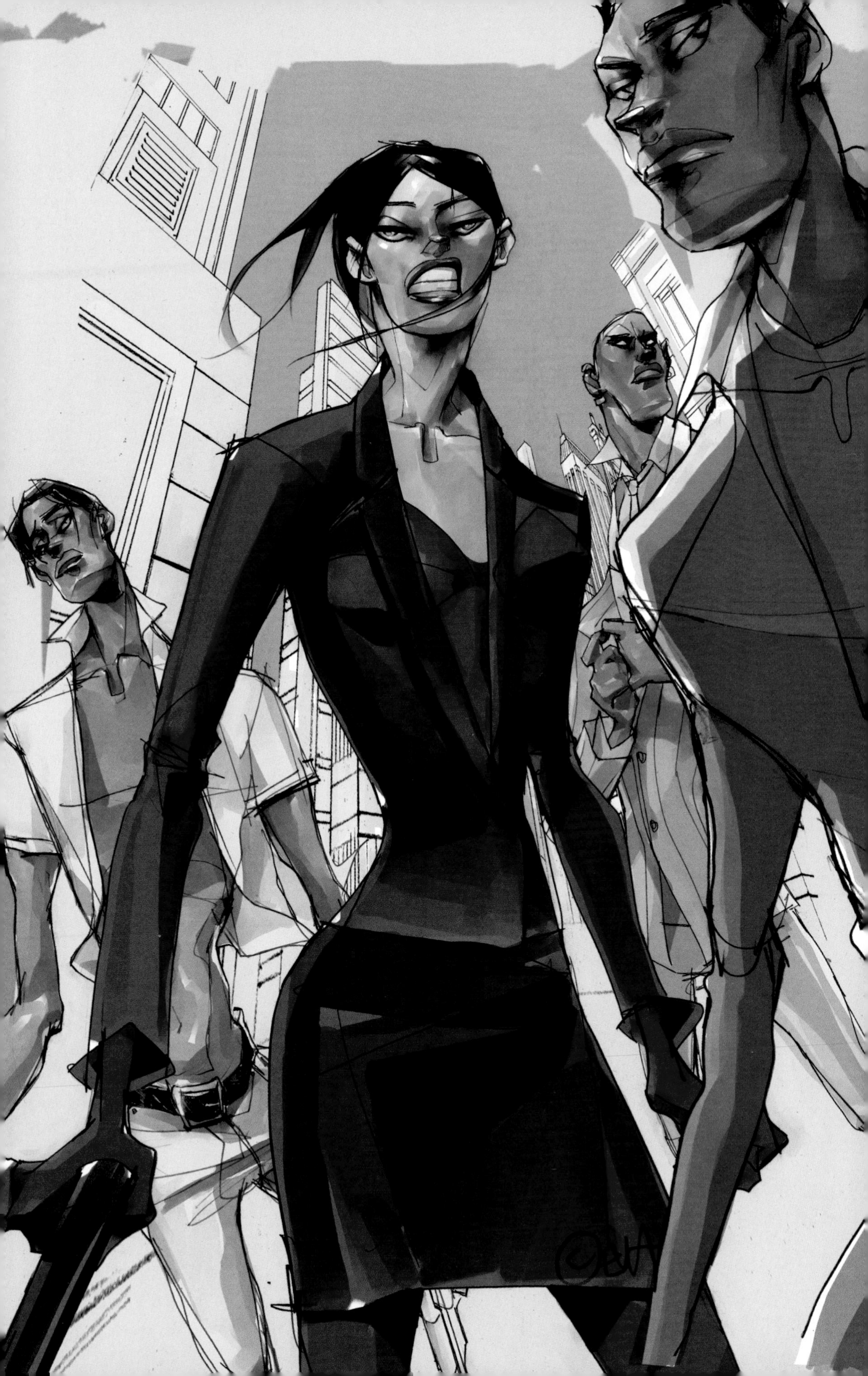

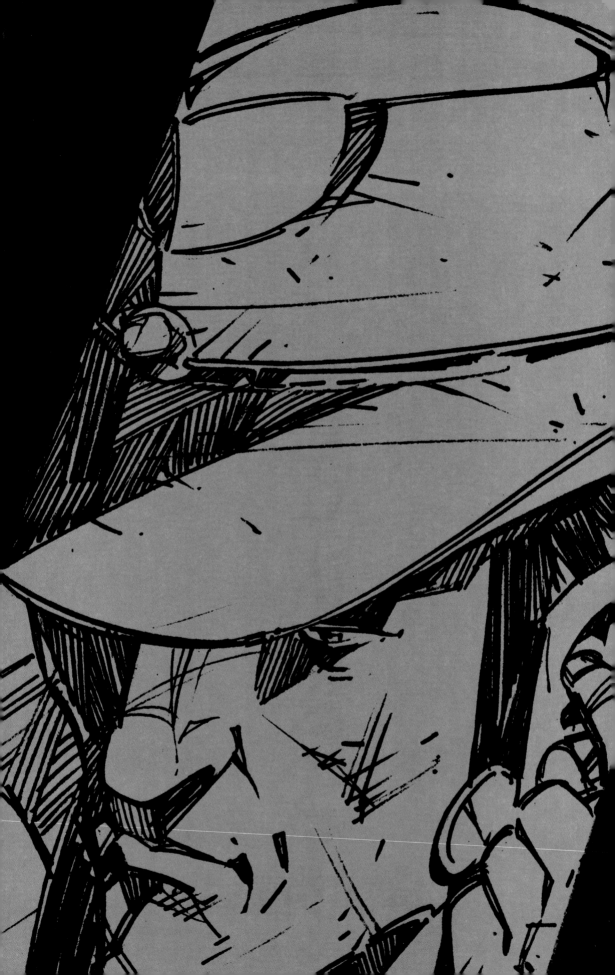

"The power you now possess is no mere tool to be wield at your pleasure. It is a gift that must be earned." — White Dragon

Chapter - 1

PREVIOUSLY

SEVEN MEN FROM SEVEN CORNERS OF THE EARTH. SEVEN DESTINIES INTERTWINED BY ONE TIE THAT BINDS THEM ALL: THE BLOOD OF AN ANCIENT CHINESE SORCERER COURSING THROUGH THEIR VEINS, THE WELLSPRING OF THEIR INCREDIBLE ABILITIES; ABILITIES THAT GO BEYOND THE NATURAL REALM....

DESPITE THEIR OBVIOUS AND NUMEROUS DIFFERENCES, THEY WERE UNITED BY THEIR SISTER, THE MYSTERIOUS RACHEL KAI. WITH HER GUIDANCE, THE SEVEN BROTHERS STOOD TOGETHER TO SAVE THE WORLD FROM CERTAIN DESTRUCTION AT THE HANDS OF THEIR ANCESTOR'S IMMORTAL ENEMY, THE SON OF HELL. AND IN SO DOING, FORGED A BOND STRONGER THAN ANY THEY'D EVER KNOWN. THEY BECAME SO MUCH MORE THAN ALLIES AND SOMETHING FAR, FAR GREATER THAN HEROES.

THEY BECAME A FAMILY.

BUT LIKE ALL FAMILIES, THIS ONE HAS ITS SHARE OF SECRETS. AND AS ONE OF THEM IS ABOUT TO DISCOVER, THOSE SECRETS CAN BE FATAL....

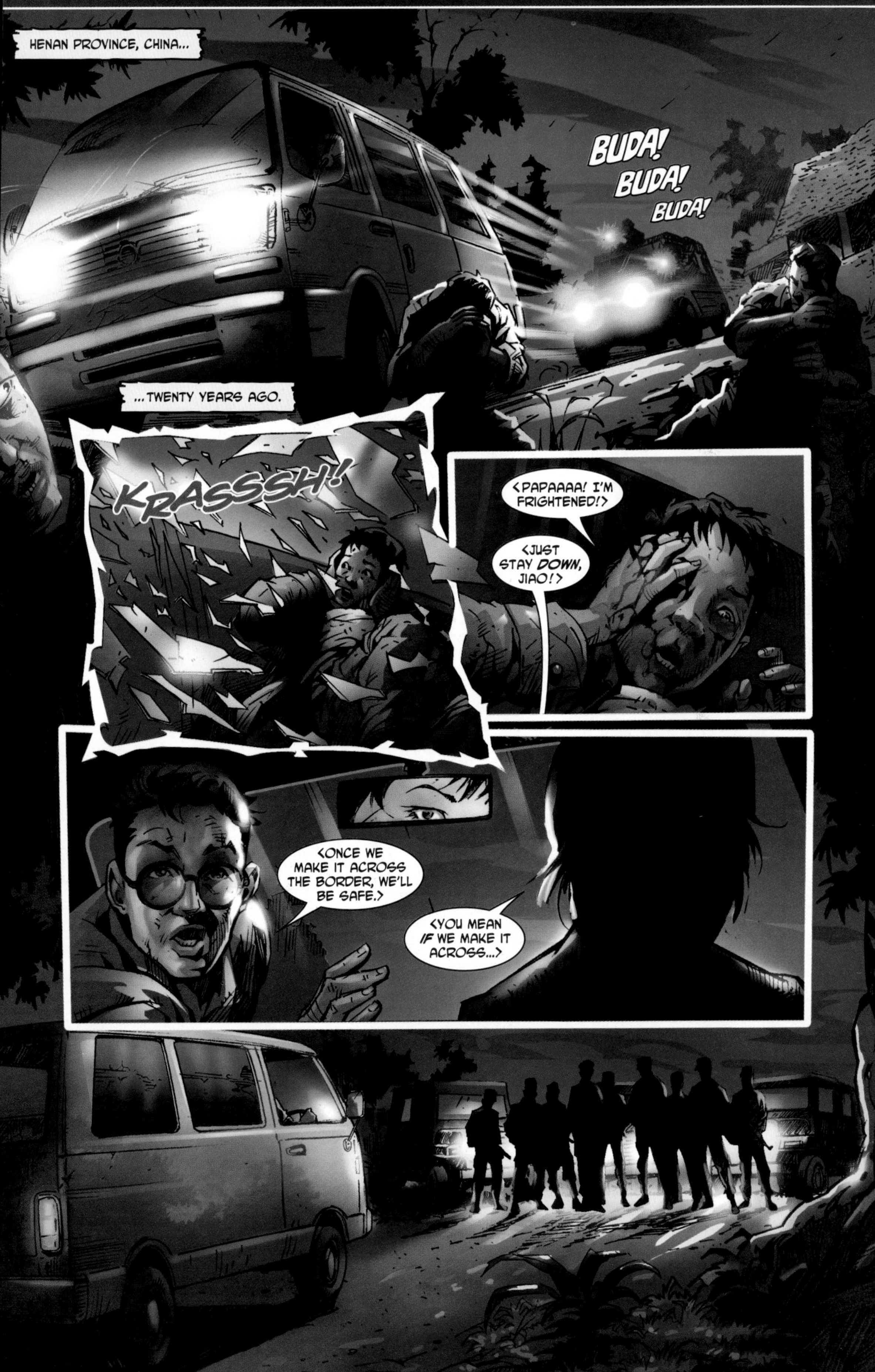
HENAN PROVINCE, CHINA...
BUDA!
BUDA!
BUDA!
...TWENTY YEARS AGO.
KRASSSH!
<PAPAAAA! I'M FRIGHTENED!>
<JUST STAY DOWN, JIAO!>
<ONCE WE MAKE IT ACROSS THE BORDER, WE'LL BE SAFE.>
<YOU MEAN IF WE MAKE IT ACROSS...>

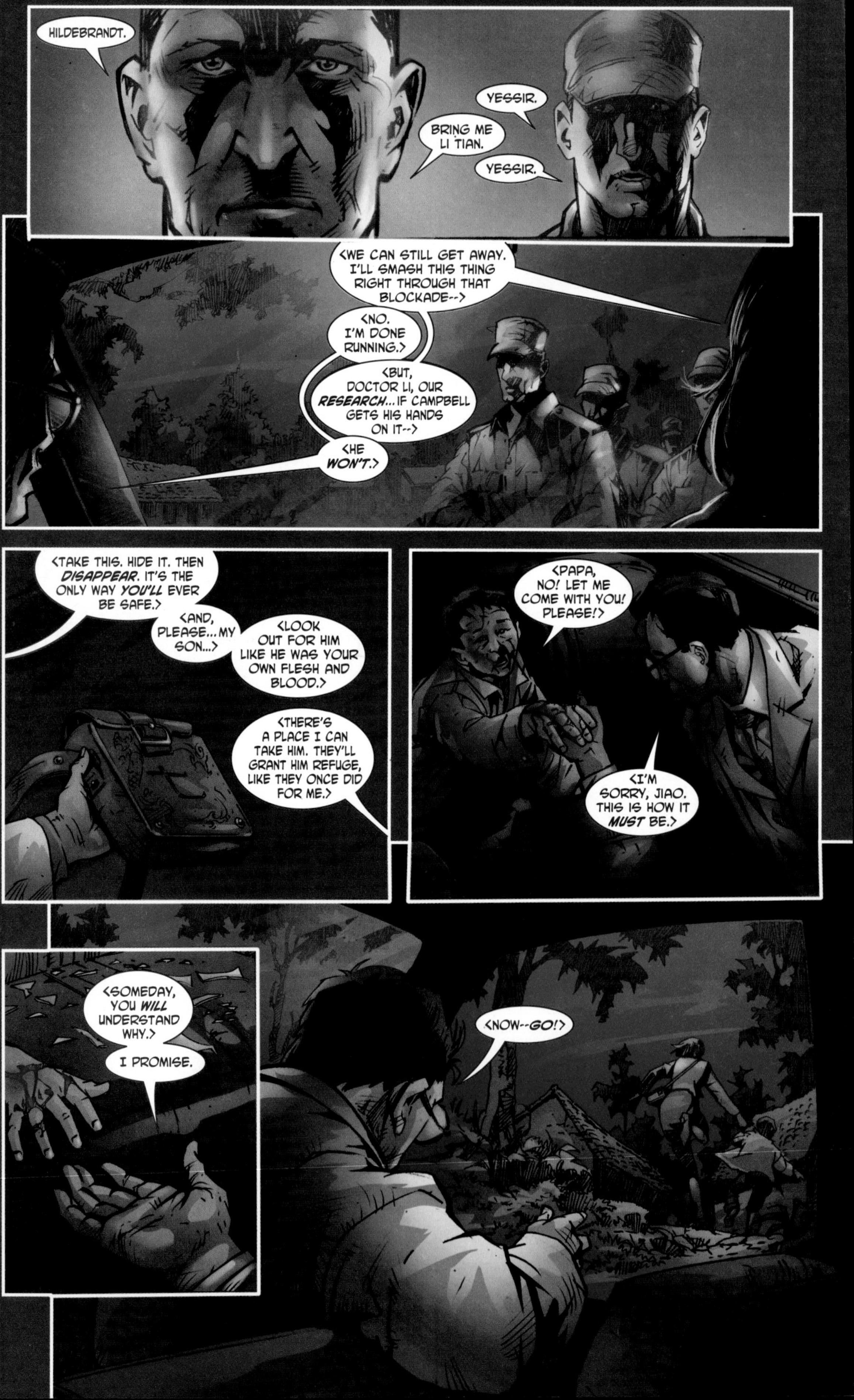
HILDEBRANDT.
YESSIR.
BRING ME LI TIAN.
YESSIR.
<WE CAN STILL GET AWAY. I'LL SMASH THIS THING RIGHT THROUGH THAT BLOCKADE-->
<NO. I'M DONE RUNNING.>
<BUT, DOCTOR LI, OUR RESEARCH...IF CAMPBELL GETS HIS HANDS ON IT-->
<HE WON'T.>
<TAKE THIS. HIDE IT. THEN DISAPPEAR. IT'S THE ONLY WAY YOU'LL EVER BE SAFE.>
<AND, PLEASE...MY SON...>
<LOOK OUT FOR HIM LIKE HE WAS YOUR OWN FLESH AND BLOOD.>
<THERE'S A PLACE I CAN TAKE HIM. THEY'LL GRANT HIM REFUGE, LIKE THEY ONCE DID FOR ME.>
<PAPA, NO! LET ME COME WITH YOU! PLEASE!>
<I'M SORRY, JIAO. THIS IS HOW IT MUST BE.>
<SOMEDAY, YOU WILL UNDERSTAND WHY.>
I PROMISE.
<NOW--GO!>

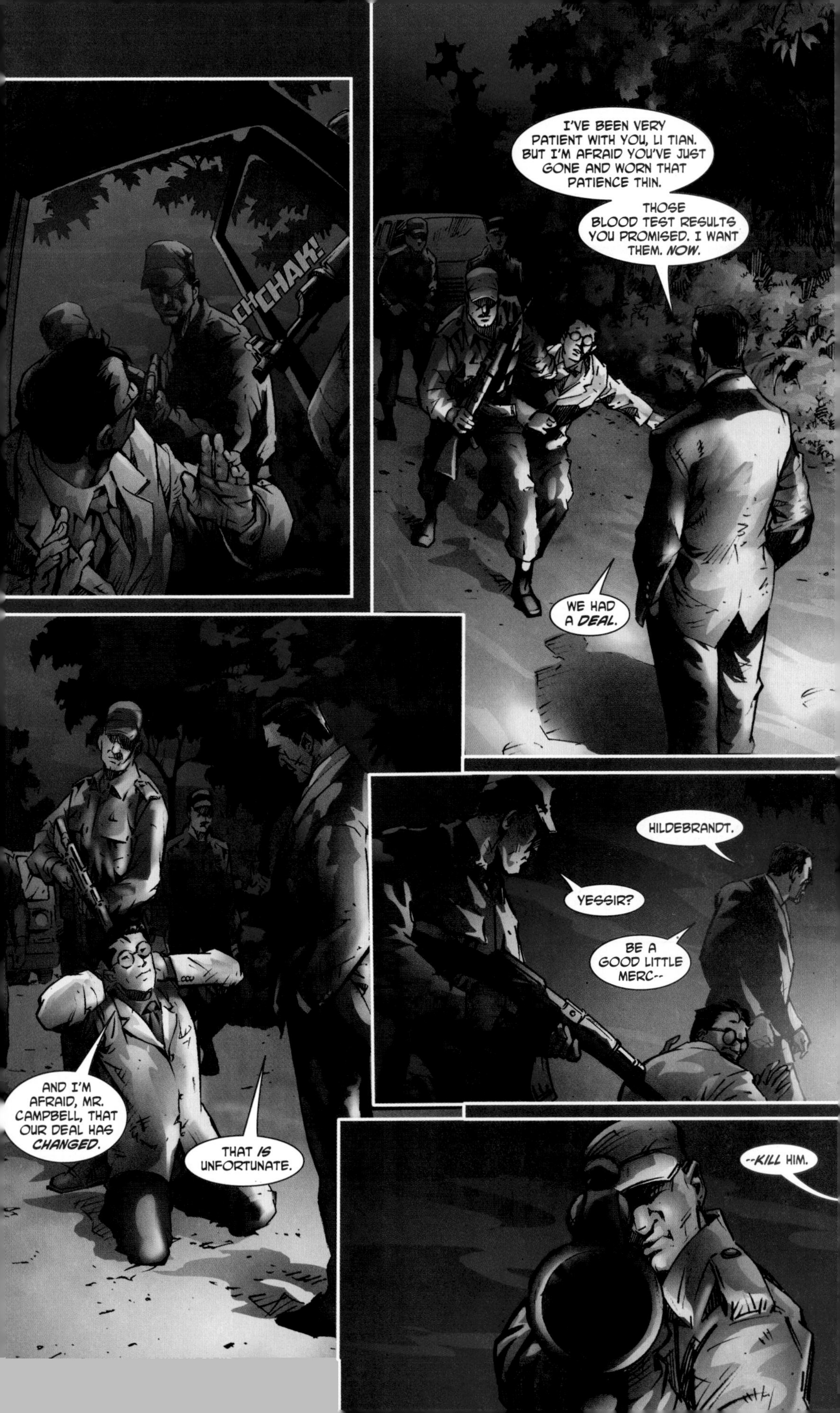
CHCHAK!
I'VE BEEN VERY PATIENT WITH YOU, LI TIAN. BUT I'M AFRAID YOU'VE JUST GONE AND WORN THAT PATIENCE THIN.
THOSE BLOOD TEST RESULTS YOU PROMISED. I WANT THEM. NOW.
WE HAD A DEAL.
AND I'M AFRAID, MR. CAMPBELL, THAT OUR DEAL HAS CHANGED.
THAT IS UNFORTUNATE.
HILDEBRANDT.
YESSIR?
BE A GOOD LITTLE MERC--
--KILL HIM.

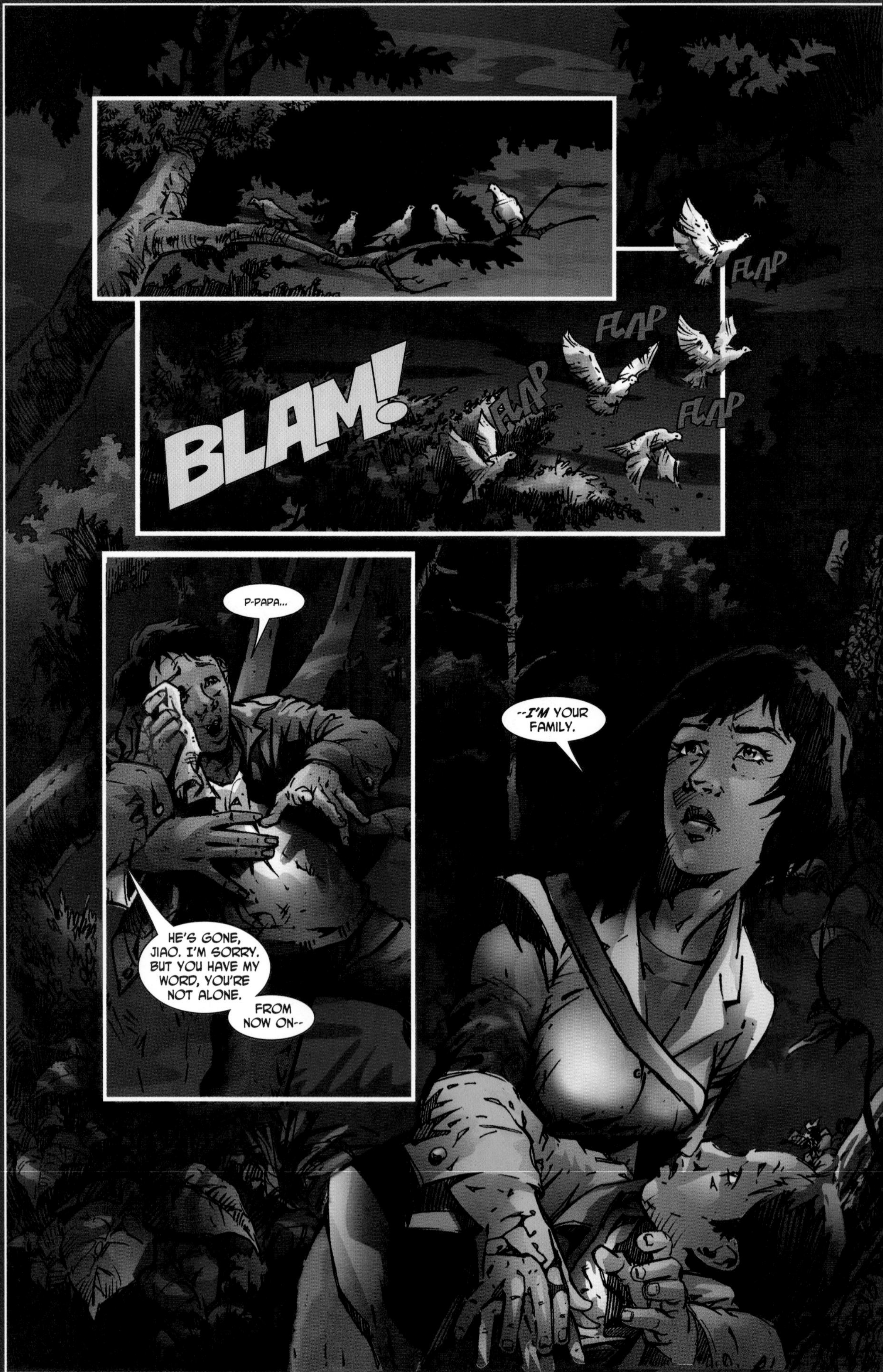
FLAP
BLAM!
FLAP
FLAP
FLAP
P-PAPA...
HE'S GONE, JIAO. I'M SORRY. BUT YOU HAVE MY WORD, YOU'RE NOT ALONE.
FROM NOW ON--
--I'M YOUR FAMILY.

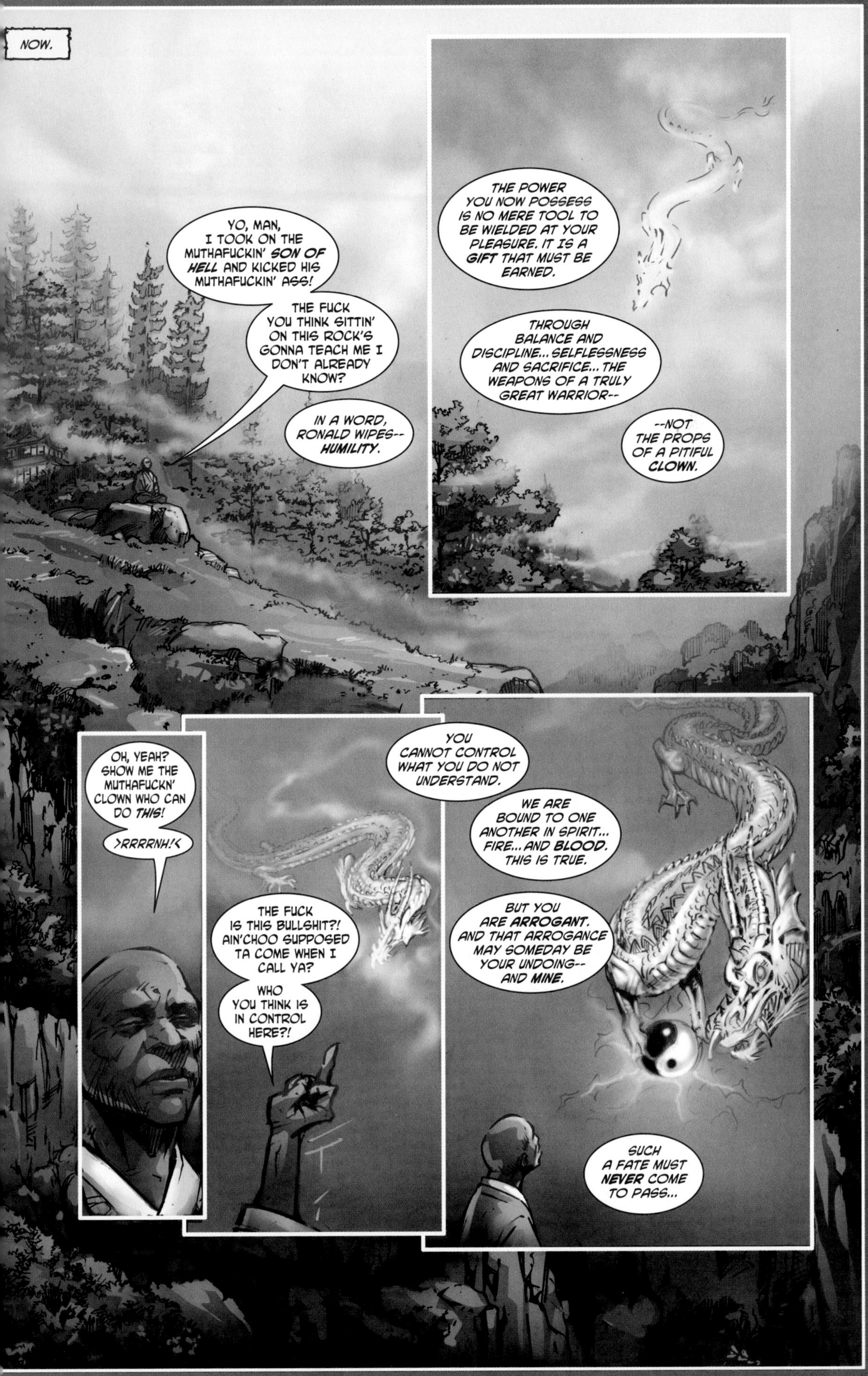
NOW.
YO, MAN, I TOOK ON THE MUTHAFUCKIN' SON OF HELL AND KICKED HIS MUTHAFUCKIN' ASS!
THE FUCK YOU THINK SITTIN' ON THIS ROCK'S GONNA TEACH ME I DON'T ALREADY KNOW?
IN A WORD, RONALD WIPES-- HUMILITY.
THE POWER YOU NOW POSSESS IS NO MERE TOOL TO BE WIELDED AT YOUR PLEASURE. IT IS A GIFT THAT MUST BE EARNED.
THROUGH BALANCE AND DISCIPLINE... SELFLESSNESS AND SACRIFICE... THE WEAPONS OF A TRULY GREAT WARRIOR--
--NOT THE PROPS OF A PITIFUL CLOWN.
OH, YEAH? SHOW ME THE MUTHAFUCKN' CLOWN WHO CAN DO THIS!
>RRRRNH!<
THE FUCK IS THIS BULLSHIT?! AIN'CHOO SUPPOSED TA COME WHEN I CALL YA?
WHO YOU THINK IS IN CONTROL HERE?!
YOU CANNOT CONTROL WHAT YOU DO NOT UNDERSTAND.
WE ARE BOUND TO ONE ANOTHER IN SPIRIT... FIRE... AND BLOOD. THIS IS TRUE.
BUT YOU ARE ARROGANT. AND THAT ARROGANCE MAY SOMEDAY BE YOUR UNDOING-- AND MINE.
SUCH A FATE MUST NEVER COME TO PASS...

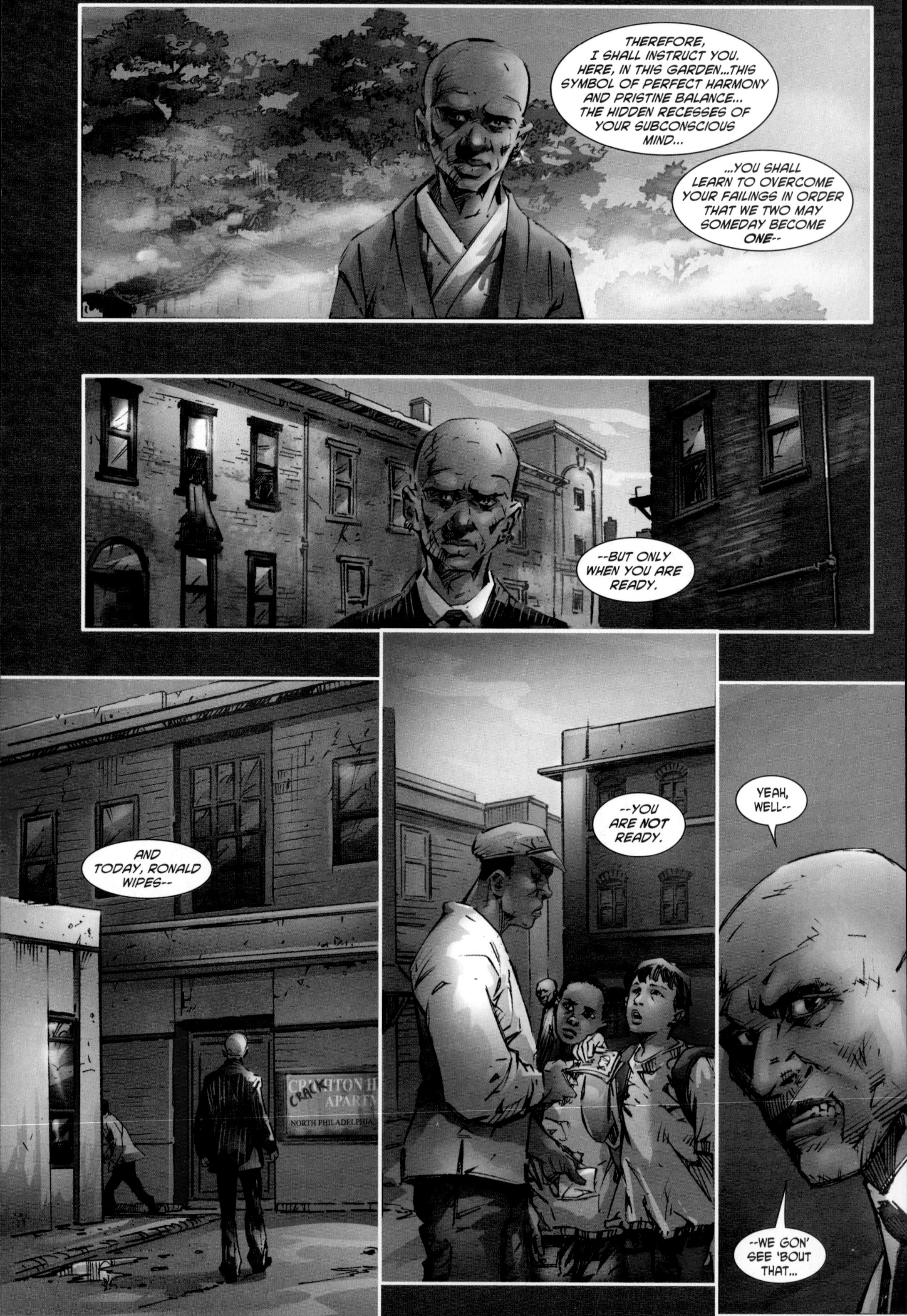
THEREFORE, I SHALL INSTRUCT YOU. HERE, IN THIS GARDEN...THIS SYMBOL OF PERFECT HARMONY AND PRISTINE BALANCE... THE HIDDEN RECESSES OF YOUR SUBCONSCIOUS MIND...
...YOU SHALL LEARN TO OVERCOME YOUR FAILINGS IN ORDER THAT WE TWO MAY SOMEDAY BECOME ONE--
--BUT ONLY WHEN YOU ARE READY.
AND TODAY, RONALD WIPES--
CRACK
NORTH PHILADELPHIA
--YOU ARE NOT READY.
YEAH, WELL--
--WE GON' SEE 'BOUT THAT...

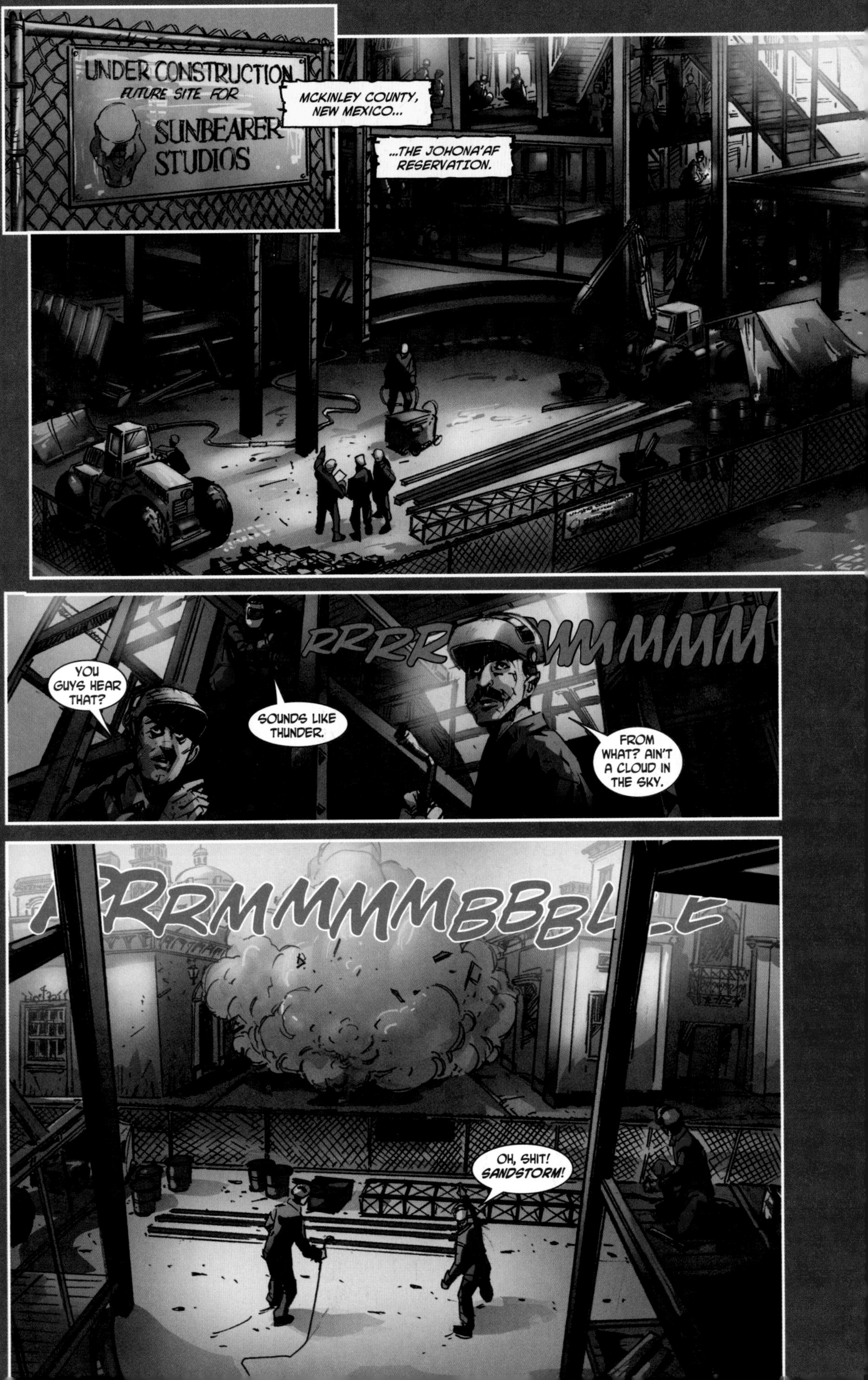
UNDER CONSTRUCTION
FUTURE SITE FOR
SUNBEARER STUDIOS
MCKINLEY COUNTY, NEW MEXICO...
...THE JOHONA'AF RESERVATION.
RRRR MMMMM
YOU GUYS HEAR THAT?
SOUNDS LIKE THUNDER.
FROM WHAT? AIN'T A CLOUD IN THE SKY.
RRRMMMMBBBLE
OH, SHIT! SANDSTORM!

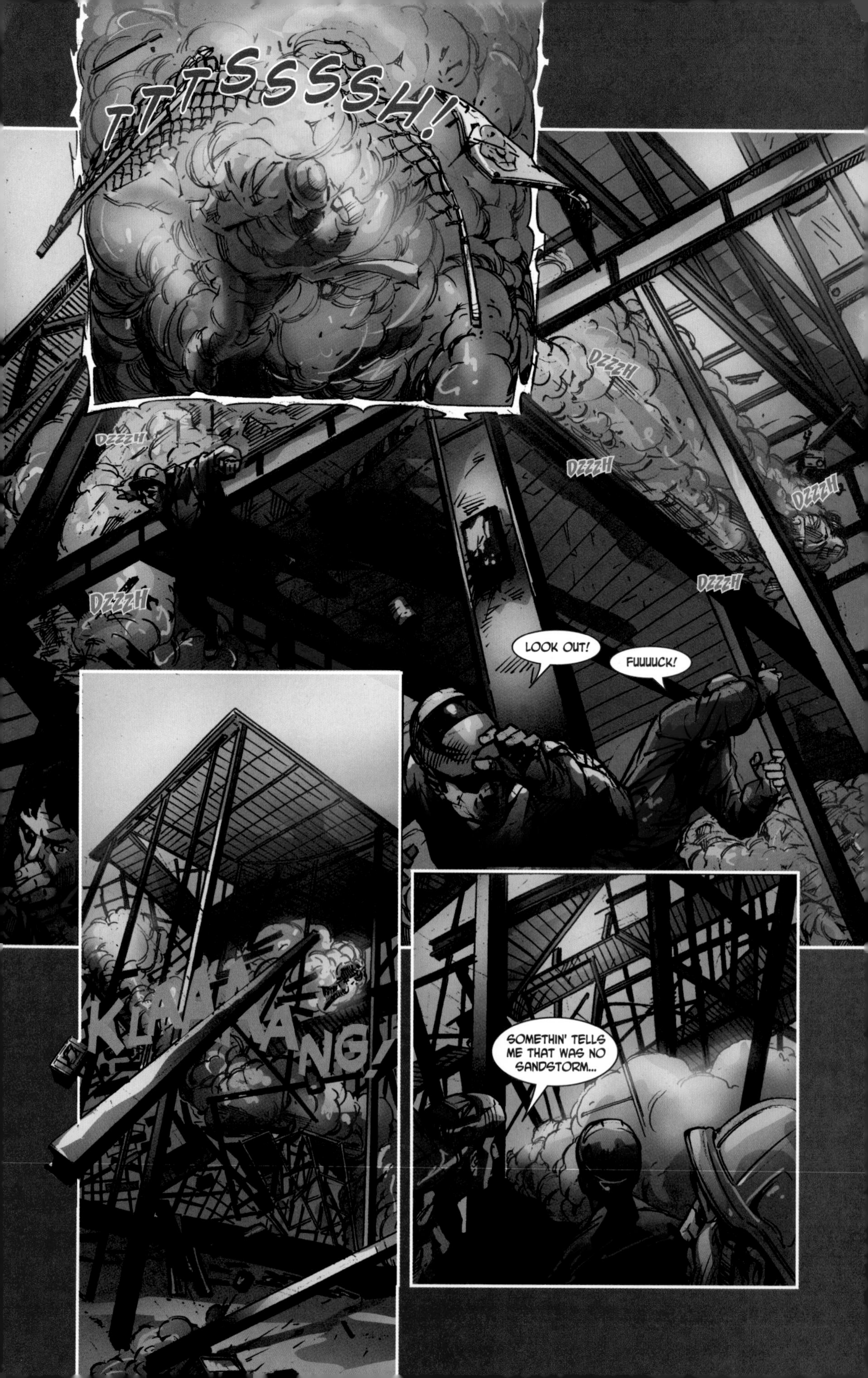
TTTSSSSSH!
DZZZH
DZZZH
DZZZH
DZZZH
DZZZH
DZZZH
LOOK OUT!
FUUUUCK!
KLAAANG!
SOMETHIN' TELLS ME THAT WAS NO SANDSTORM...

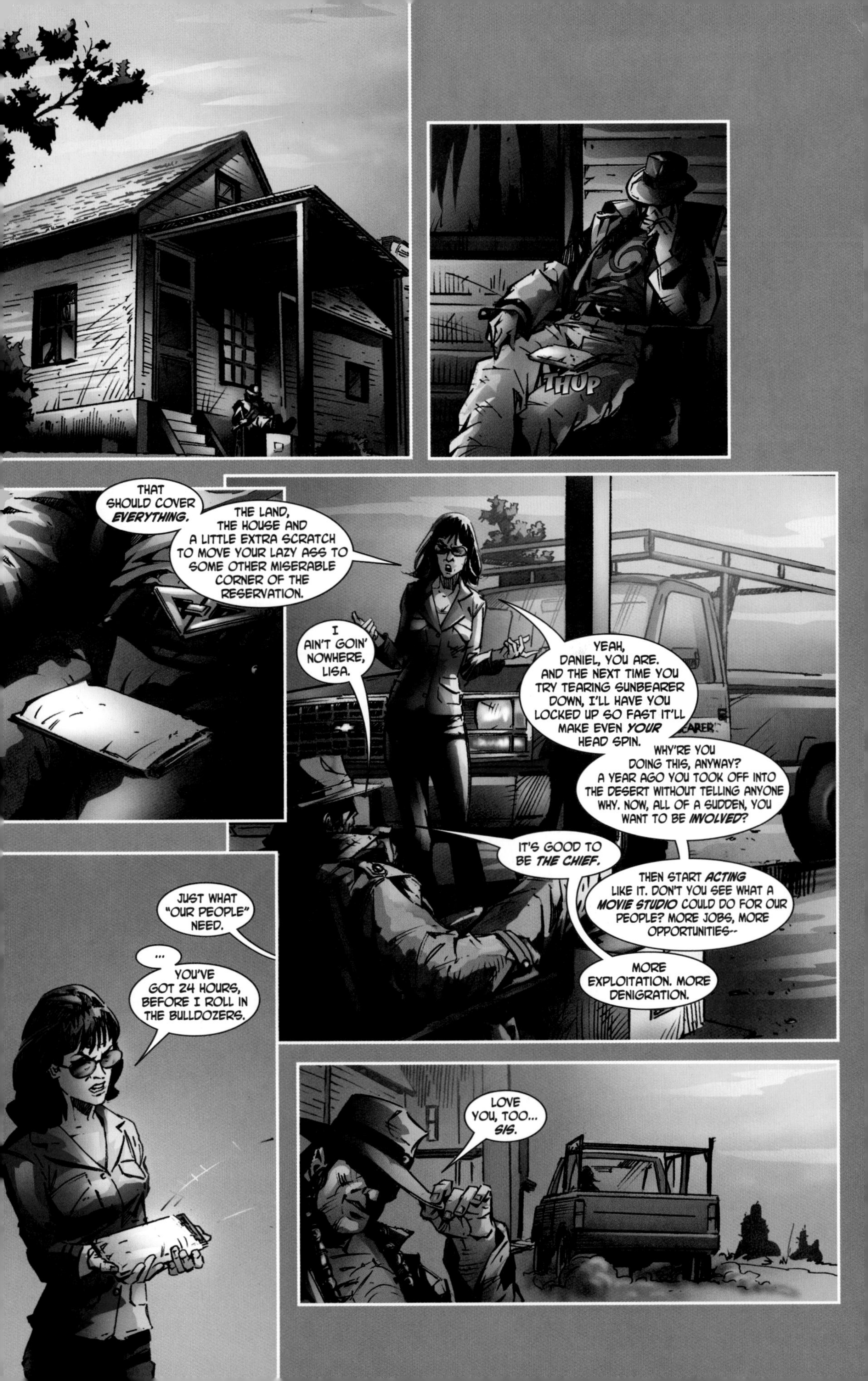
THUP
THAT SHOULD COVER EVERYTHING.
THE LAND, THE HOUSE AND A LITTLE EXTRA SCRATCH TO MOVE YOUR LAZY ASS TO SOME OTHER MISERABLE CORNER OF THE RESERVATION.
I AIN'T GOIN' NOWHERE, LISA.
YEAH, DANIEL, YOU ARE. AND THE NEXT TIME YOU TRY TEARING SUNBEARER DOWN, I'LL HAVE YOU LOCKED UP SO FAST IT'LL MAKE EVEN YOUR HEAD SPIN.
WHY'RE YOU DOING THIS, ANYWAY? A YEAR AGO YOU TOOK OFF INTO THE DESERT WITHOUT TELLING ANYONE WHY. NOW, ALL OF A SUDDEN, YOU WANT TO BE INVOLVED?
IT'S GOOD TO BE THE CHIEF.
THEN START ACTING LIKE IT. DON'T YOU SEE WHAT A MOVIE STUDIO COULD DO FOR OUR PEOPLE? MORE JOBS, MORE OPPORTUNITIES--
MORE EXPLOITATION. MORE DENIGRATION.
JUST WHAT "OUR PEOPLE" NEED.
...
YOU'VE GOT 24 HOURS, BEFORE I ROLL IN THE BULLDOZERS.
LOVE YOU, TOO... SIS.

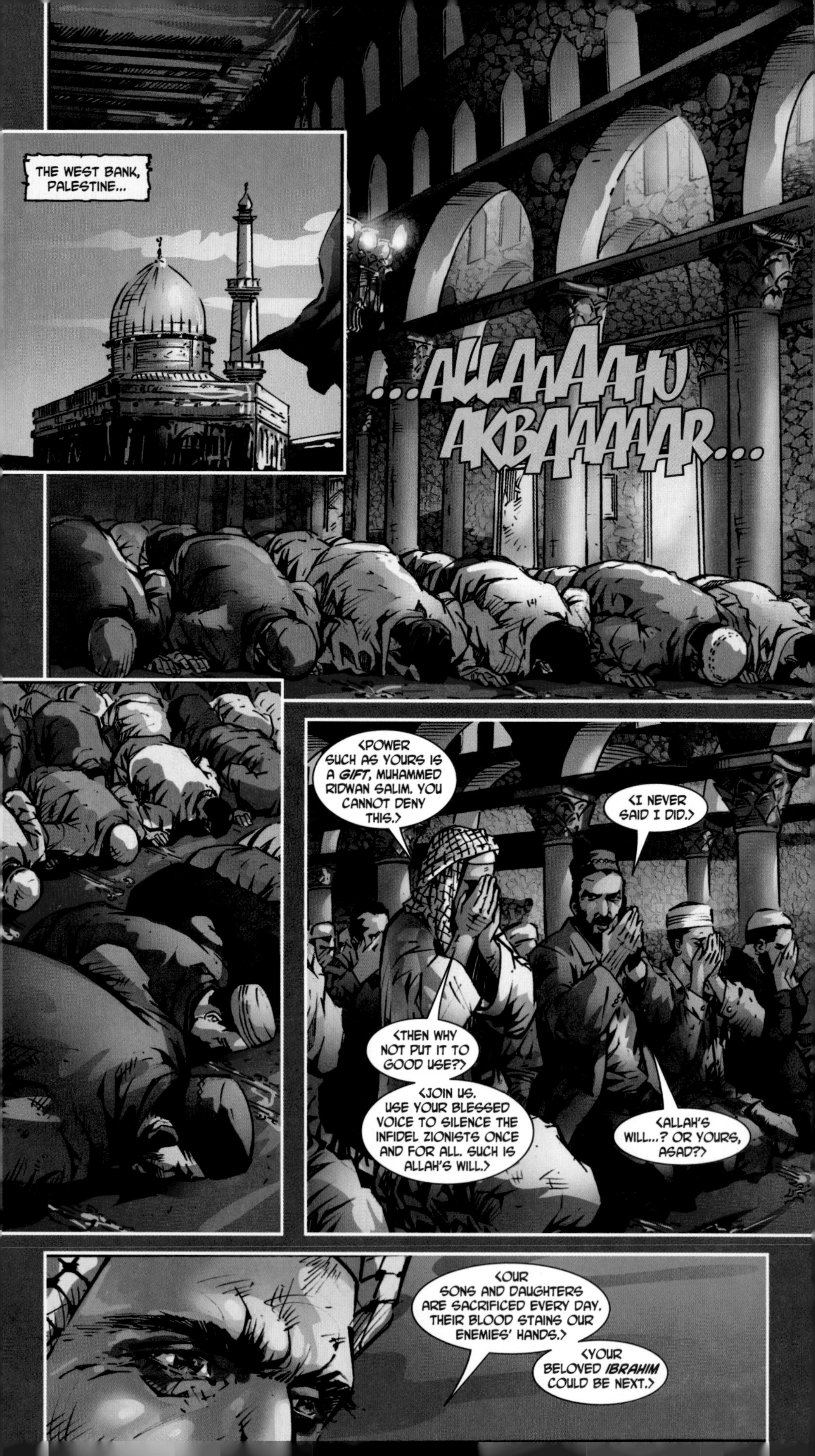
THE WEST BANK, PALESTINE...
...ALLAAAAHU AKBAAAAAR...
<POWER SUCH AS YOURS IS A *GIFT*, MUHAMMED RIDWAN SALIM. YOU CANNOT DENY THIS.>
<I NEVER SAID I DID.>
<THEN WHY NOT PUT IT TO GOOD USE?>
<JOIN US. USE YOUR BLESSED VOICE TO SILENCE THE INFIDEL ZIONISTS ONCE AND FOR ALL. SUCH IS ALLAH'S WILL.>
<ALLAH'S WILL...? OR YOURS, ASAD?>
<OUR SONS AND DAUGHTERS ARE SACRIFICED EVERY DAY. THEIR BLOOD STAINS OUR ENEMIES' HANDS.>
<YOUR BELOVED *IBRAHIM* COULD BE NEXT.>

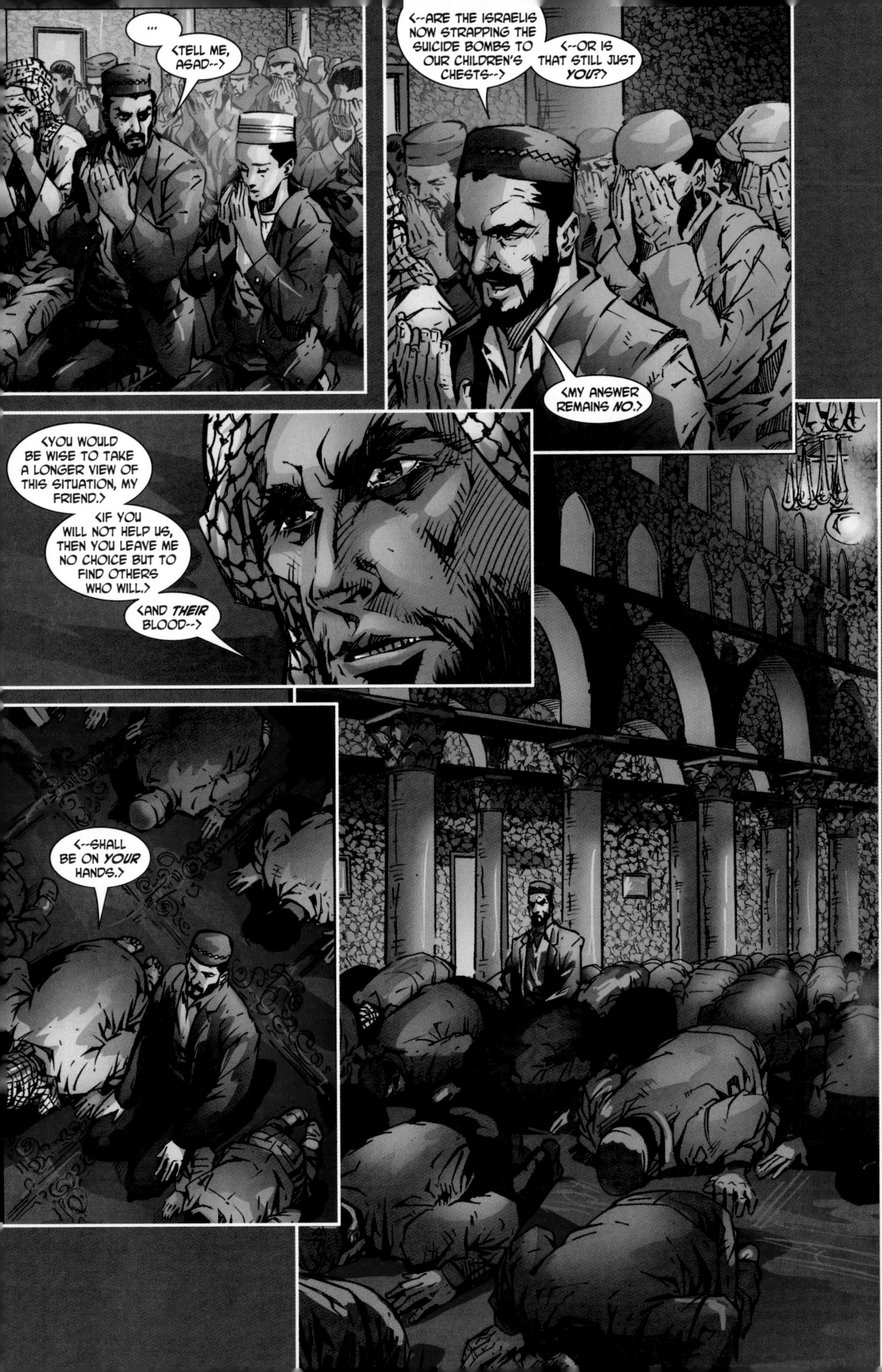
...
<TELL ME, ASAD-->
<--ARE THE ISRAELIS NOW STRAPPING THE SUICIDE BOMBS TO OUR CHILDREN'S CHESTS-->
<--OR IS THAT STILL JUST *YOU*?>
<MY ANSWER REMAINS *NO*.>
<YOU WOULD BE WISE TO TAKE A LONGER VIEW OF THIS SITUATION, MY FRIEND.>
<IF YOU WILL NOT HELP US, THEN YOU LEAVE ME NO CHOICE BUT TO FIND OTHERS WHO WILL.>
<AND *THEIR* BLOOD-->
<--SHALL BE ON *YOUR* HANDS.>

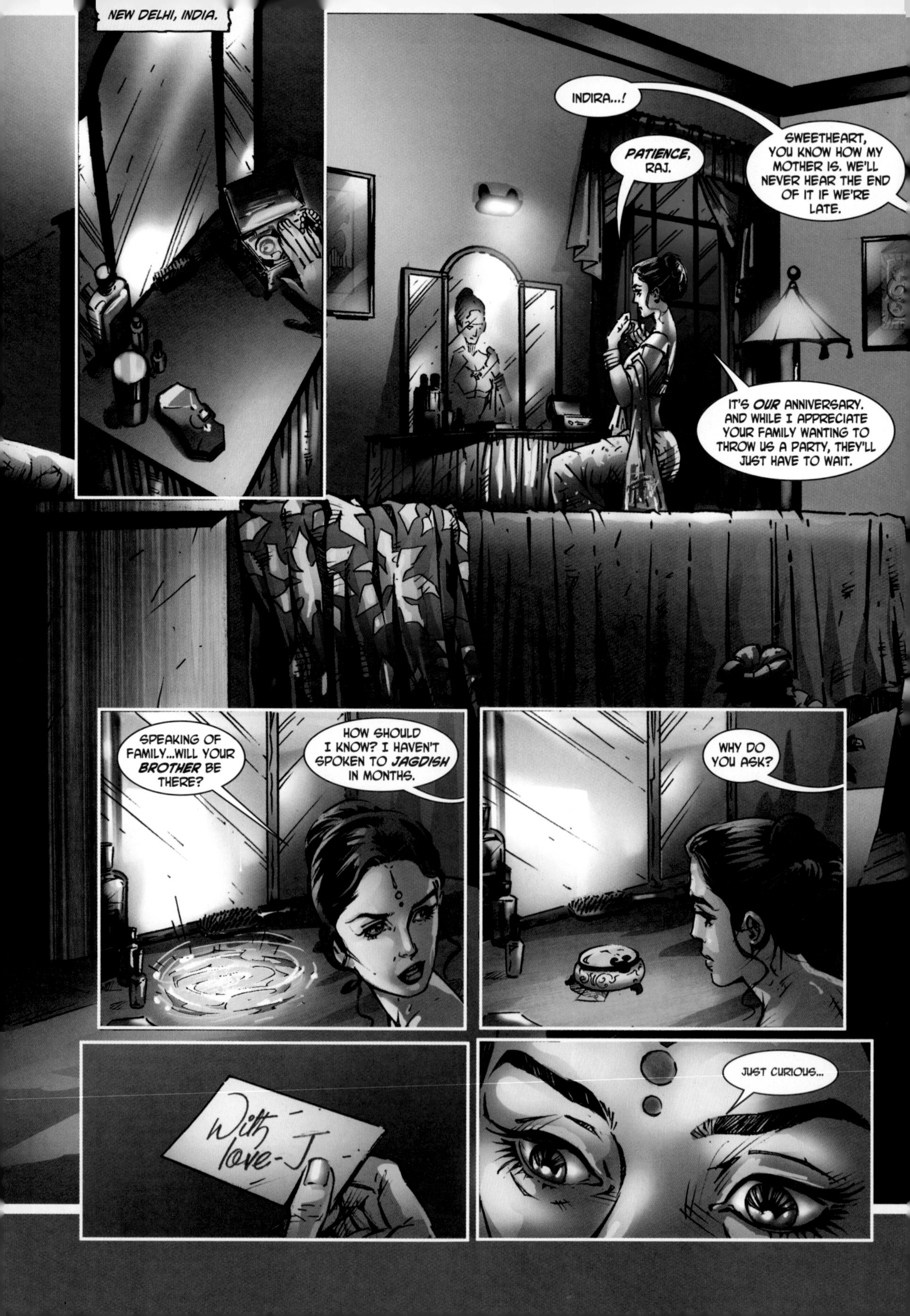
NEW DELHI, INDIA.
INDIRA...!
PATIENCE, RAJ.
SWEETHEART, YOU KNOW HOW MY MOTHER IS. WE'LL NEVER HEAR THE END OF IT IF WE'RE LATE.
IT'S OUR ANNIVERSARY. AND WHILE I APPRECIATE YOUR FAMILY WANTING TO THROW US A PARTY, THEY'LL JUST HAVE TO WAIT.
SPEAKING OF FAMILY...WILL YOUR BROTHER BE THERE?
HOW SHOULD I KNOW? I HAVEN'T SPOKEN TO JAGDISH IN MONTHS.
WHY DO YOU ASK?
With love-J
JUST CURIOUS...

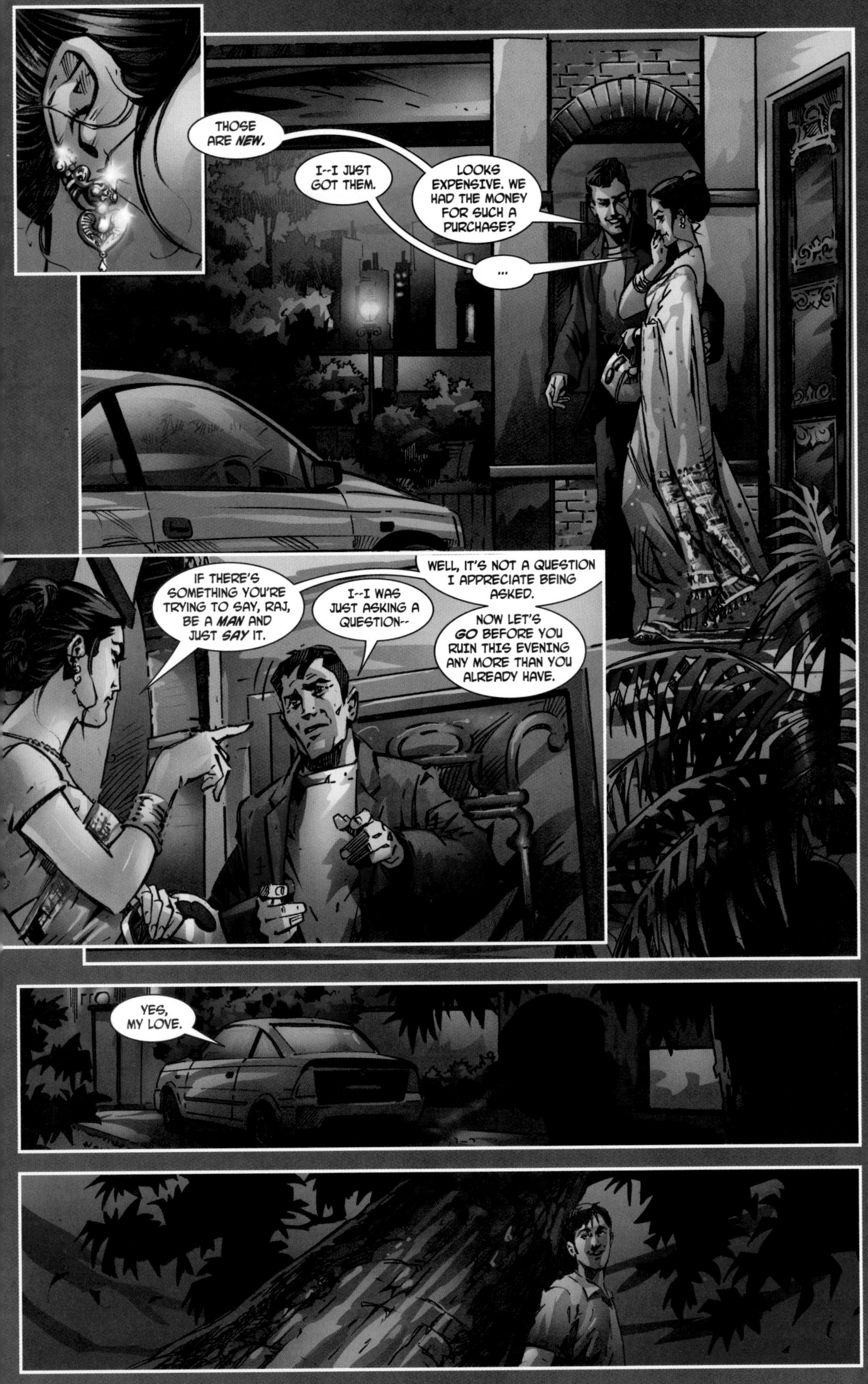
THOSE ARE NEW.
I--I JUST GOT THEM.
LOOKS EXPENSIVE. WE HAD THE MONEY FOR SUCH A PURCHASE?
...
IF THERE'S SOMETHING YOU'RE TRYING TO SAY, RAJ, BE A MAN AND JUST SAY IT.
I--I WAS JUST ASKING A QUESTION--
WELL, IT'S NOT A QUESTION I APPRECIATE BEING ASKED.
NOW LET'S GO BEFORE YOU RUIN THIS EVENING ANY MORE THAN YOU ALREADY HAVE.
YES, MY LOVE.

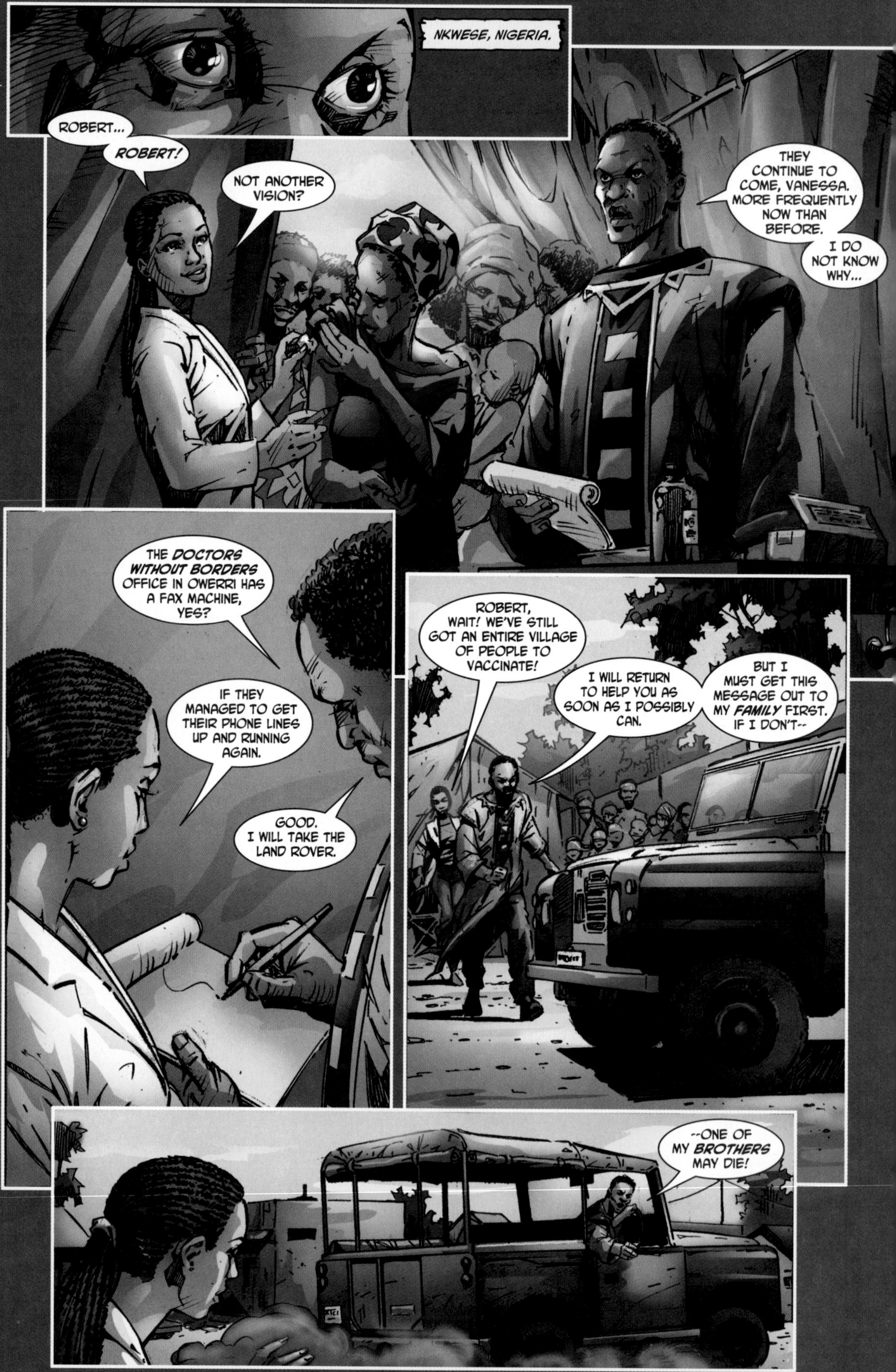
NKWESE, NIGERIA.
ROBERT... ROBERT!
NOT ANOTHER VISION?
THEY CONTINUE TO COME, VANESSA. MORE FREQUENTLY NOW THAN BEFORE.
I DO NOT KNOW WHY...
THE DOCTORS WITHOUT BORDERS OFFICE IN OWERRI HAS A FAX MACHINE, YES?
IF THEY MANAGED TO GET THEIR PHONE LINES UP AND RUNNING AGAIN.
GOOD. I WILL TAKE THE LAND ROVER.
ROBERT, WAIT! WE'VE STILL GOT AN ENTIRE VILLAGE OF PEOPLE TO VACCINATE!
I WILL RETURN TO HELP YOU AS SOON AS I POSSIBLY CAN.
BUT I MUST GET THIS MESSAGE OUT TO MY FAMILY FIRST. IF I DON'T--
--ONE OF MY BROTHERS MAY DIE!

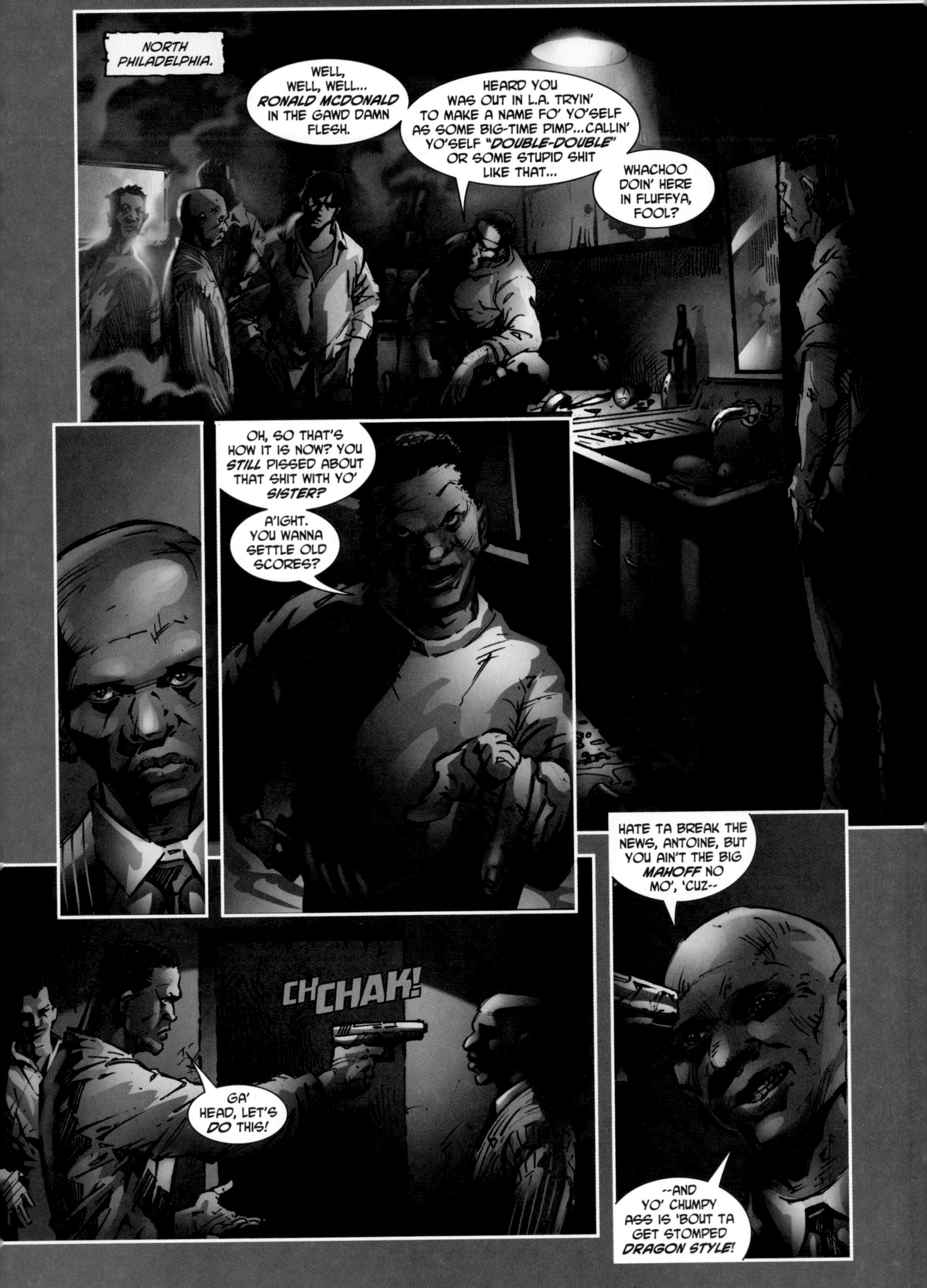
NORTH PHILADELPHIA.
WELL, WELL, WELL... RONALD MCDONALD IN THE GAWD DAMN FLESH.
HEARD YOU WAS OUT IN L.A. TRYIN' TO MAKE A NAME FO' YO'SELF AS SOME BIG-TIME PIMP...CALLIN' YO'SELF "DOUBLE-DOUBLE" OR SOME STUPID SHIT LIKE THAT...
WHACHOO DOIN' HERE IN FLUFFYA, FOOL?
OH, SO THAT'S HOW IT IS NOW? YOU STILL PISSED ABOUT THAT SHIT WITH YO' SISTER?
A'IGHT. YOU WANNA SETTLE OLD SCORES?
CHCHAK!
GA' HEAD, LET'S DO THIS!
HATE TA BREAK THE NEWS, ANTOINE, BUT YOU AIN'T THE BIG MAHOFF NO MO', 'CUZ--
--AND YO' CHUMPY ASS IS 'BOUT TA GET STOMPED DRAGON STYLE!

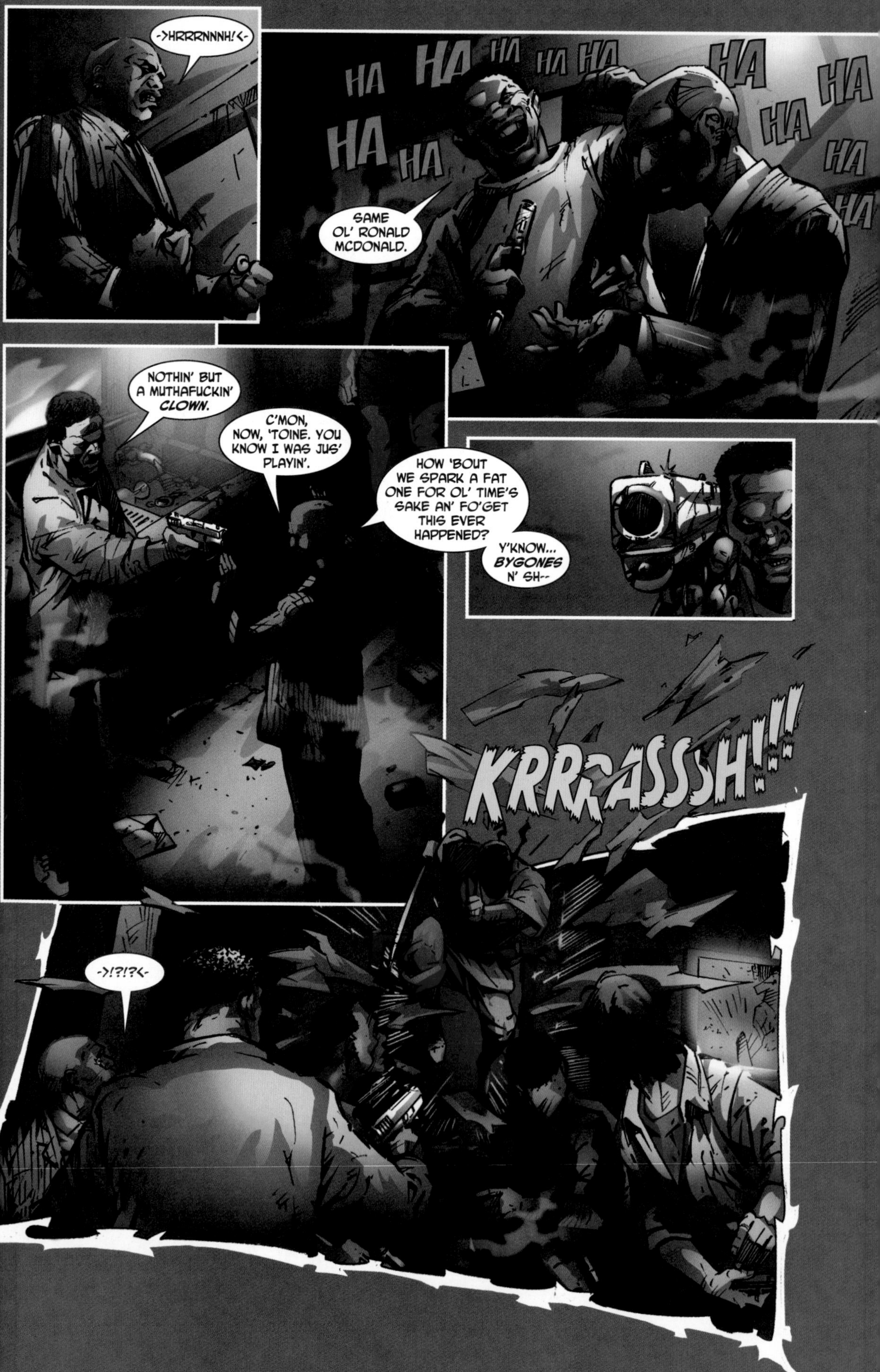
->HRRRNNNH!<-
HA HA HA HA HA HA HA HA HA HA HA HA HA
SAME OL' RONALD MCDONALD.
NOTHIN' BUT A MUTHAFUCKIN' *CLOWN.*
C'MON, NOW, 'TOINE. YOU KNOW I WAS JUS' PLAYIN'.
HOW 'BOUT WE SPARK A FAT ONE FOR OL' TIME'S SAKE AN' FO'GET THIS EVER HAPPENED?
Y'KNOW... *BYGONES* N' SH--
KRRRASSSH!!!
->!?!?<-

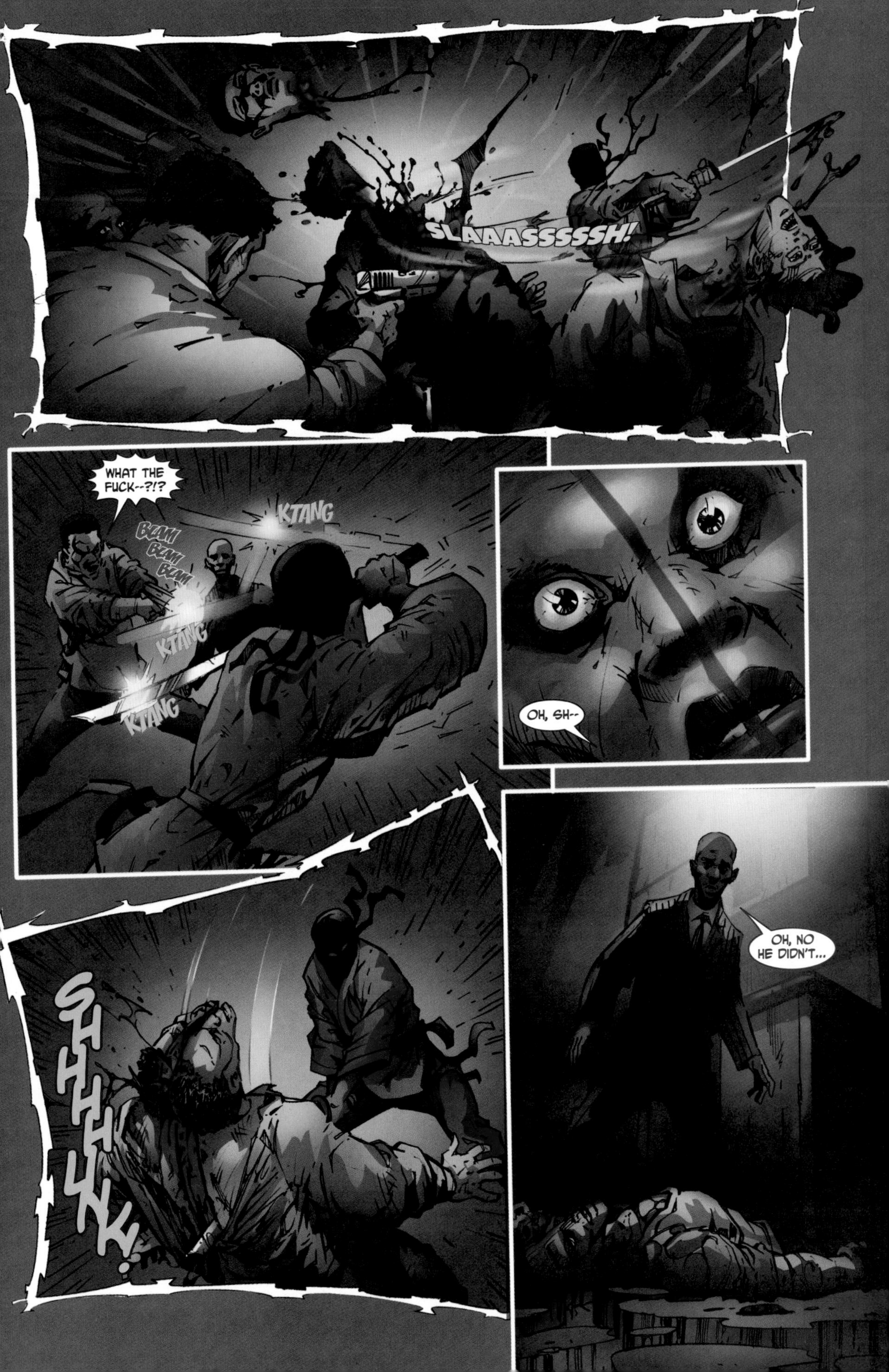
SLAAASSSSSH!
WHAT THE FUCK--?!?
KTANG
BLAM BLAM BLAM
KTANG
KTANG
OH, SH--
SHHHUNK!
OH, NO HE DIDN'T...

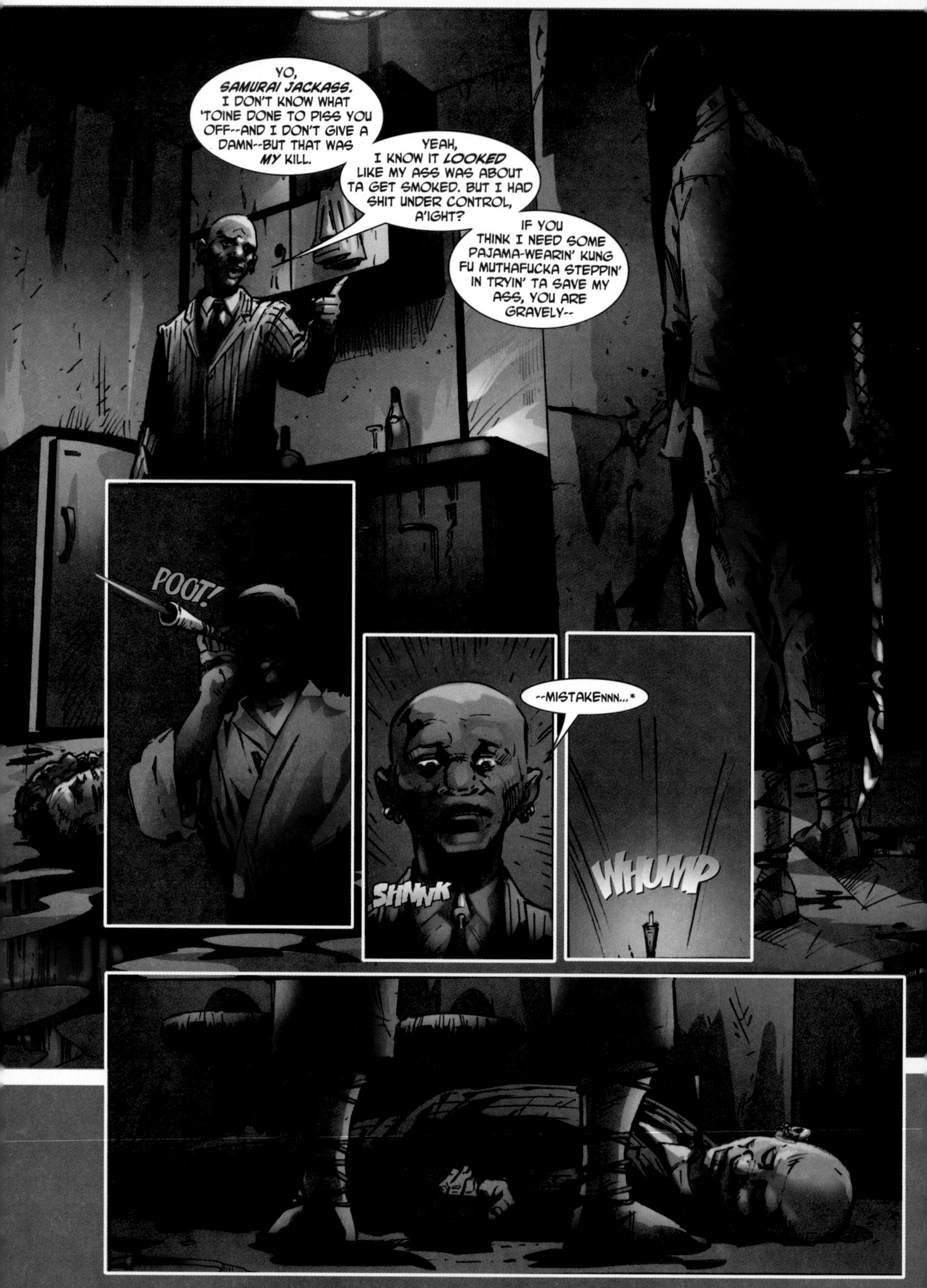
YO, SAMURAI JACKASS. I DON'T KNOW WHAT 'TOINE DONE TO PISS YOU OFF--AND I DON'T GIVE A DAMN--BUT THAT WAS MY KILL.
YEAH, I KNOW IT LOOKED LIKE MY ASS WAS ABOUT TA GET SMOKED. BUT I HAD SHIT UNDER CONTROL, A'IGHT?
IF YOU THINK I NEED SOME PAJAMA-WEARIN' KUNG FU MUTHAFUCKA STEPPIN' IN TRYIN' TA SAVE MY ASS, YOU ARE GRAVELY--
POOT!
SHNNK
--MISTAKENNN...*
WHUMP

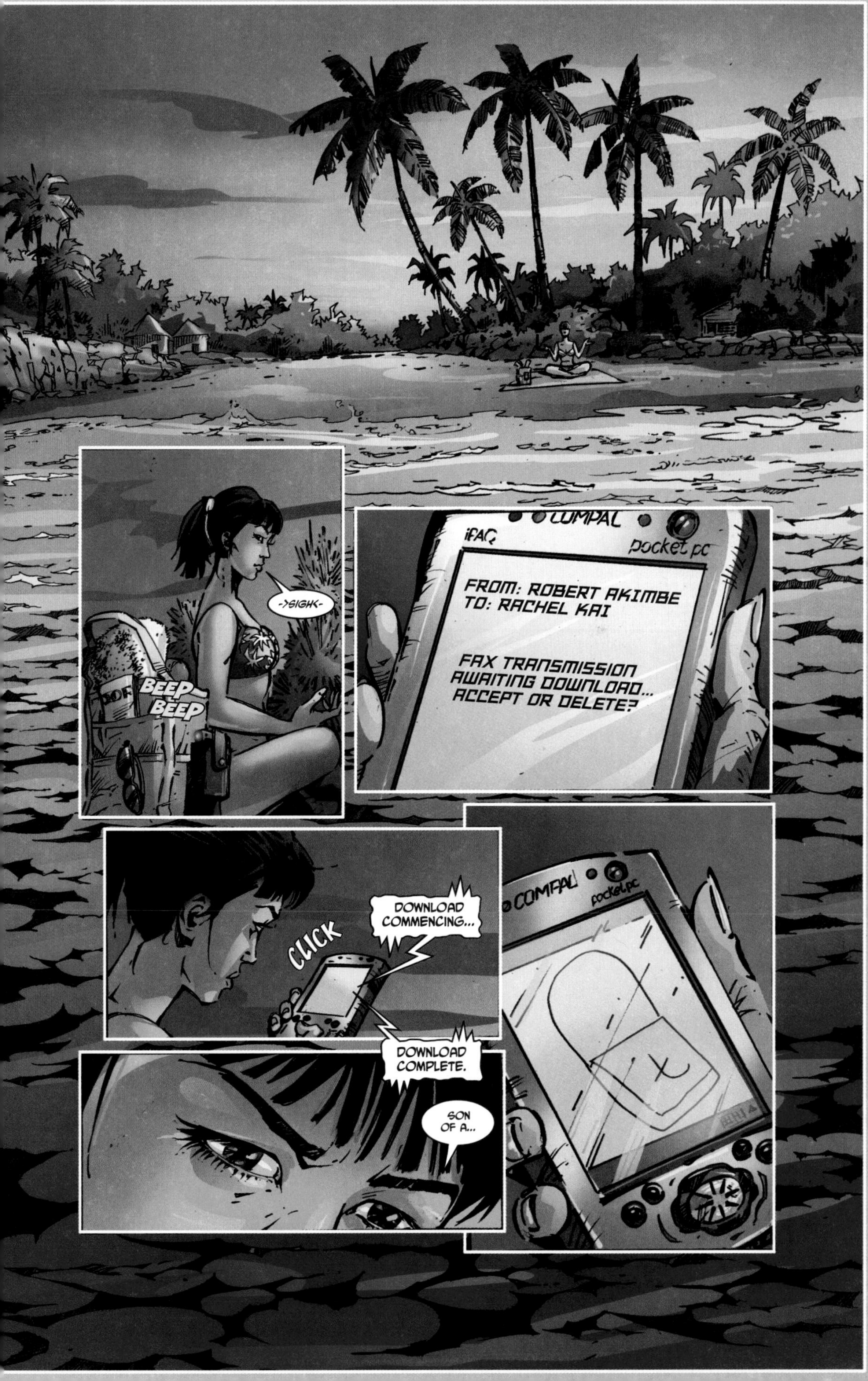
->SIGH<-
BEEP BEEP
DIOR
COMPAL
iPAQ
pocket pc
FROM: ROBERT AKIMBE
TO: RACHEL KAI
FAX TRANSMISSION
AWAITING DOWNLOAD...
ACCEPT OR DELETE?
CLICK
DOWNLOAD COMMENCING...
DOWNLOAD COMPLETE.
COMPAL
pocket pc
SON OF A...

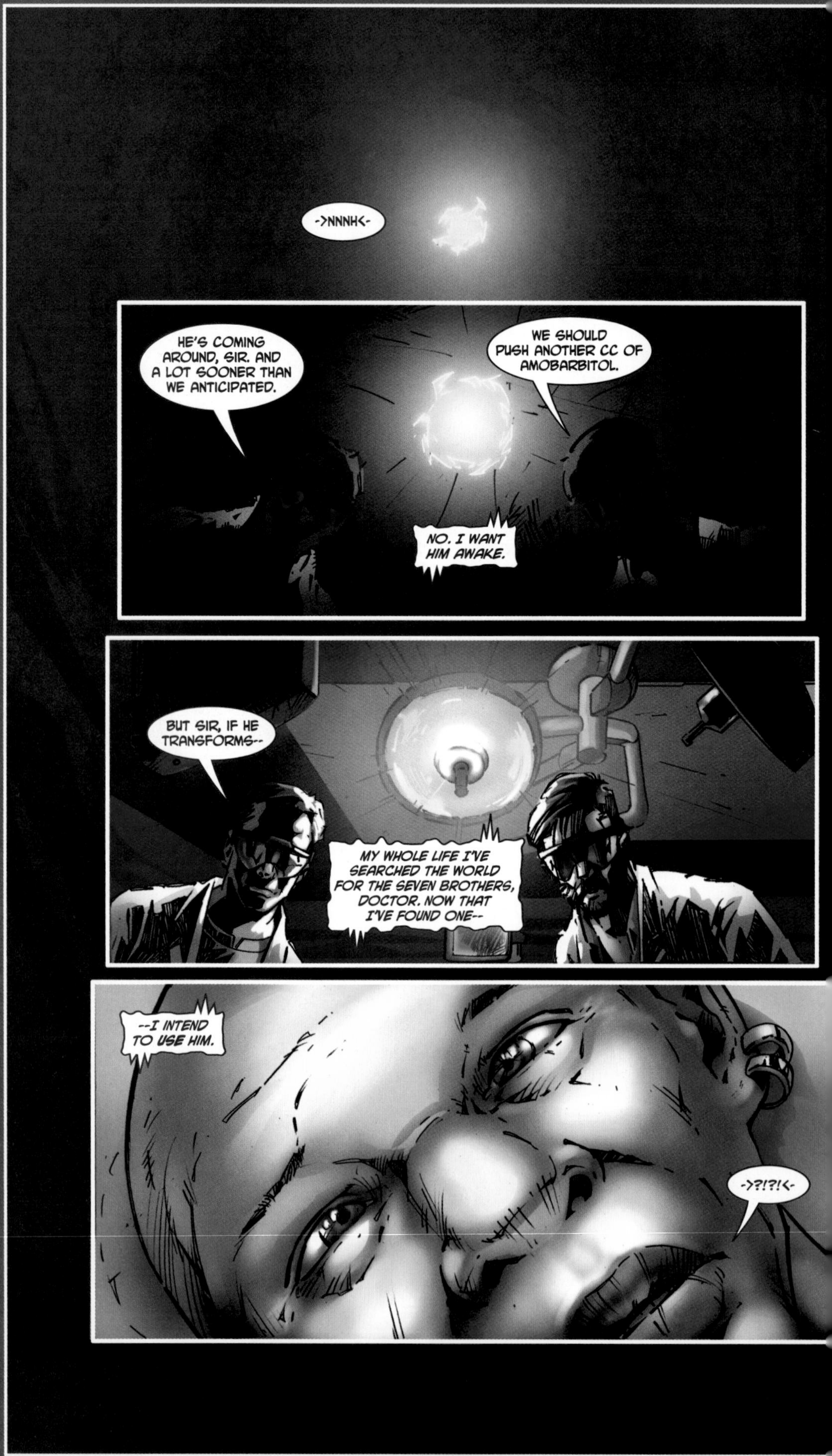

->NNNH<-
HE'S COMING AROUND, SIR. AND A LOT SOONER THAN WE ANTICIPATED.
WE SHOULD PUSH ANOTHER CC OF AMOBARBITOL.
NO. I WANT HIM AWAKE.
BUT SIR, IF HE TRANSFORMS--
MY WHOLE LIFE I'VE SEARCHED THE WORLD FOR THE SEVEN BROTHERS, DOCTOR. NOW THAT I'VE FOUND ONE--
--I INTEND TO USE HIM.
->?!?!<-

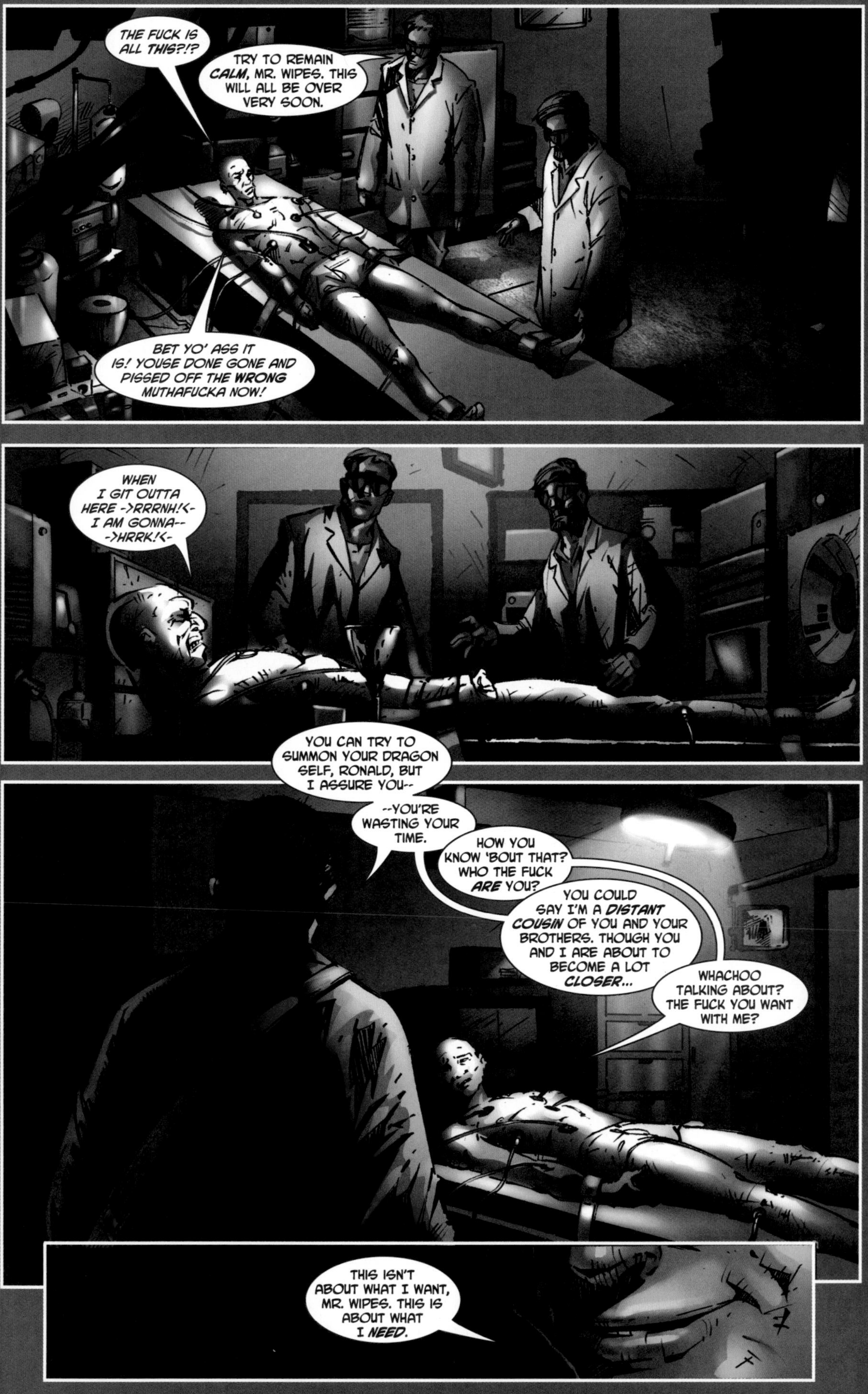
THE FUCK IS ALL THIS?!?
TRY TO REMAIN CALM, MR. WIPES. THIS WILL ALL BE OVER VERY SOON.
BET YO' ASS IT IS! YOUSE DONE GONE AND PISSED OFF THE WRONG MUTHAFUCKA NOW!
WHEN I GIT OUTTA HERE ->RRRNH!<- I AM GONNA-- ->HRRK!<-
YOU CAN TRY TO SUMMON YOUR DRAGON SELF, RONALD, BUT I ASSURE YOU--
--YOU'RE WASTING YOUR TIME.
HOW YOU KNOW 'BOUT THAT? WHO THE FUCK ARE YOU?
YOU COULD SAY I'M A DISTANT COUSIN OF YOU AND YOUR BROTHERS. THOUGH YOU AND I ARE ABOUT TO BECOME A LOT CLOSER...
WHACHOO TALKING ABOUT? THE FUCK YOU WANT WITH ME?
THIS ISN'T ABOUT WHAT I WANT, MR. WIPES. THIS IS ABOUT WHAT I NEED.

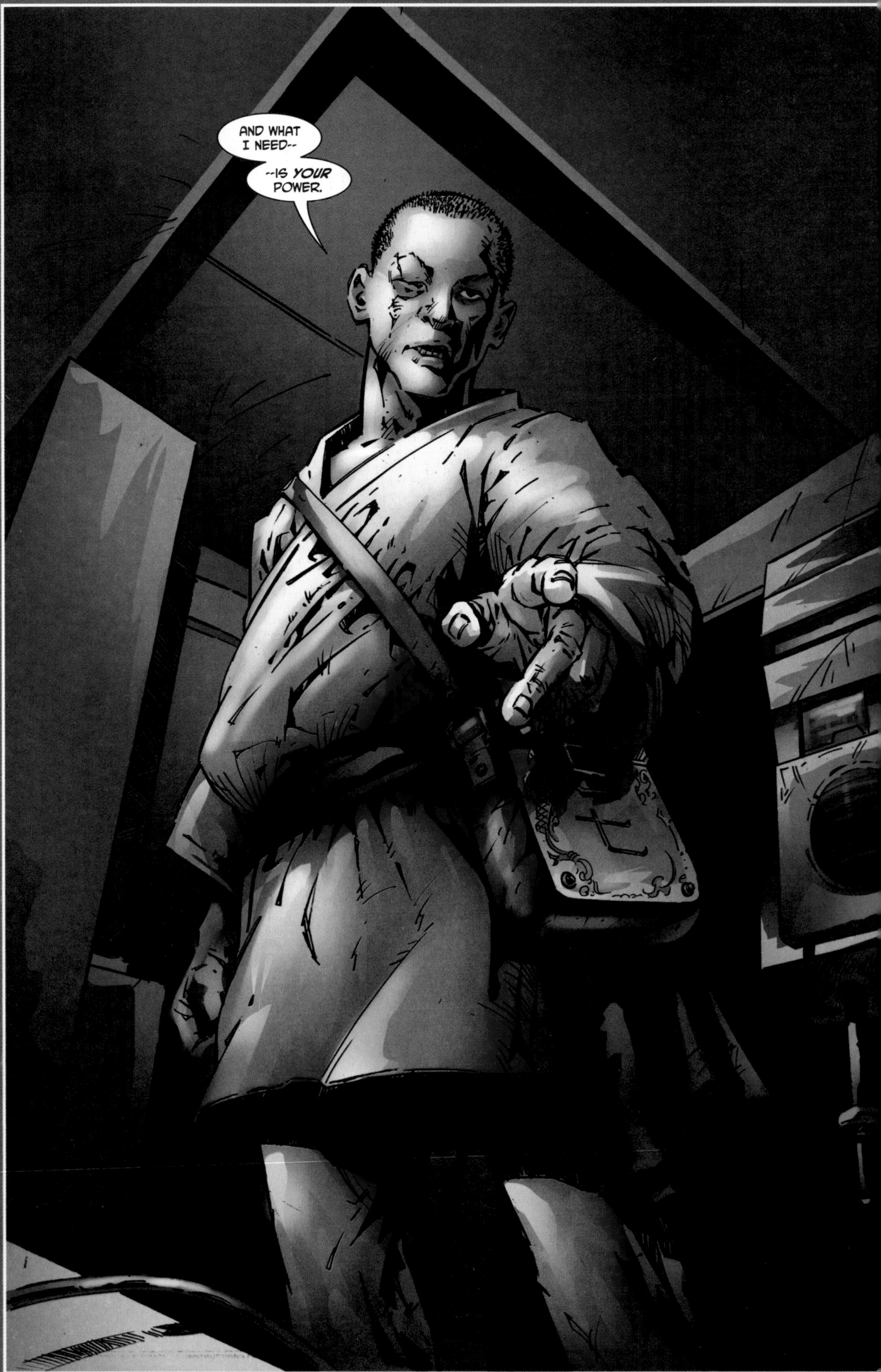
AND WHAT I NEED--
--IS *YOUR* POWER.

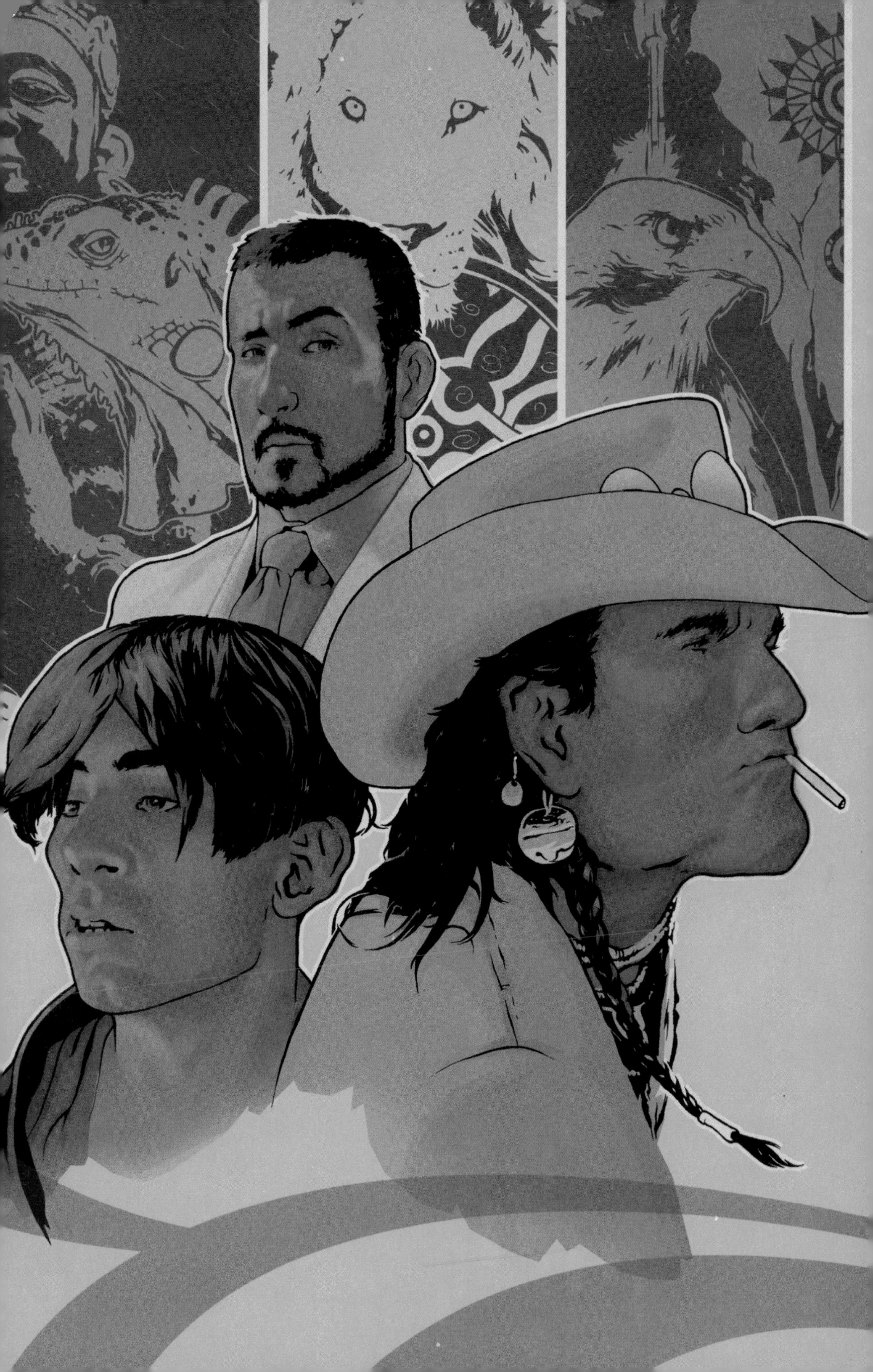

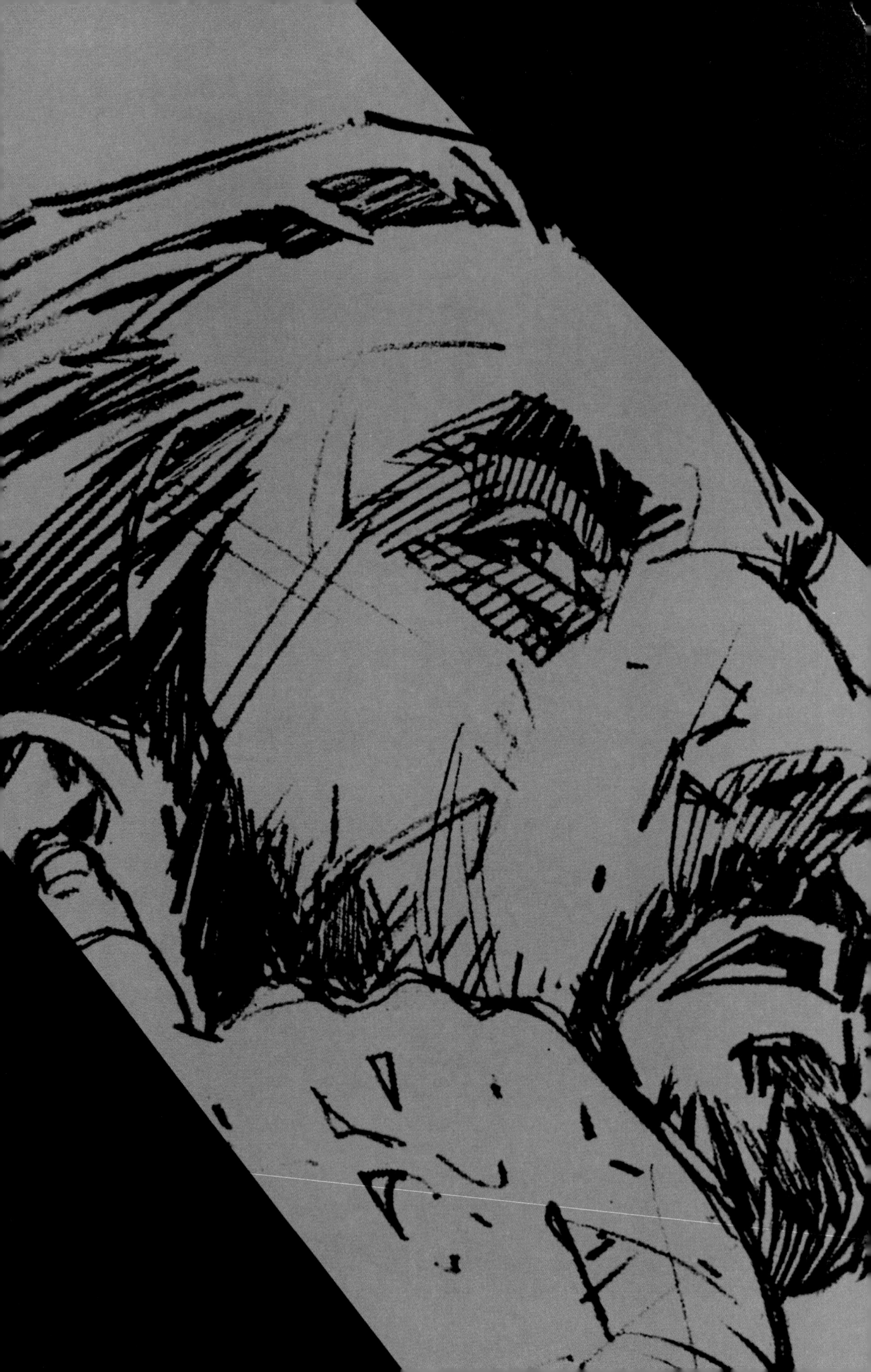

"Family.
The one thing in life
we **don't** get
to choose..." — Rachel Kai

Chapter - 2

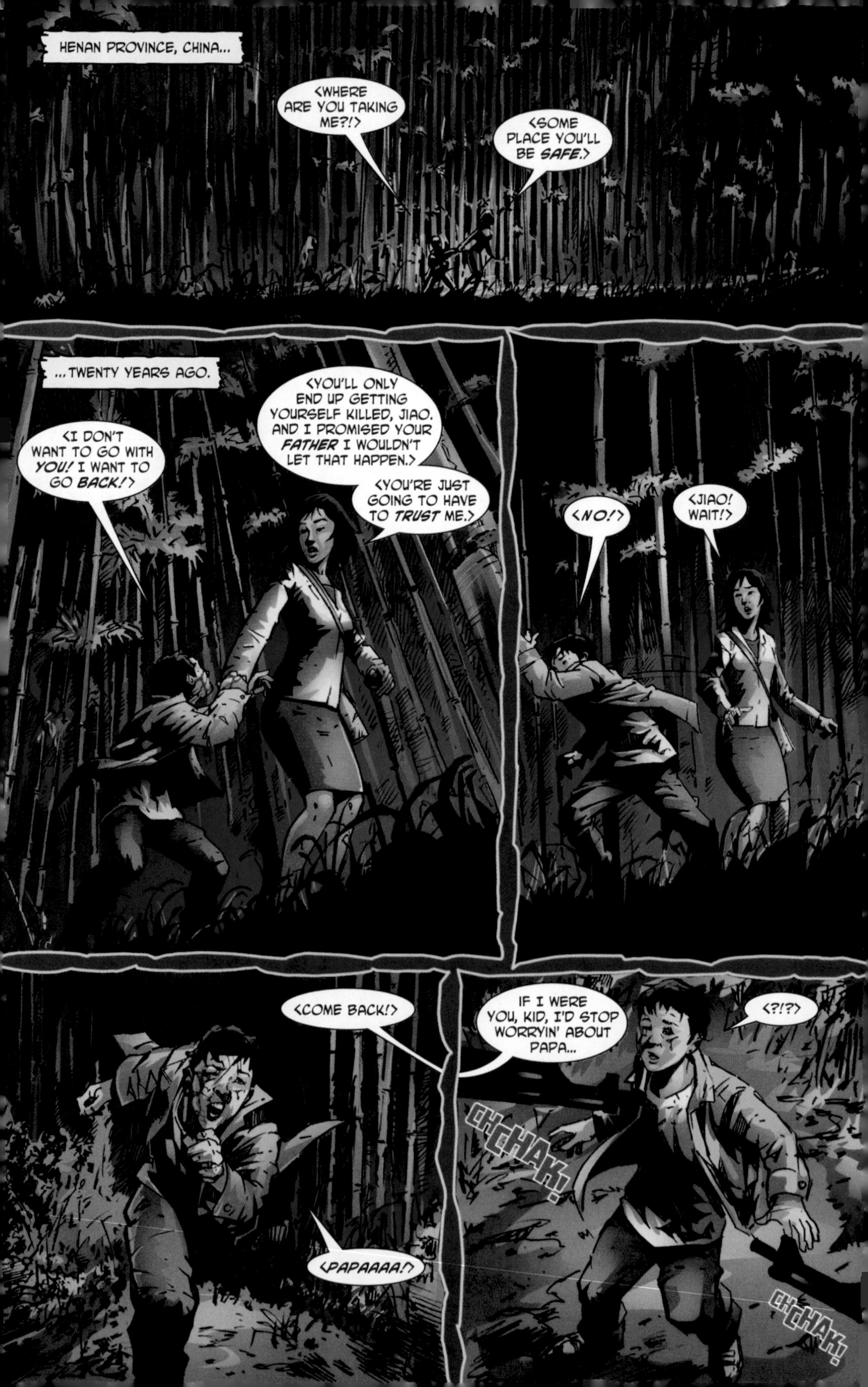
HENAN PROVINCE, CHINA...
<WHERE ARE YOU TAKING ME?!>
<SOME PLACE YOU'LL BE SAFE.>
...TWENTY YEARS AGO.
<I DON'T WANT TO GO WITH YOU! I WANT TO GO BACK!>
<YOU'LL ONLY END UP GETTING YOURSELF KILLED, JIAO. AND I PROMISED YOUR FATHER I WOULDN'T LET THAT HAPPEN.>
<YOU'RE JUST GOING TO HAVE TO TRUST ME.>
<NO!>
<JIAO! WAIT!>
<COME BACK!>
<PAPAAAA!>
IF I WERE YOU, KID, I'D STOP WORRYIN' ABOUT PAPA...
<?!?>
CHCHAK!
CHCHAK!

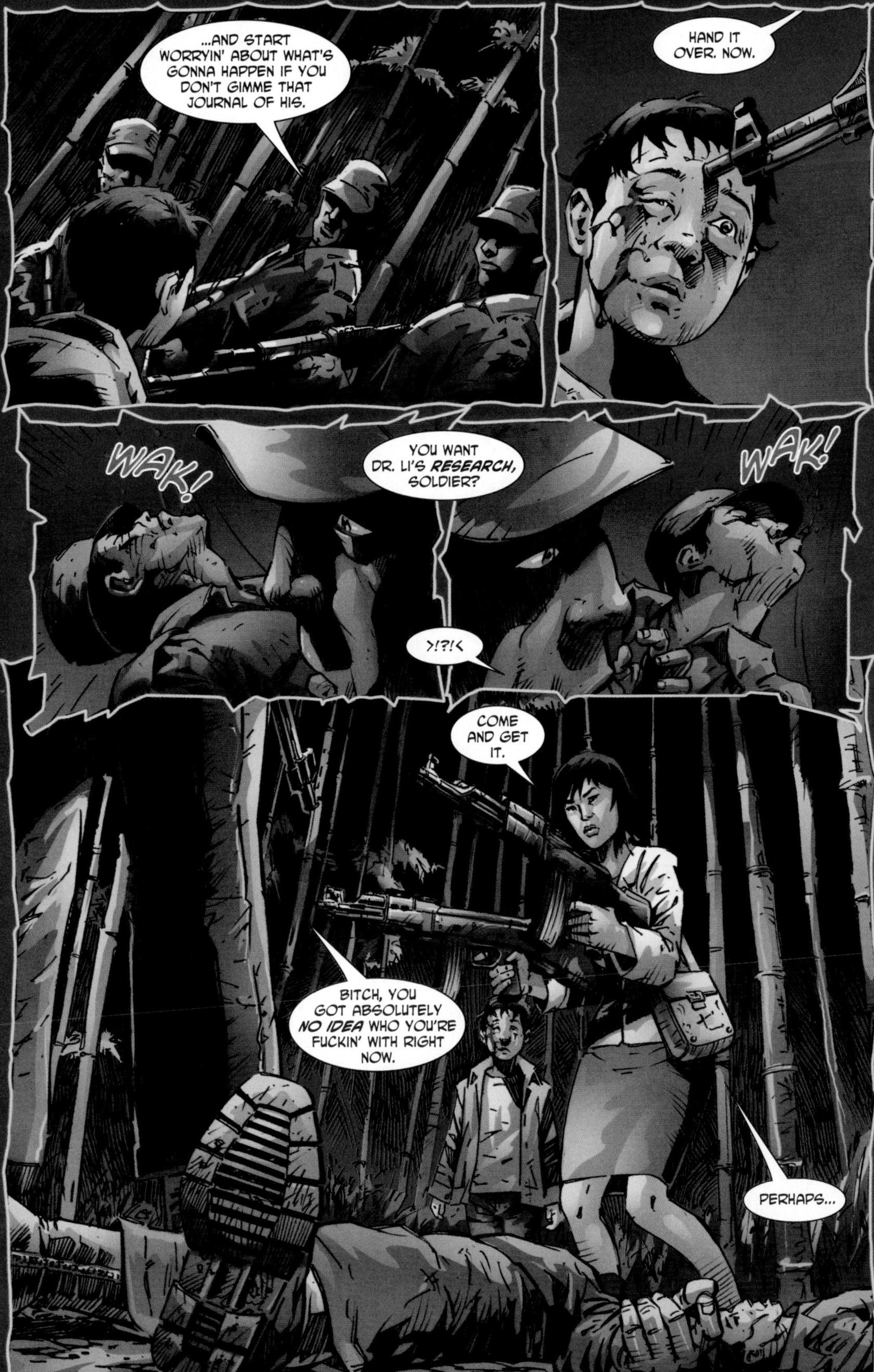
...AND START WORRYIN' ABOUT WHAT'S GONNA HAPPEN IF YOU DON'T GIMME THAT JOURNAL OF HIS.
HAND IT OVER. NOW.
WAK!
YOU WANT DR. LI'S RESEARCH, SOLDIER?
WAK!
>!?!<
COME AND GET IT.
BITCH, YOU GOT ABSOLUTELY NO IDEA WHO YOU'RE FUCKIN' WITH RIGHT NOW.
PERHAPS...

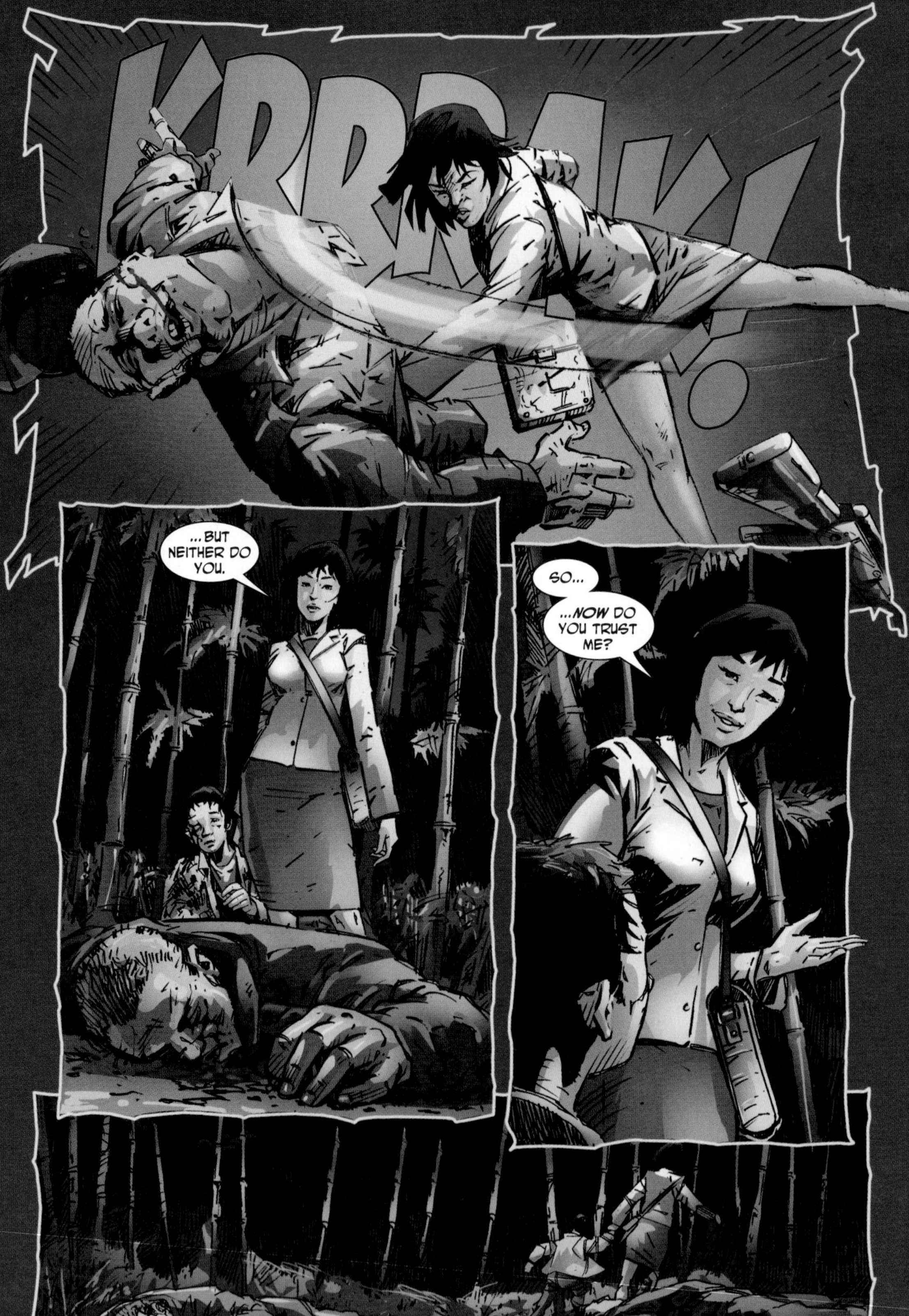
KRRAK!!
...BUT NEITHER DO YOU.
SO...
...NOW DO YOU TRUST ME?

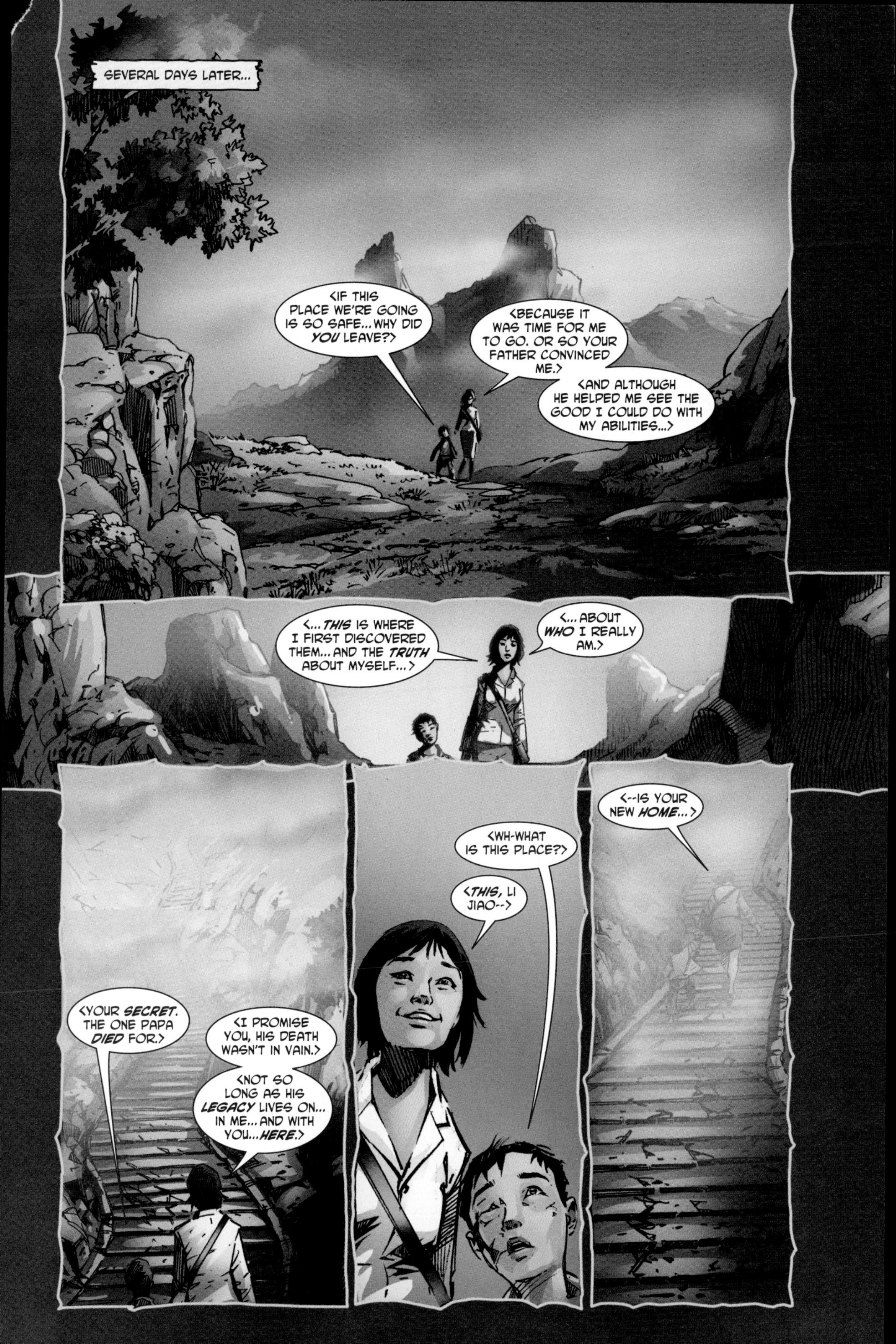
SEVERAL DAYS LATER...
<IF THIS PLACE WE'RE GOING IS SO SAFE... WHY DID *YOU* LEAVE?>
<BECAUSE IT WAS TIME FOR ME TO GO. OR SO YOUR FATHER CONVINCED ME.>
<AND ALTHOUGH HE HELPED ME SEE THE GOOD I COULD DO WITH MY ABILITIES...>
<...*THIS* IS WHERE I FIRST DISCOVERED THEM... AND THE *TRUTH* ABOUT MYSELF...>
<... ABOUT *WHO* I REALLY AM.>
<YOUR *SECRET*. THE ONE PAPA *DIED* FOR.>
<I PROMISE YOU, HIS DEATH WASN'T IN VAIN.>
<NOT SO LONG AS HIS *LEGACY* LIVES ON... IN ME... AND WITH YOU... *HERE*.>
<WH-WHAT IS THIS PLACE?>
<*THIS*, LI JIAO-->
<--IS YOUR NEW *HOME*...>

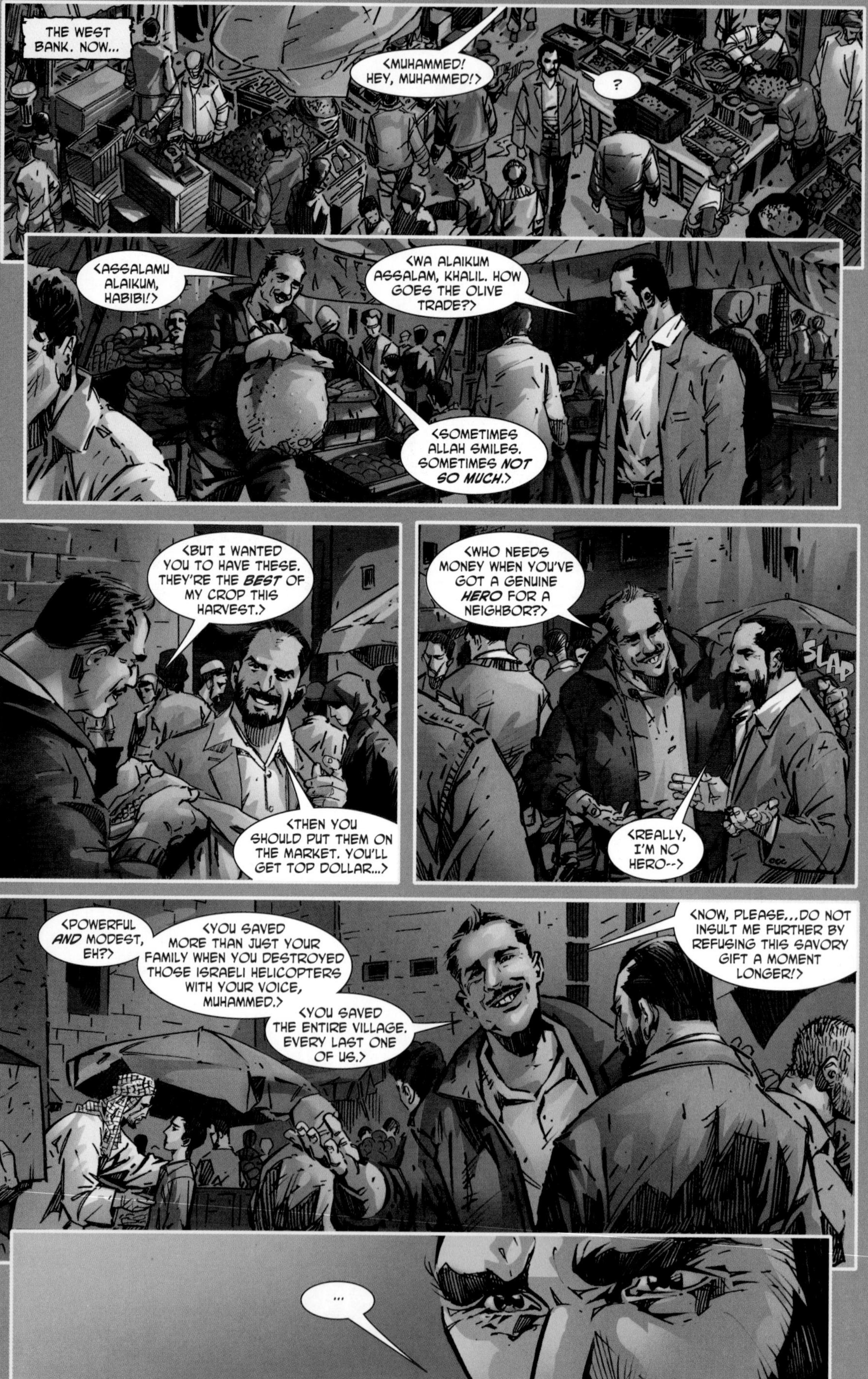

THE WEST BANK. NOW...
<MUHAMMED! HEY, MUHAMMED!>
?
<ASSALAMU ALAIKUM, HABIBI!>
<WA ALAIKUM ASSALAM, KHALIL. HOW GOES THE OLIVE TRADE?>
<SOMETIMES ALLAH SMILES. SOMETIMES NOT SO MUCH.>
<BUT I WANTED YOU TO HAVE THESE. THEY'RE THE BEST OF MY CROP THIS HARVEST.>
<THEN YOU SHOULD PUT THEM ON THE MARKET. YOU'LL GET TOP DOLLAR...>
<WHO NEEDS MONEY WHEN YOU'VE GOT A GENUINE HERO FOR A NEIGHBOR?>
SLAP
<REALLY, I'M NO HERO-->
<POWERFUL AND MODEST, EH?>
<YOU SAVED MORE THAN JUST YOUR FAMILY WHEN YOU DESTROYED THOSE ISRAELI HELICOPTERS WITH YOUR VOICE, MUHAMMED.>
<YOU SAVED THE ENTIRE VILLAGE. EVERY LAST ONE OF US.>
<NOW, PLEASE...DO NOT INSULT ME FURTHER BY REFUSING THIS SAVORY GIFT A MOMENT LONGER!>
...

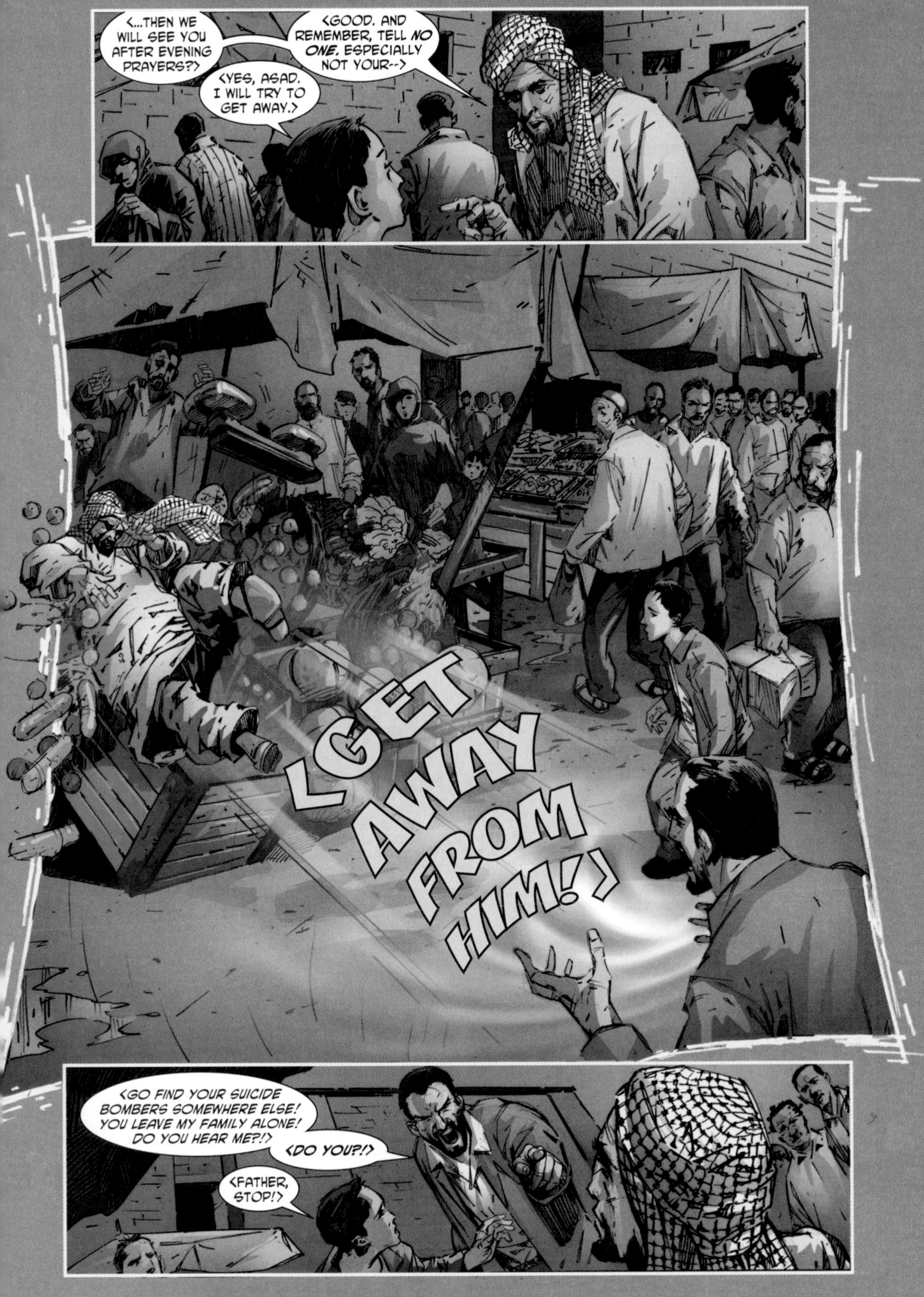

<...THEN WE WILL SEE YOU AFTER EVENING PRAYERS?>
<GOOD. AND REMEMBER, TELL NO ONE. ESPECIALLY NOT YOUR-->
<YES, ASAD. I WILL TRY TO GET AWAY.>
<GET AWAY FROM HIM!>
<GO FIND YOUR SUICIDE BOMBERS SOMEWHERE ELSE! YOU LEAVE MY FAMILY ALONE! DO YOU HEAR ME?!>
<DO YOU?!>
<FATHER, STOP!>

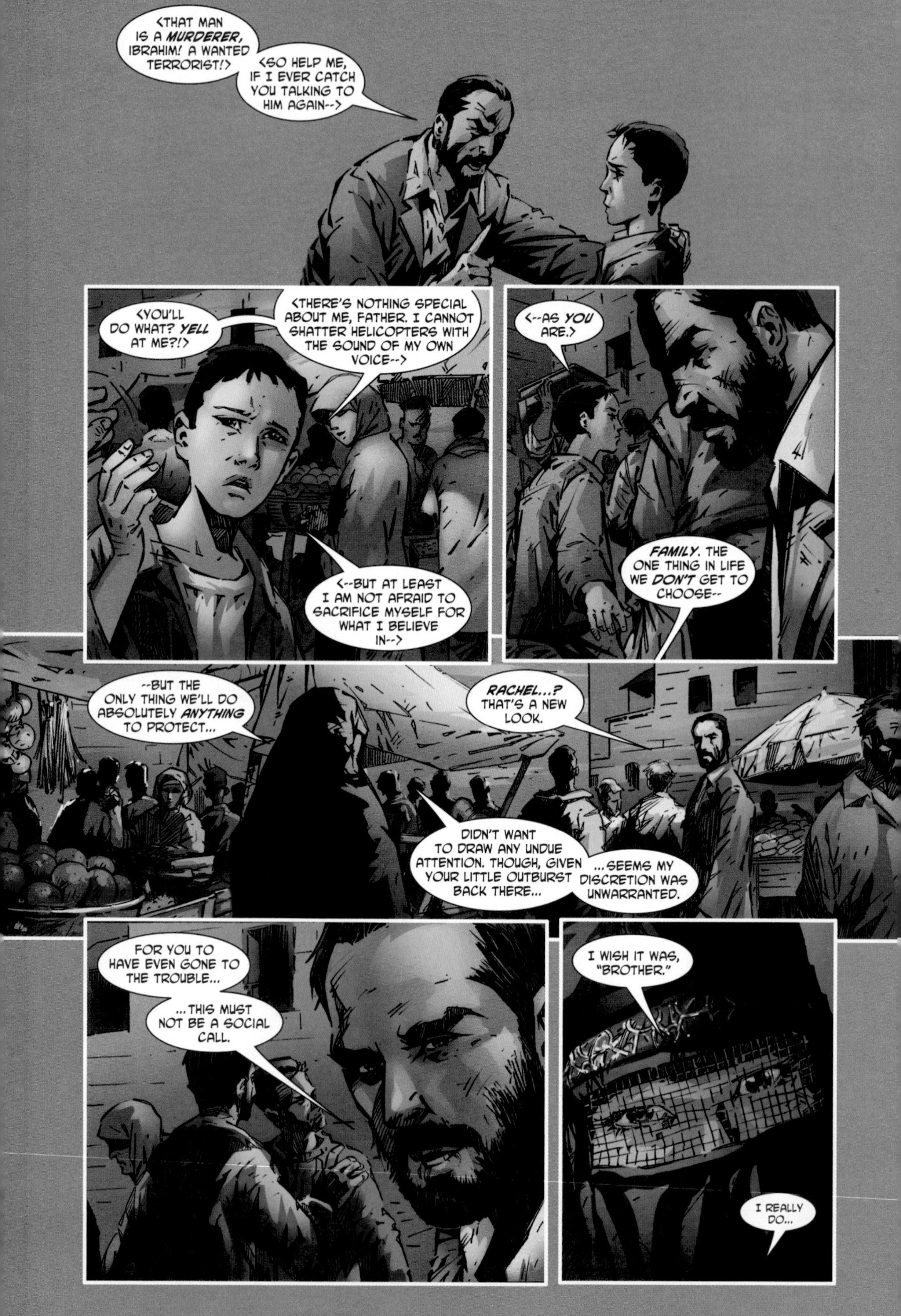
<THAT MAN IS A *MURDERER,* IBRAHIM! A WANTED TERRORIST!>
<SO HELP ME, IF I EVER CATCH YOU TALKING TO HIM AGAIN-->
<YOU'LL DO WHAT? *YELL* AT ME?!>
<THERE'S NOTHING SPECIAL ABOUT ME, FATHER. I CANNOT SHATTER HELICOPTERS WITH THE SOUND OF MY OWN VOICE-->
<--BUT AT LEAST I AM NOT AFRAID TO SACRIFICE MYSELF FOR WHAT I BELIEVE IN-->
<--AS *YOU* ARE.>
FAMILY. THE ONE THING IN LIFE WE *DON'T* GET TO CHOOSE--
--BUT THE ONLY THING WE'LL DO ABSOLUTELY *ANYTHING* TO PROTECT...
RACHEL...? THAT'S A NEW LOOK.
DIDN'T WANT TO DRAW ANY UNDUE ATTENTION. THOUGH, GIVEN YOUR LITTLE OUTBURST BACK THERE...
...SEEMS MY DISCRETION WAS UNWARRANTED.
FOR YOU TO HAVE EVEN GONE TO THE TROUBLE...
...THIS MUST NOT BE A SOCIAL CALL.
I WISH IT WAS, "BROTHER."
I REALLY DO...

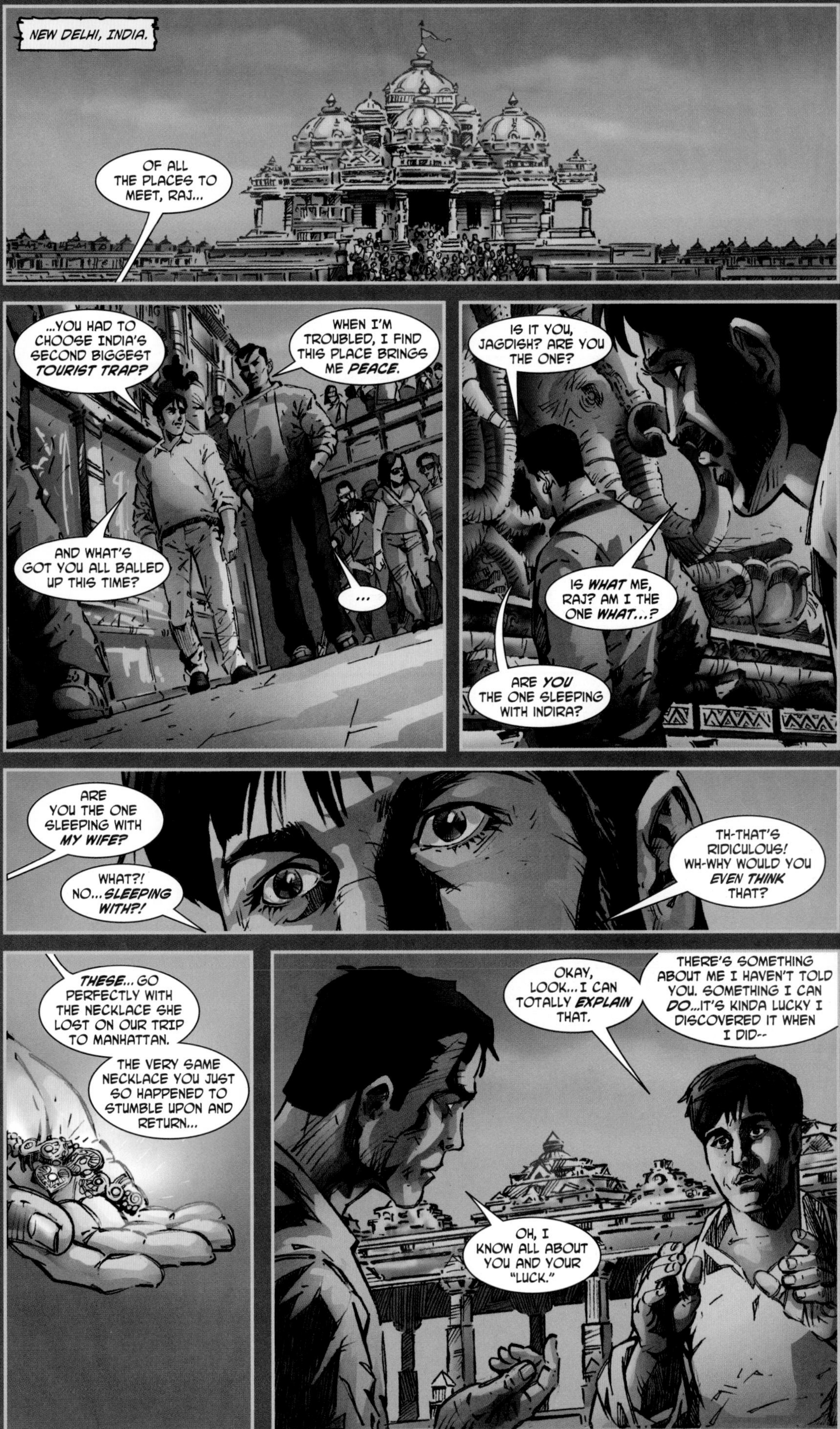
NEW DELHI, INDIA.
OF ALL THE PLACES TO MEET, RAJ...
...YOU HAD TO CHOOSE INDIA'S SECOND BIGGEST TOURIST TRAP?
WHEN I'M TROUBLED, I FIND THIS PLACE BRINGS ME PEACE.
AND WHAT'S GOT YOU ALL BALLED UP THIS TIME?
...
IS IT YOU, JAGDISH? ARE YOU THE ONE?
IS WHAT ME, RAJ? AM I THE ONE WHAT...?
ARE YOU THE ONE SLEEPING WITH INDIRA?
ARE YOU THE ONE SLEEPING WITH MY WIFE?
WHAT?! NO...SLEEPING WITH?!
TH-THAT'S RIDICULOUS! WH-WHY WOULD YOU EVEN THINK THAT?
THESE...GO PERFECTLY WITH THE NECKLACE SHE LOST ON OUR TRIP TO MANHATTAN.
THE VERY SAME NECKLACE YOU JUST SO HAPPENED TO STUMBLE UPON AND RETURN...
OKAY, LOOK...I CAN TOTALLY EXPLAIN THAT.
THERE'S SOMETHING ABOUT ME I HAVEN'T TOLD YOU. SOMETHING I CAN DO...IT'S KINDA LUCKY I DISCOVERED IT WHEN I DID--
OH, I KNOW ALL ABOUT YOU AND YOUR "LUCK."

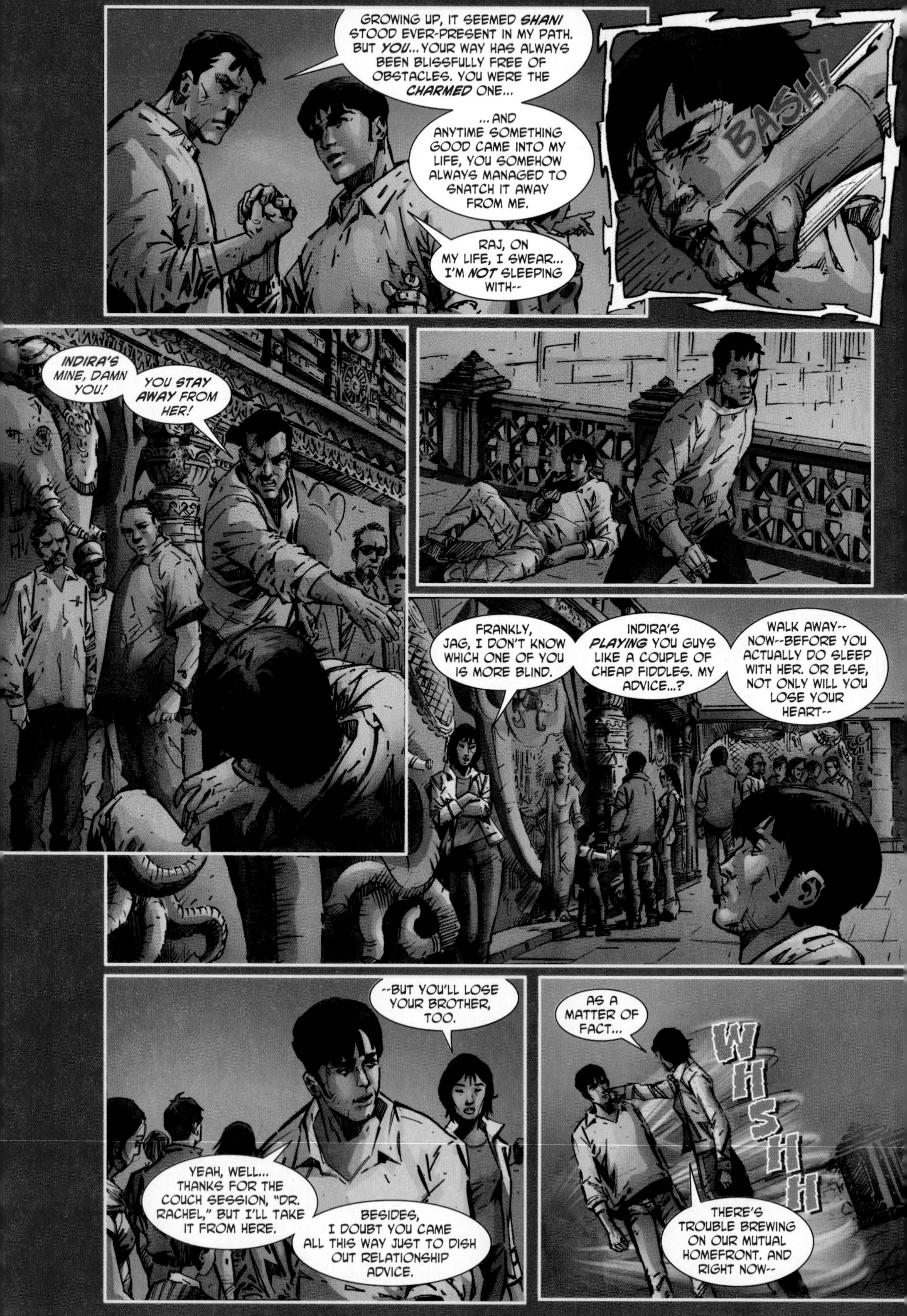
GROWING UP, IT SEEMED SHANI STOOD EVER-PRESENT IN MY PATH. BUT YOU... YOUR WAY HAS ALWAYS BEEN BLISSFULLY FREE OF OBSTACLES. YOU WERE THE CHARMED ONE...
...AND ANYTIME SOMETHING GOOD CAME INTO MY LIFE, YOU SOMEHOW ALWAYS MANAGED TO SNATCH IT AWAY FROM ME.
RAJ, ON MY LIFE, I SWEAR... I'M NOT SLEEPING WITH--
BASH!
INDIRA'S MINE, DAMN YOU!
YOU STAY AWAY FROM HER!
FRANKLY, JAG, I DON'T KNOW WHICH ONE OF YOU IS MORE BLIND.
INDIRA'S PLAYING YOU GUYS LIKE A COUPLE OF CHEAP FIDDLES. MY ADVICE...?
WALK AWAY-- NOW--BEFORE YOU ACTUALLY DO SLEEP WITH HER. OR ELSE, NOT ONLY WILL YOU LOSE YOUR HEART--
--BUT YOU'LL LOSE YOUR BROTHER, TOO.
YEAH, WELL... THANKS FOR THE COUCH SESSION, "DR. RACHEL," BUT I'LL TAKE IT FROM HERE.
BESIDES, I DOUBT YOU CAME ALL THIS WAY JUST TO DISH OUT RELATIONSHIP ADVICE.
AS A MATTER OF FACT...
WHSHH
THERE'S TROUBLE BREWING ON OUR MUTUAL HOMEFRONT. AND RIGHT NOW--

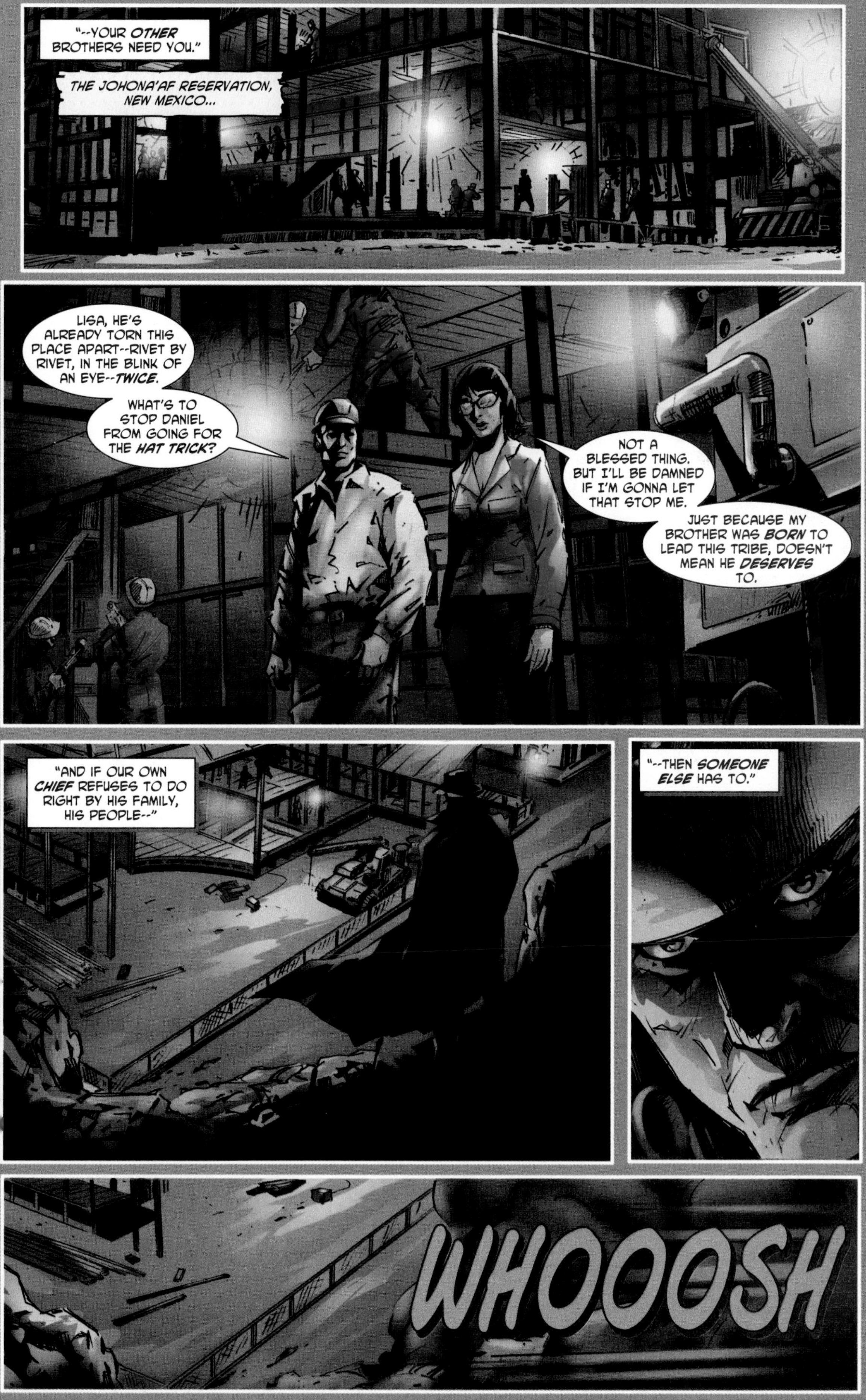
"--YOUR OTHER BROTHERS NEED YOU."
THE JOHONA'AF RESERVATION, NEW MEXICO...
LISA, HE'S ALREADY TORN THIS PLACE APART--RIVET BY RIVET, IN THE BLINK OF AN EYE--TWICE.
WHAT'S TO STOP DANIEL FROM GOING FOR THE HAT TRICK?
NOT A BLESSED THING. BUT I'LL BE DAMNED IF I'M GONNA LET THAT STOP ME.
JUST BECAUSE MY BROTHER WAS BORN TO LEAD THIS TRIBE, DOESN'T MEAN HE DESERVES TO.
"AND IF OUR OWN CHIEF REFUSES TO DO RIGHT BY HIS FAMILY, HIS PEOPLE--"
"--THEN SOMEONE ELSE HAS TO."
WHOOOSH

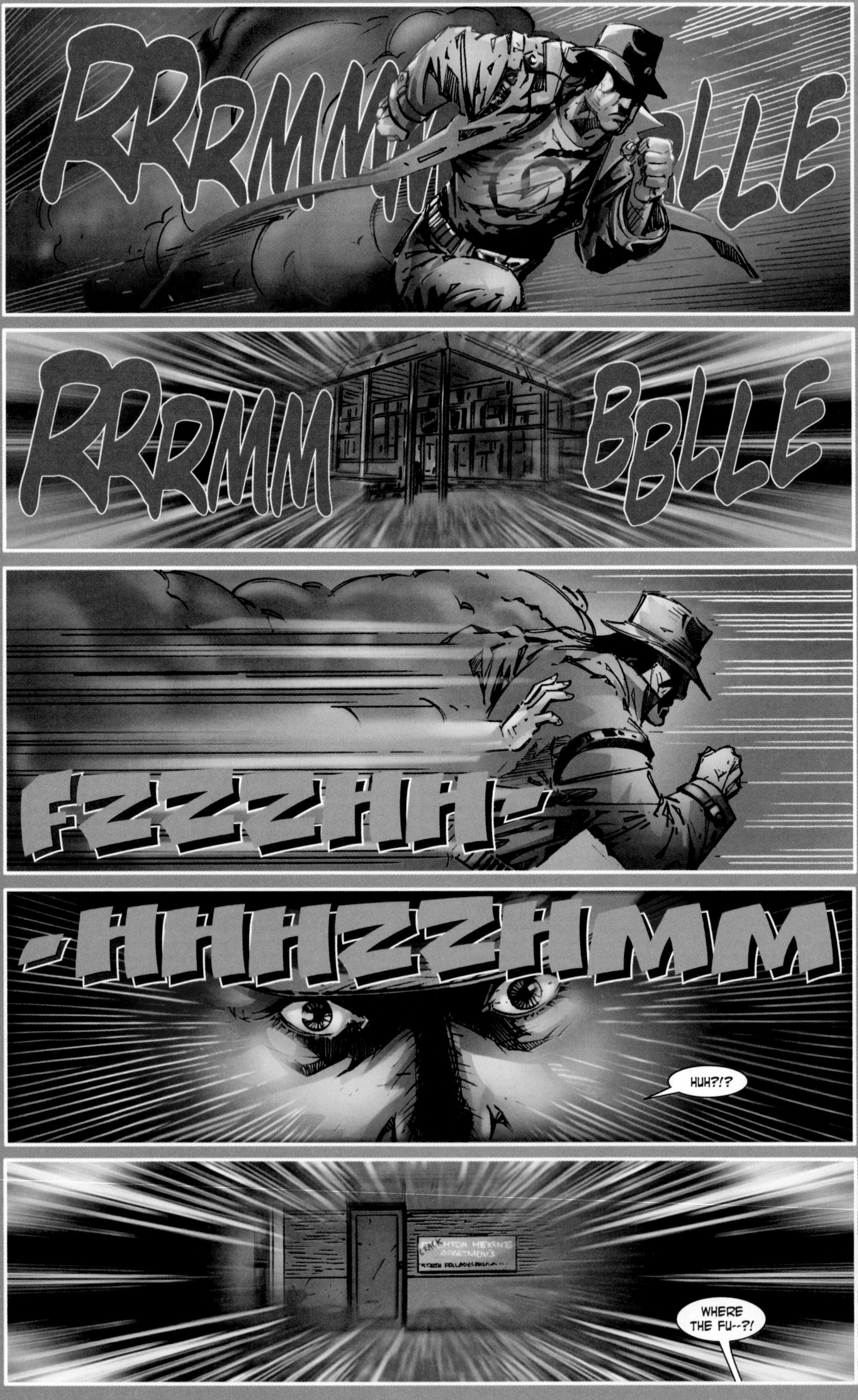
RRRMMMBBLLE
RRRMM BBLLE
FZZZHH-
-HHHZZHMM
HUH?!?
CRACK
WHERE THE FU--?!

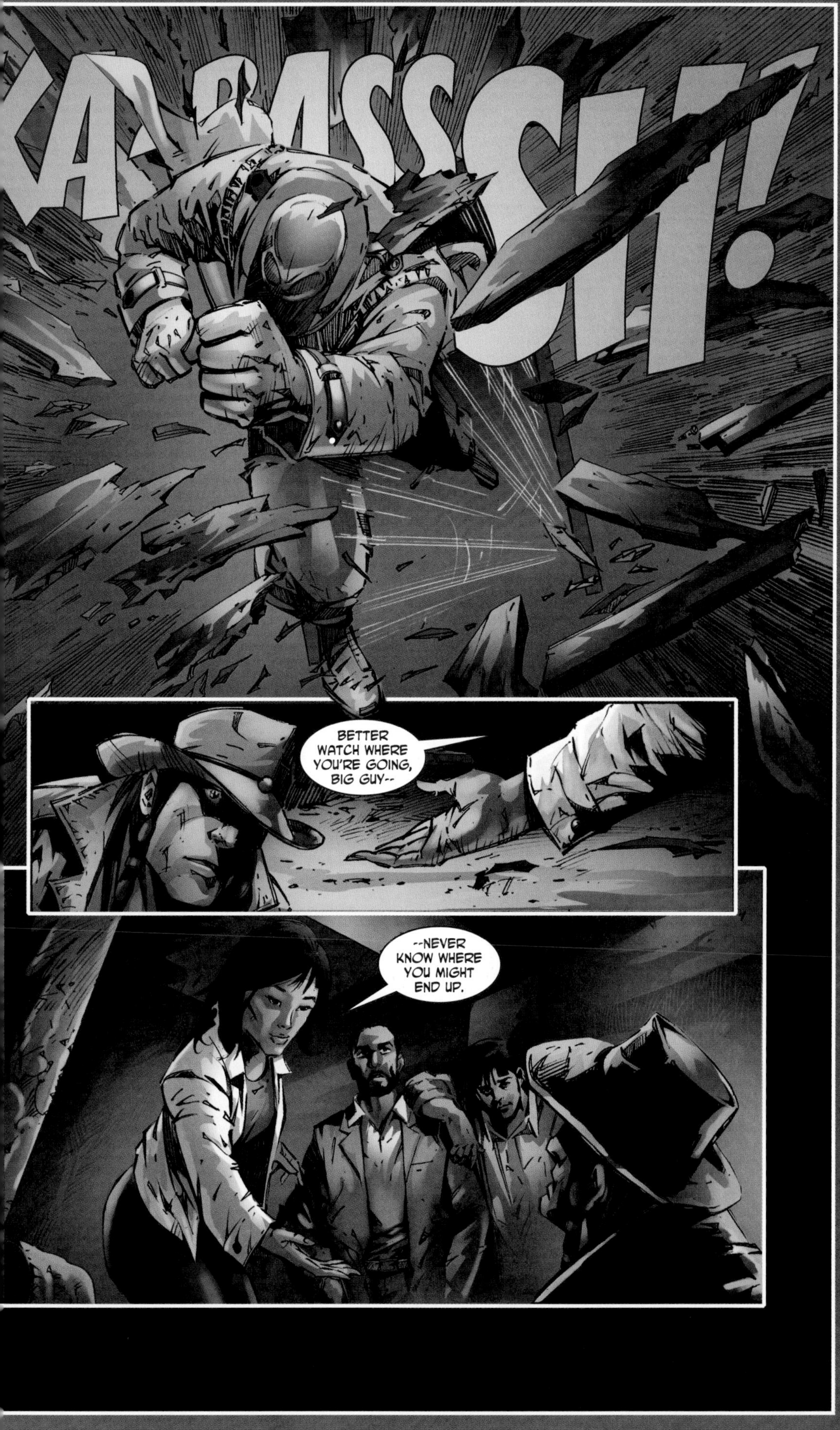
BETTER WATCH WHERE YOU'RE GOING, BIG GUY--
--NEVER KNOW WHERE YOU MIGHT END UP.

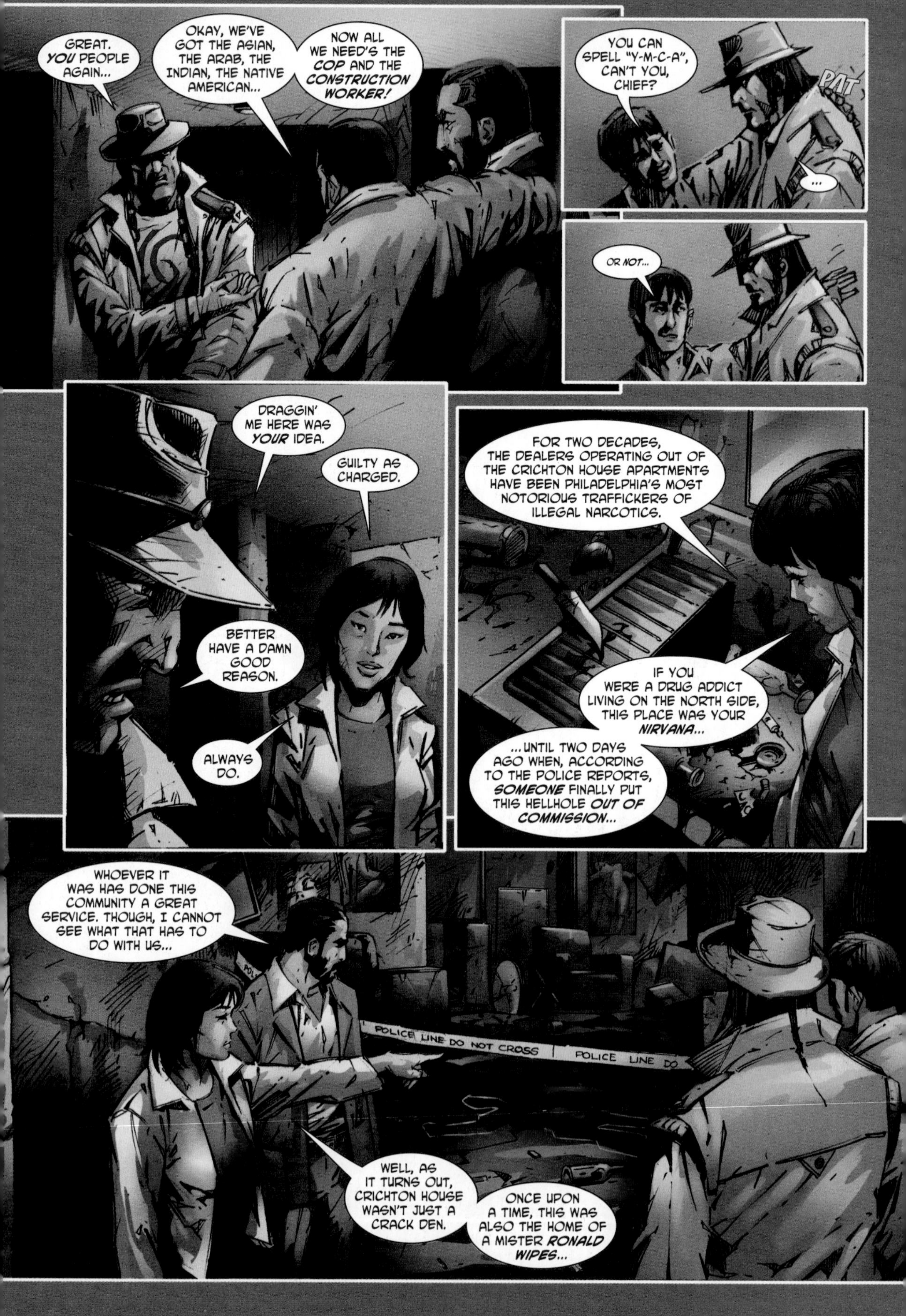
GREAT. YOU PEOPLE AGAIN...
OKAY, WE'VE GOT THE ASIAN, THE ARAB, THE INDIAN, THE NATIVE AMERICAN...
NOW ALL WE NEED'S THE COP AND THE CONSTRUCTION WORKER!
YOU CAN SPELL "Y-M-C-A", CAN'T YOU, CHIEF?
PAT
...
OR NOT...
DRAGGIN' ME HERE WAS YOUR IDEA.
GUILTY AS CHARGED.
BETTER HAVE A DAMN GOOD REASON.
ALWAYS DO.
FOR TWO DECADES, THE DEALERS OPERATING OUT OF THE CRICHTON HOUSE APARTMENTS HAVE BEEN PHILADELPHIA'S MOST NOTORIOUS TRAFFICKERS OF ILLEGAL NARCOTICS.
IF YOU WERE A DRUG ADDICT LIVING ON THE NORTH SIDE, THIS PLACE WAS YOUR NIRVANA...
...UNTIL TWO DAYS AGO WHEN, ACCORDING TO THE POLICE REPORTS, SOMEONE FINALLY PUT THIS HELLHOLE OUT OF COMMISSION...
WHOEVER IT WAS HAS DONE THIS COMMUNITY A GREAT SERVICE. THOUGH, I CANNOT SEE WHAT THAT HAS TO DO WITH US...
POLICE LINE DO NOT CROSS
POLICE LINE DO
WELL, AS IT TURNS OUT, CRICHTON HOUSE WASN'T JUST A CRACK DEN.
ONCE UPON A TIME, THIS WAS ALSO THE HOME OF A MISTER RONALD WIPES...

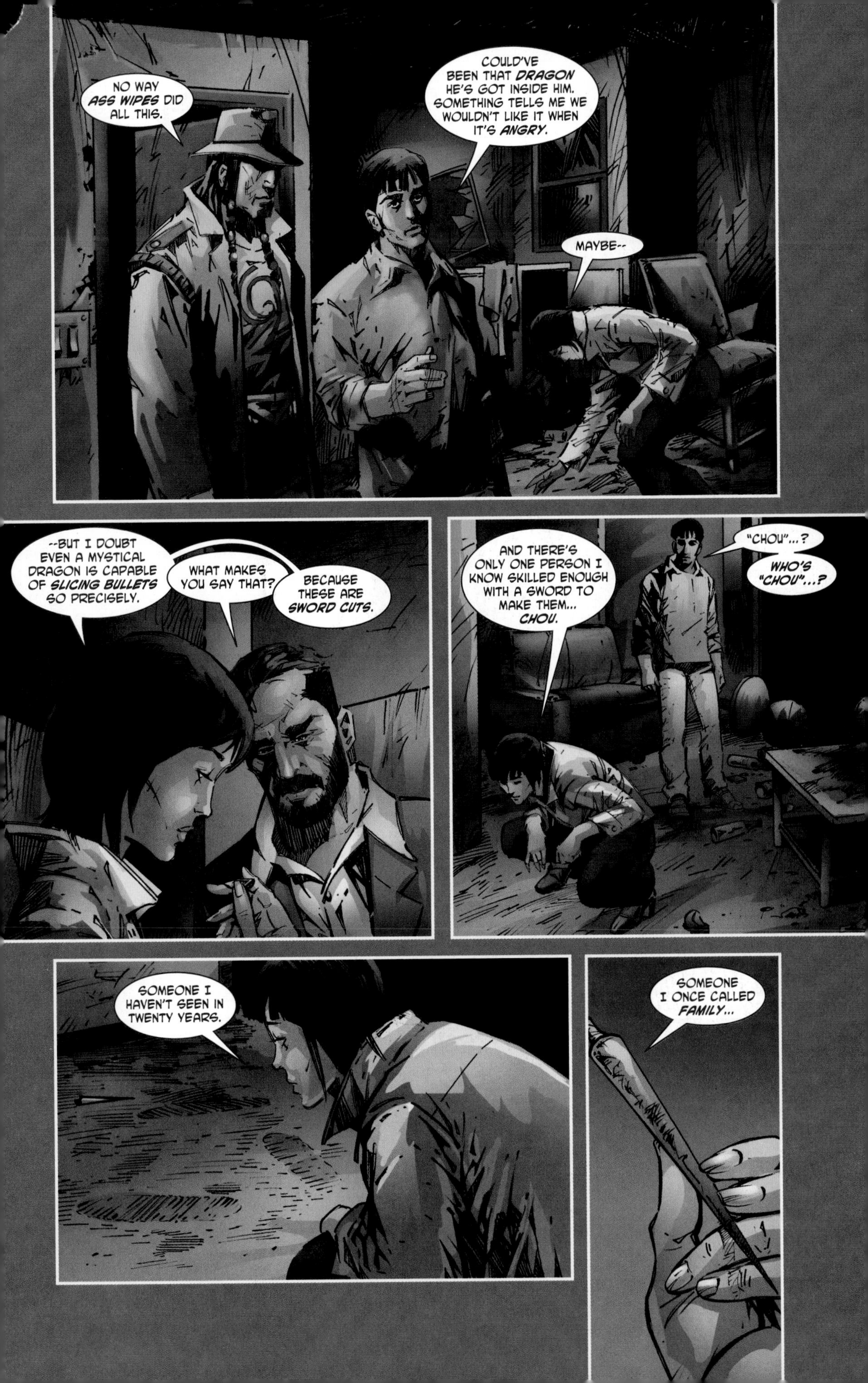
NO WAY *ASS WIPES* DID ALL THIS.
COULD'VE BEEN THAT *DRAGON* HE'S GOT INSIDE HIM. SOMETHING TELLS ME WE WOULDN'T LIKE IT WHEN IT'S *ANGRY*.
MAYBE--
--BUT I DOUBT EVEN A MYSTICAL DRAGON IS CAPABLE OF *SLICING BULLETS* SO PRECISELY.
WHAT MAKES YOU SAY THAT?
BECAUSE THESE ARE *SWORD CUTS*.
AND THERE'S ONLY ONE PERSON I KNOW SKILLED ENOUGH WITH A SWORD TO MAKE THEM... *CHOU*.
"CHOU"...?
WHO'S "CHOU"...?
SOMEONE I HAVEN'T SEEN IN TWENTY YEARS.
SOMEONE I ONCE CALLED *FAMILY*...

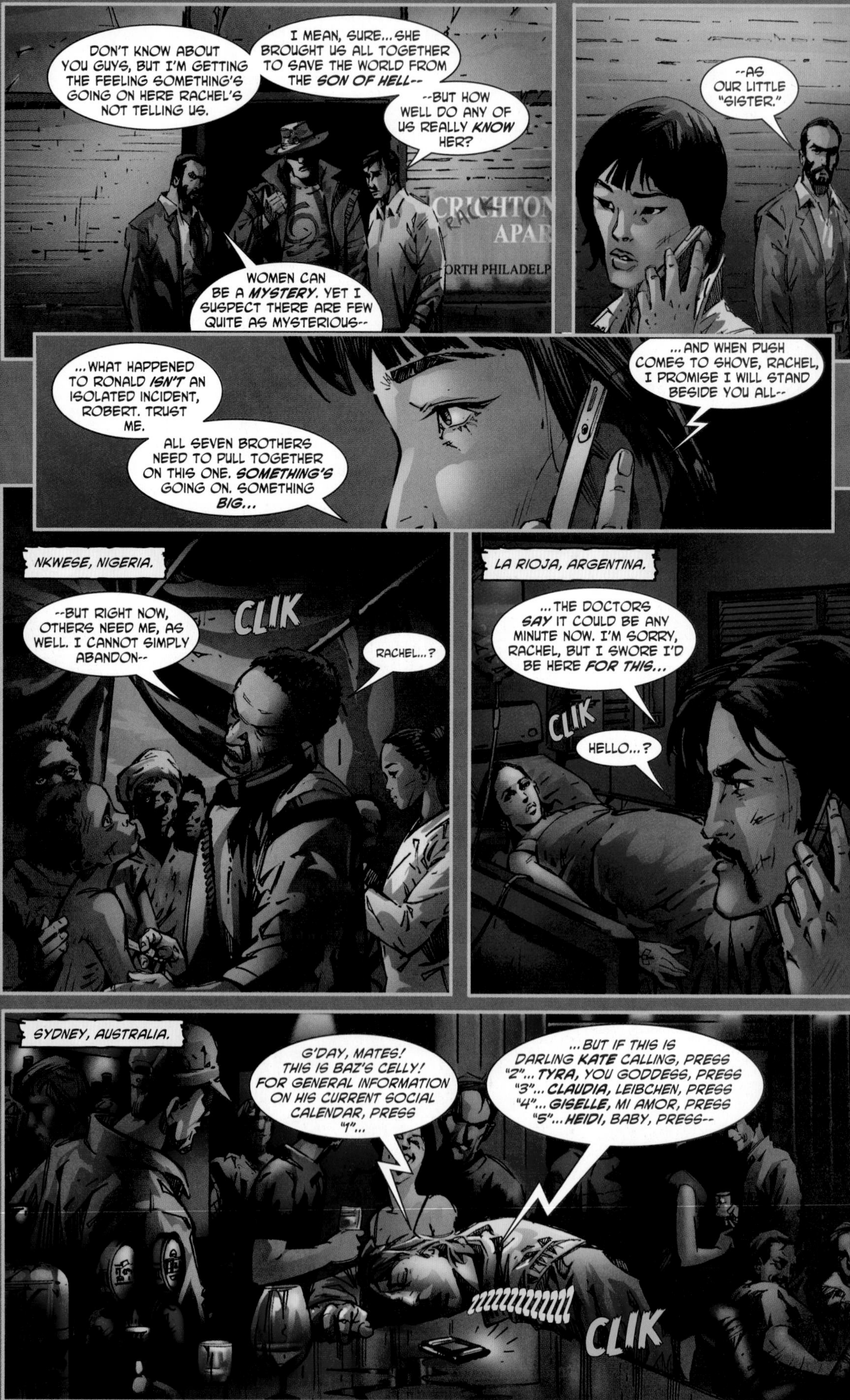
DON'T KNOW ABOUT YOU GUYS, BUT I'M GETTING THE FEELING SOMETHING'S GOING ON HERE RACHEL'S NOT TELLING US.
I MEAN, SURE... SHE BROUGHT US ALL TOGETHER TO SAVE THE WORLD FROM THE SON OF HELL--
--BUT HOW WELL DO ANY OF US REALLY KNOW HER?
CRICHTON APAR
ORTH PHILADELP
WOMEN CAN BE A MYSTERY. YET I SUSPECT THERE ARE FEW QUITE AS MYSTERIOUS--
--AS OUR LITTLE "SISTER."
...WHAT HAPPENED TO RONALD ISN'T AN ISOLATED INCIDENT, ROBERT. TRUST ME.
ALL SEVEN BROTHERS NEED TO PULL TOGETHER ON THIS ONE. SOMETHING'S GOING ON. SOMETHING BIG...
...AND WHEN PUSH COMES TO SHOVE, RACHEL, I PROMISE I WILL STAND BESIDE YOU ALL--
NKWESE, NIGERIA.
--BUT RIGHT NOW, OTHERS NEED ME, AS WELL. I CANNOT SIMPLY ABANDON--
CLIK
RACHEL...?
LA RIOJA, ARGENTINA.
...THE DOCTORS SAY IT COULD BE ANY MINUTE NOW. I'M SORRY, RACHEL, BUT I SWORE I'D BE HERE FOR THIS...
CLIK
HELLO...?
SYDNEY, AUSTRALIA.
G'DAY, MATES! THIS IS BAZ'S CELLY! FOR GENERAL INFORMATION ON HIS CURRENT SOCIAL CALENDAR, PRESS "1"...
...BUT IF THIS IS DARLING KATE CALLING, PRESS "2"... TYRA, YOU GODDESS, PRESS "3"... CLAUDIA, LEIBCHEN, PRESS "4"... GISELLE, MI AMOR, PRESS "5"... HEIDI, BABY, PRESS--
ZZZZZZZZZZZZZ
CLIK

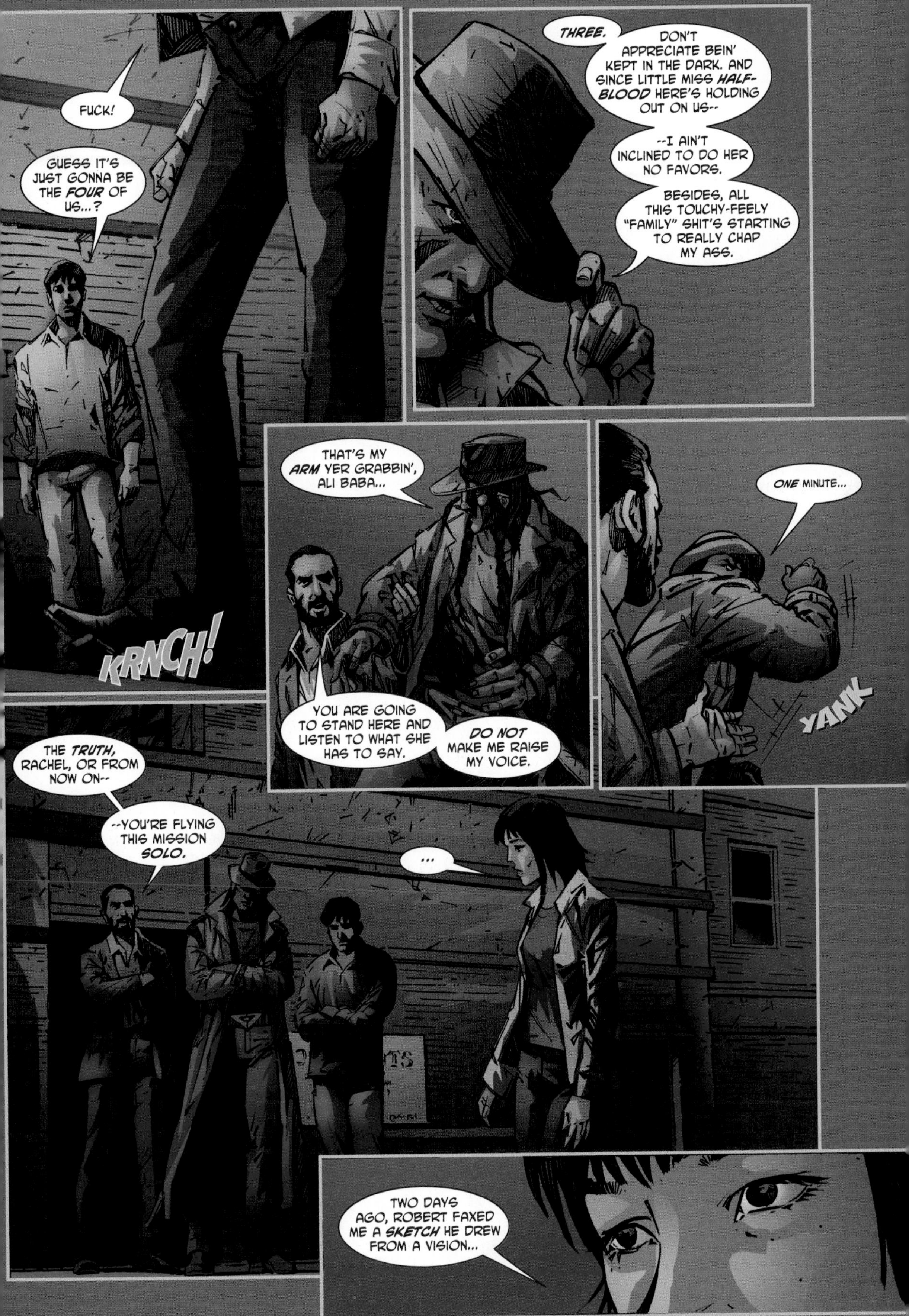
FUCK!
GUESS IT'S JUST GONNA BE THE FOUR OF US...?
KRNCH!
THREE.
DON'T APPRECIATE BEIN' KEPT IN THE DARK. AND SINCE LITTLE MISS HALF-BLOOD HERE'S HOLDING OUT ON US--
--I AIN'T INCLINED TO DO HER NO FAVORS.
BESIDES, ALL THIS TOUCHY-FEELY "FAMILY" SHIT'S STARTING TO REALLY CHAP MY ASS.
THAT'S MY ARM YER GRABBIN', ALI BABA...
YOU ARE GOING TO STAND HERE AND LISTEN TO WHAT SHE HAS TO SAY.
DO NOT MAKE ME RAISE MY VOICE.
ONE MINUTE...
YANK
THE TRUTH, RACHEL, OR FROM NOW ON--
--YOU'RE FLYING THIS MISSION SOLO.
...
TWO DAYS AGO, ROBERT FAXED ME A SKETCH HE DREW FROM A VISION...

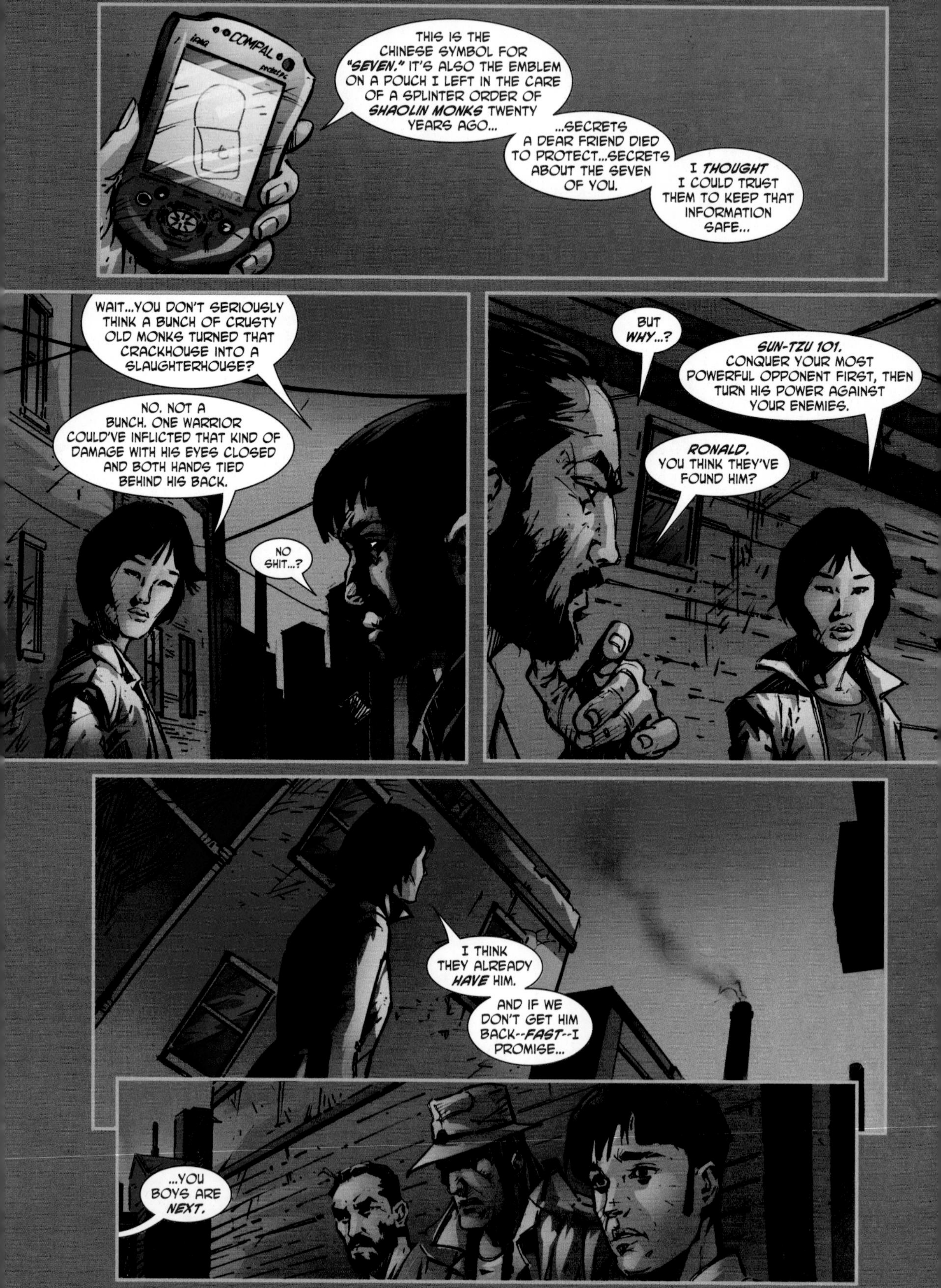
THIS IS THE CHINESE SYMBOL FOR "SEVEN." IT'S ALSO THE EMBLEM ON A POUCH I LEFT IN THE CARE OF A SPLINTER ORDER OF SHAOLIN MONKS TWENTY YEARS AGO...
...SECRETS A DEAR FRIEND DIED TO PROTECT...SECRETS ABOUT THE SEVEN OF YOU.
I THOUGHT I COULD TRUST THEM TO KEEP THAT INFORMATION SAFE...
WAIT...YOU DON'T SERIOUSLY THINK A BUNCH OF CRUSTY OLD MONKS TURNED THAT CRACKHOUSE INTO A SLAUGHTERHOUSE?
NO. NOT A BUNCH. ONE WARRIOR COULD'VE INFLICTED THAT KIND OF DAMAGE WITH HIS EYES CLOSED AND BOTH HANDS TIED BEHIND HIS BACK.
NO SHIT...?
BUT WHY...?
SUN-TZU 101. CONQUER YOUR MOST POWERFUL OPPONENT FIRST, THEN TURN HIS POWER AGAINST YOUR ENEMIES.
RONALD. YOU THINK THEY'VE FOUND HIM?
I THINK THEY ALREADY HAVE HIM.
AND IF WE DON'T GET HIM BACK--FAST--I PROMISE...
...YOU BOYS ARE NEXT.

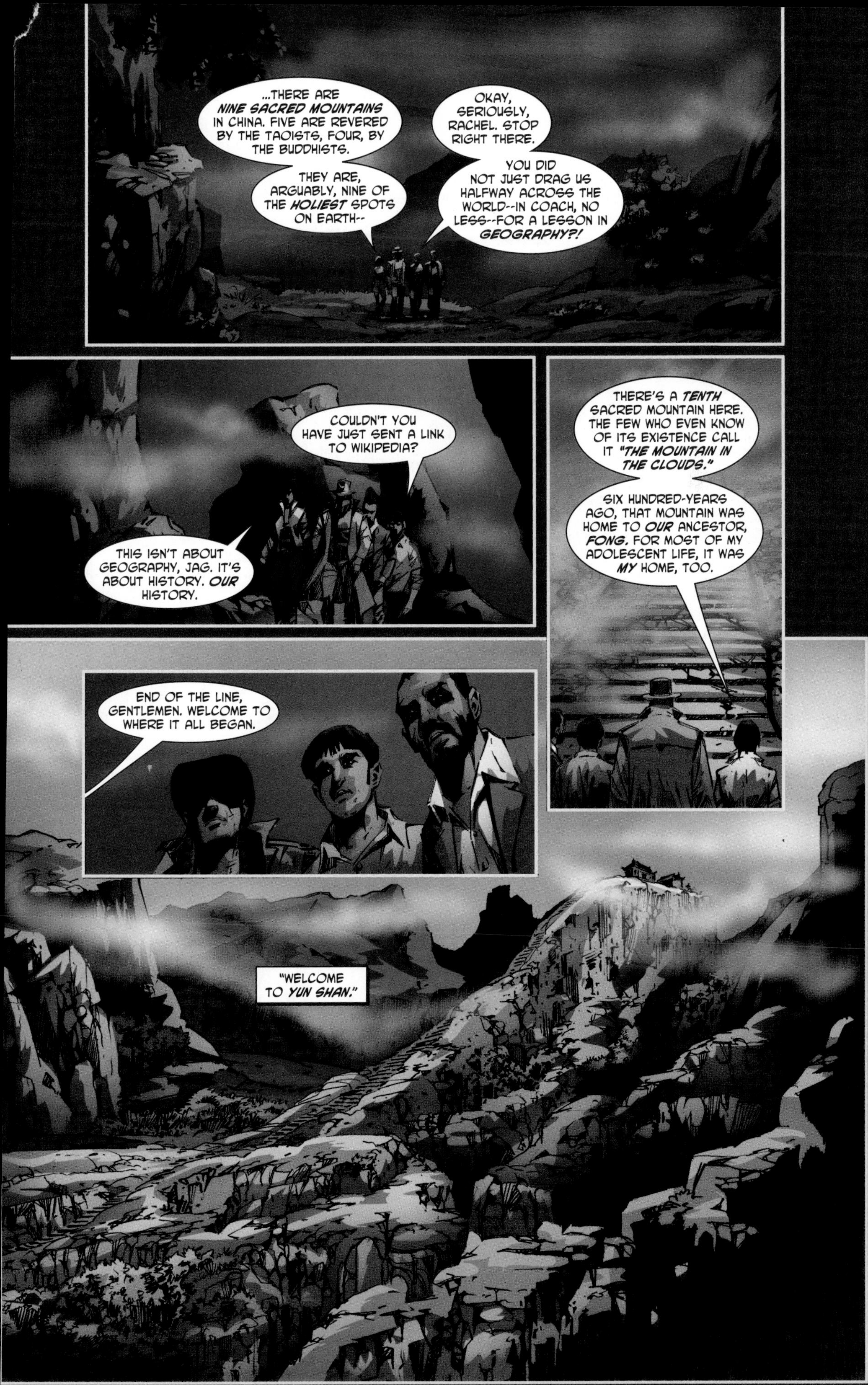
...THERE ARE NINE SACRED MOUNTAINS IN CHINA. FIVE ARE REVERED BY THE TAOISTS, FOUR, BY THE BUDDHISTS.
THEY ARE, ARGUABLY, NINE OF THE HOLIEST SPOTS ON EARTH--
OKAY, SERIOUSLY, RACHEL. STOP RIGHT THERE.
YOU DID NOT JUST DRAG US HALFWAY ACROSS THE WORLD--IN COACH, NO LESS--FOR A LESSON IN GEOGRAPHY?!
COULDN'T YOU HAVE JUST SENT A LINK TO WIKIPEDIA?
THIS ISN'T ABOUT GEOGRAPHY, JAG. IT'S ABOUT HISTORY. OUR HISTORY.
THERE'S A TENTH SACRED MOUNTAIN HERE. THE FEW WHO EVEN KNOW OF ITS EXISTENCE CALL IT "THE MOUNTAIN IN THE CLOUDS."
SIX HUNDRED-YEARS AGO, THAT MOUNTAIN WAS HOME TO OUR ANCESTOR, FONG. FOR MOST OF MY ADOLESCENT LIFE, IT WAS MY HOME, TOO.
END OF THE LINE, GENTLEMEN. WELCOME TO WHERE IT ALL BEGAN.
"WELCOME TO YUN SHAN."

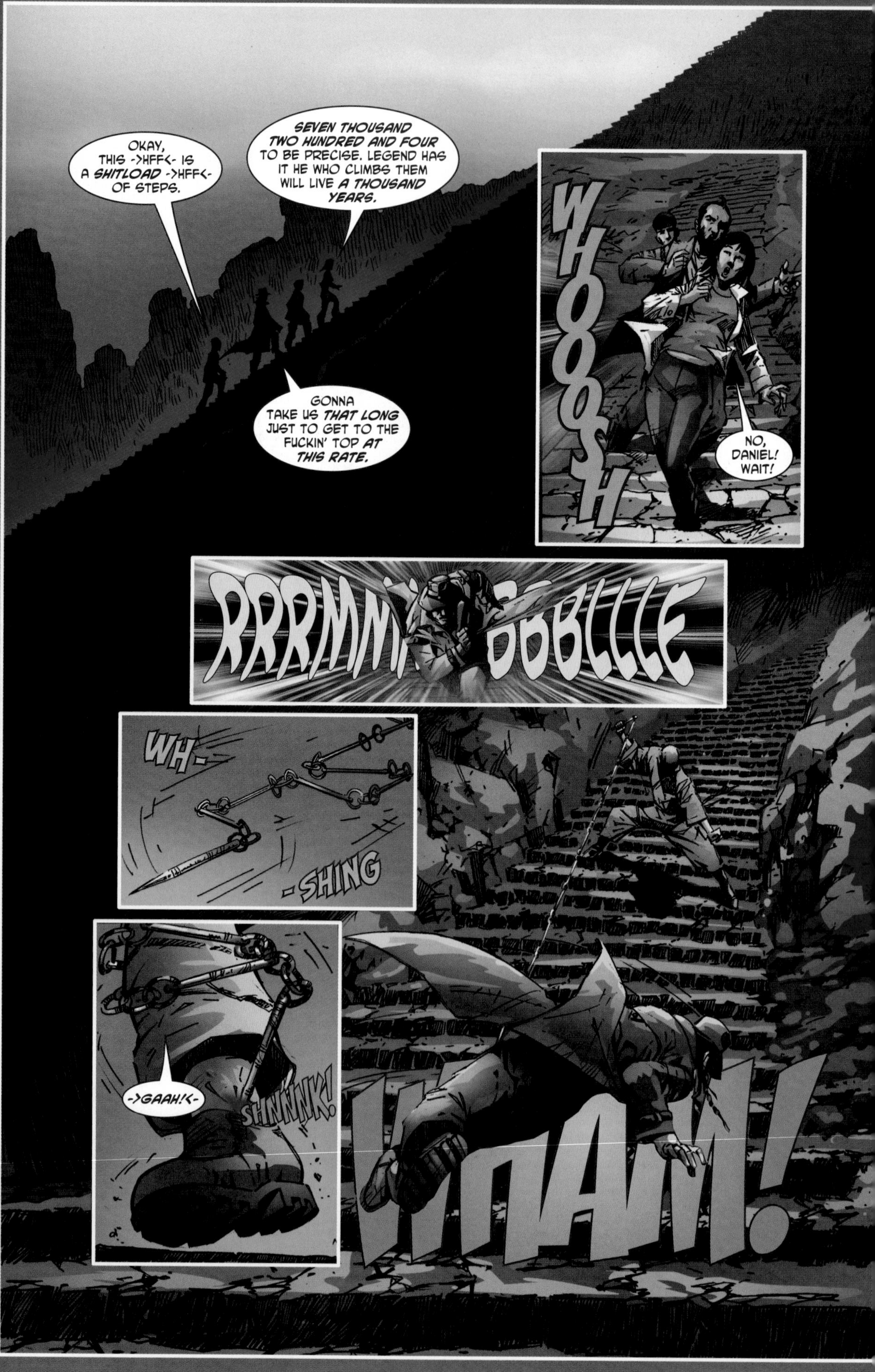
OKAY, THIS ->HFF<- IS A SHITLOAD ->HFF<- OF STEPS.
SEVEN THOUSAND TWO HUNDRED AND FOUR TO BE PRECISE. LEGEND HAS IT HE WHO CLIMBS THEM WILL LIVE A THOUSAND YEARS.
GONNA TAKE US THAT LONG JUST TO GET TO THE FUCKIN' TOP AT THIS RATE.
WHOOOSH
NO, DANIEL! WAIT!
RRRMN DDBLLLE
WH-
-SHING
->GAAH!<-
SHNNNK!
WHAM!

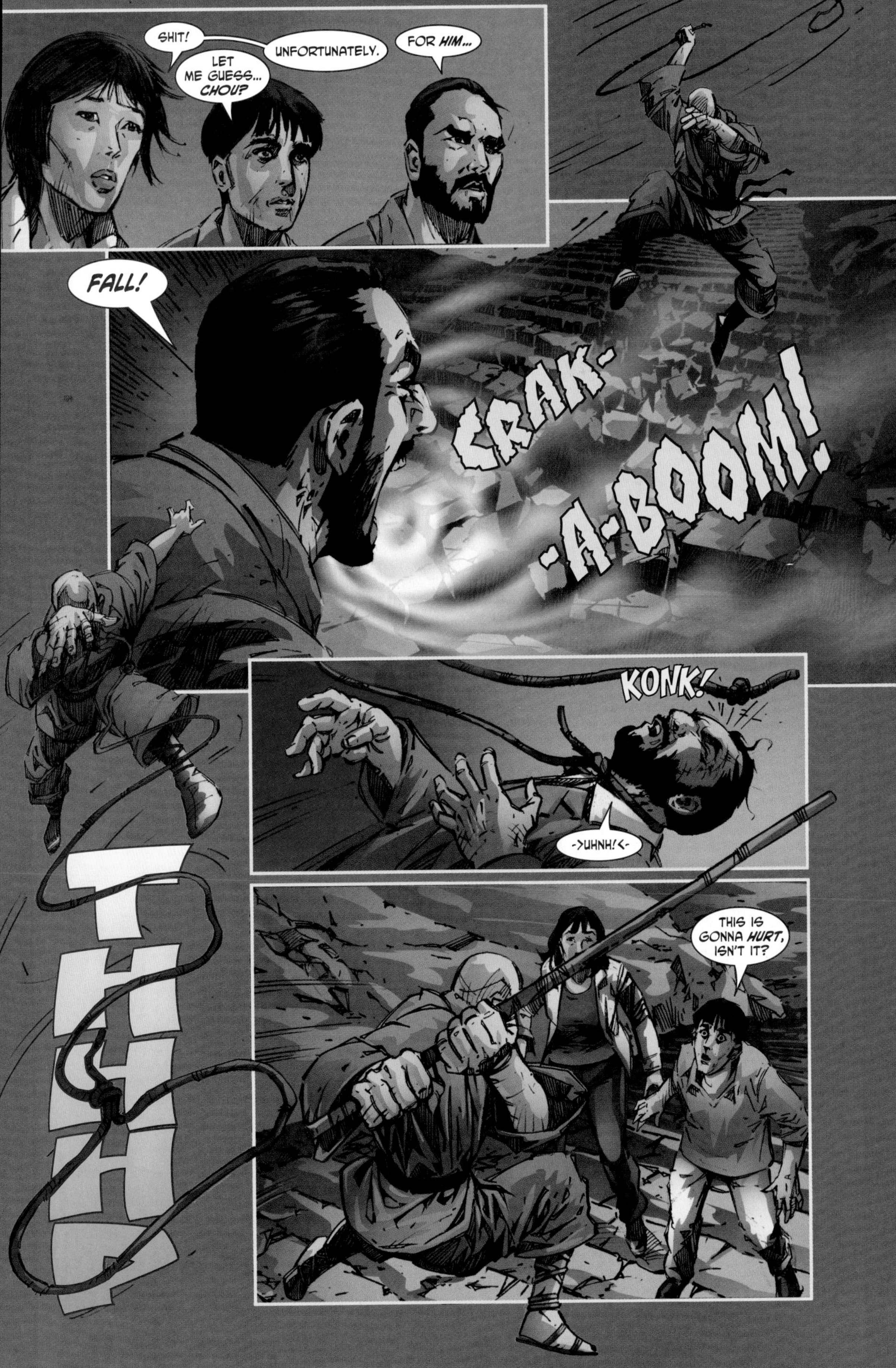
SHIT!
LET ME GUESS... CHOU?
UNFORTUNATELY.
FOR HIM...
FALL!
CRAK-
-A-BOOM!
KONK!
->UHNH!<-
THIS IS GONNA HURT, ISN'T IT?

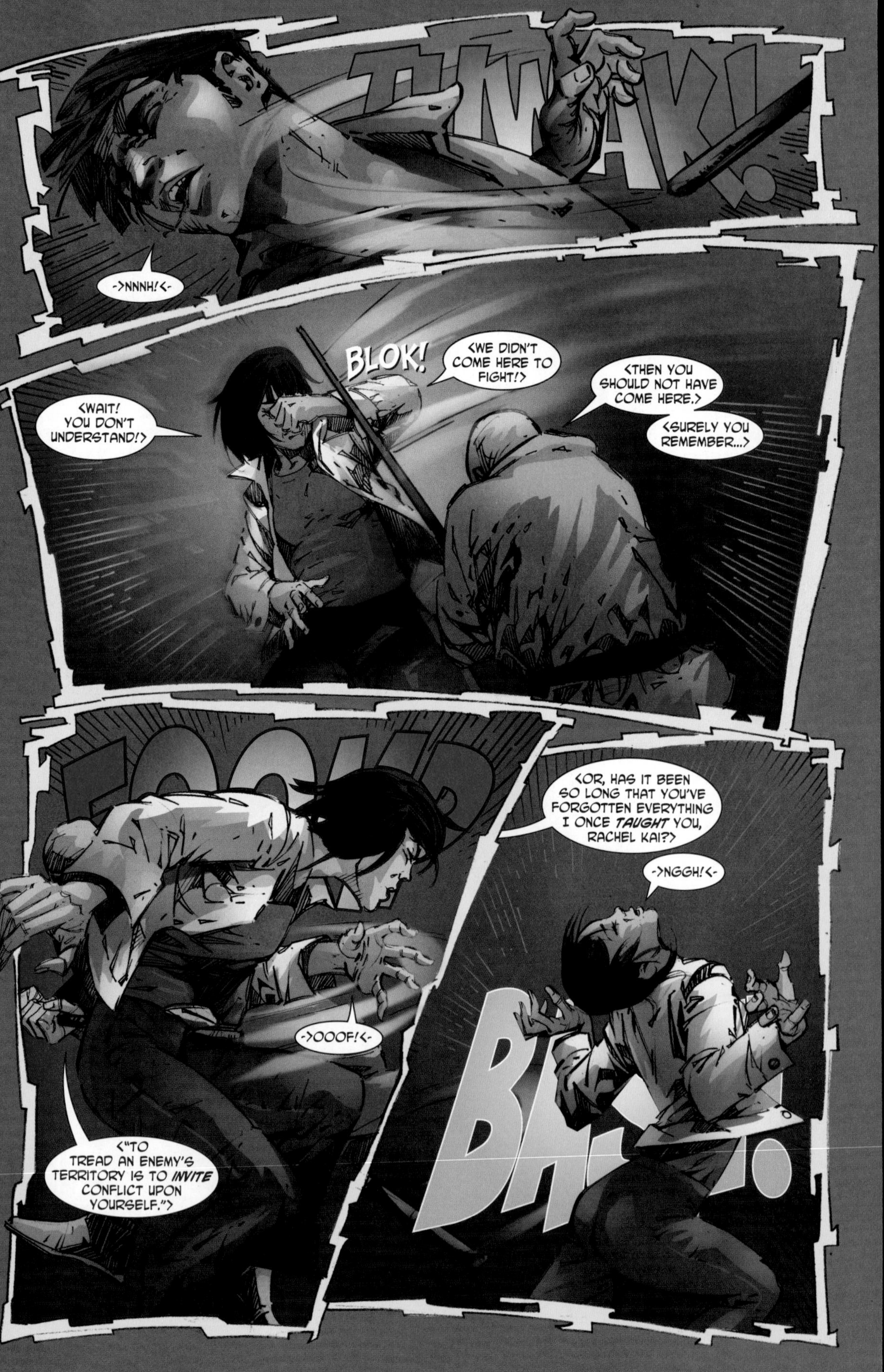
THWAK!
->NNNH!<-
BLOK!
<WE DIDN'T COME HERE TO FIGHT!>
<WAIT! YOU DON'T UNDERSTAND!>
<THEN YOU SHOULD NOT HAVE COME HERE.>
<SURELY YOU REMEMBER...>
->OOOF!<-
<"TO TREAD AN ENEMY'S TERRITORY IS TO *INVITE* CONFLICT UPON YOURSELF.">
<OR, HAS IT BEEN SO LONG THAT YOU'VE FORGOTTEN EVERYTHING I ONCE *TAUGHT* YOU, RACHEL KAI?>
->NGGH!<-

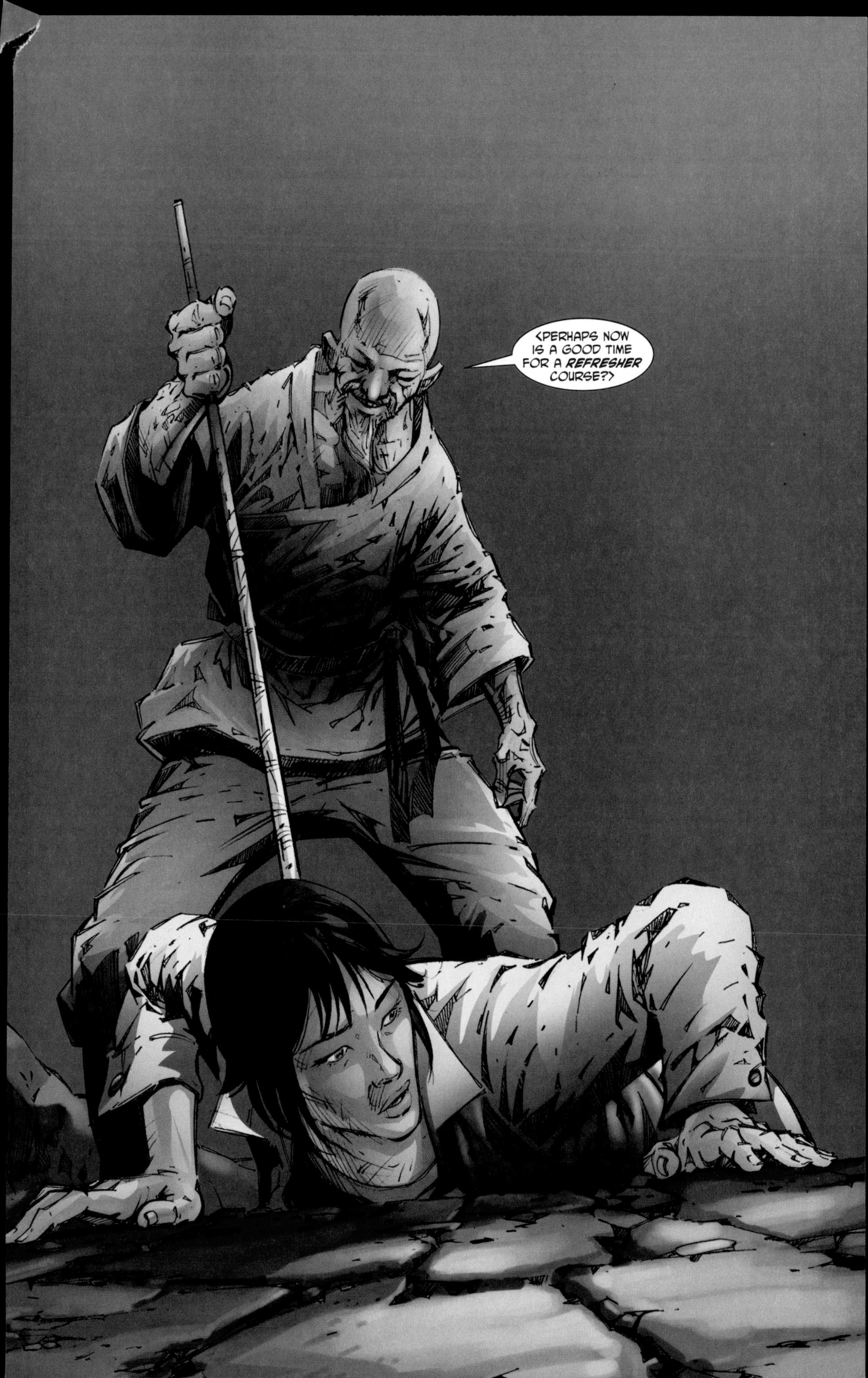
<PERHAPS NOW IS A GOOD TIME FOR A *REFRESHER* COURSE?>

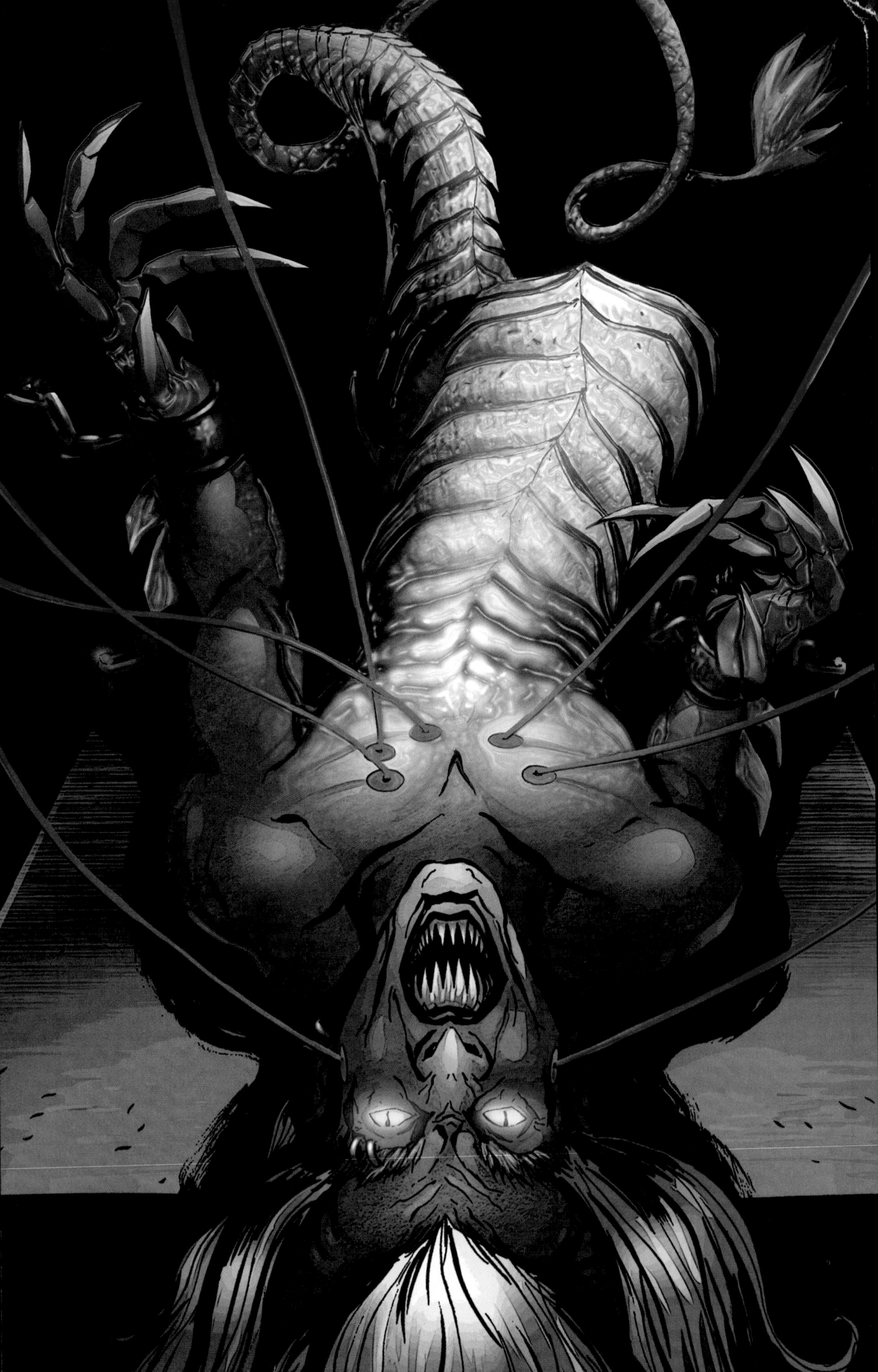

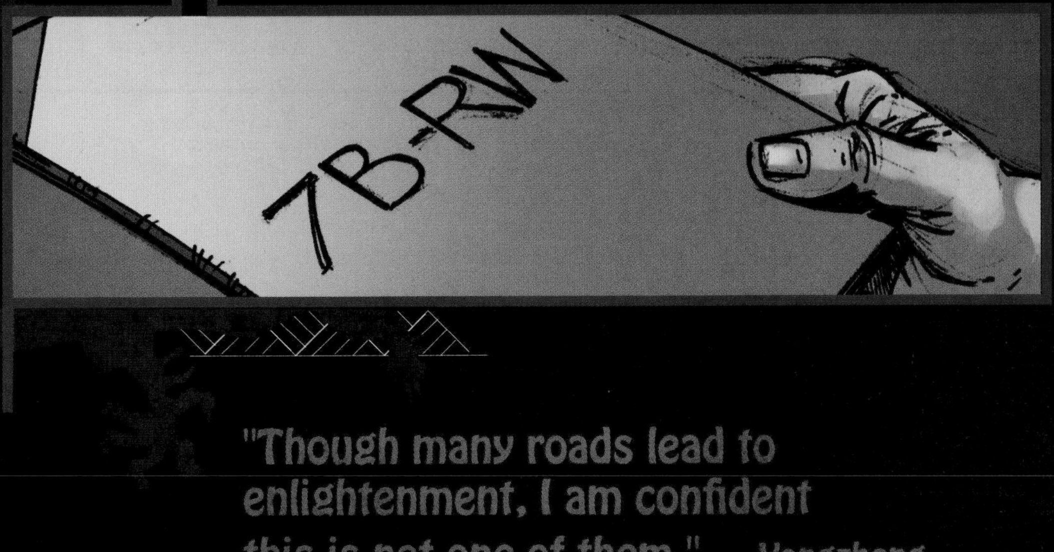
7B-RW

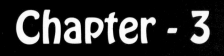

"Though many roads lead to enlightenment, I am confident this is not one of them." — Yongzheng

Chapter - 3

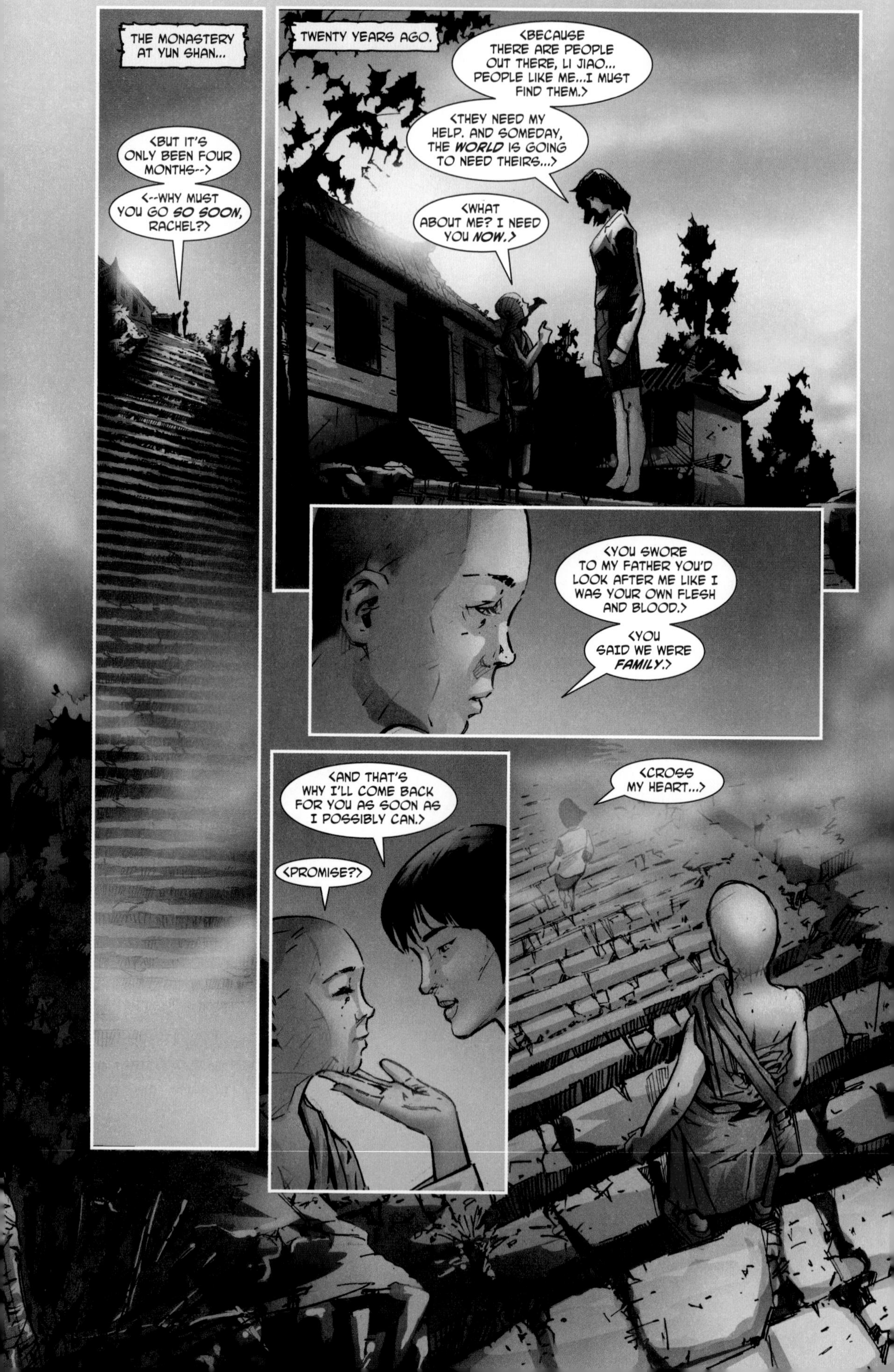
THE MONASTERY AT YUN SHAN...
<BUT IT'S ONLY BEEN FOUR MONTHS-->
<--WHY MUST YOU GO SO SOON, RACHEL?>
TWENTY YEARS AGO.
<BECAUSE THERE ARE PEOPLE OUT THERE, LI JIAO... PEOPLE LIKE ME...I MUST FIND THEM.>
<THEY NEED MY HELP. AND SOMEDAY, THE WORLD IS GOING TO NEED THEIRS...>
<WHAT ABOUT ME? I NEED YOU NOW.>
<YOU SWORE TO MY FATHER YOU'D LOOK AFTER ME LIKE I WAS YOUR OWN FLESH AND BLOOD.>
<YOU SAID WE WERE FAMILY.>
<AND THAT'S WHY I'LL COME BACK FOR YOU AS SOON AS I POSSIBLY CAN.>
<PROMISE?>
<CROSS MY HEART...>

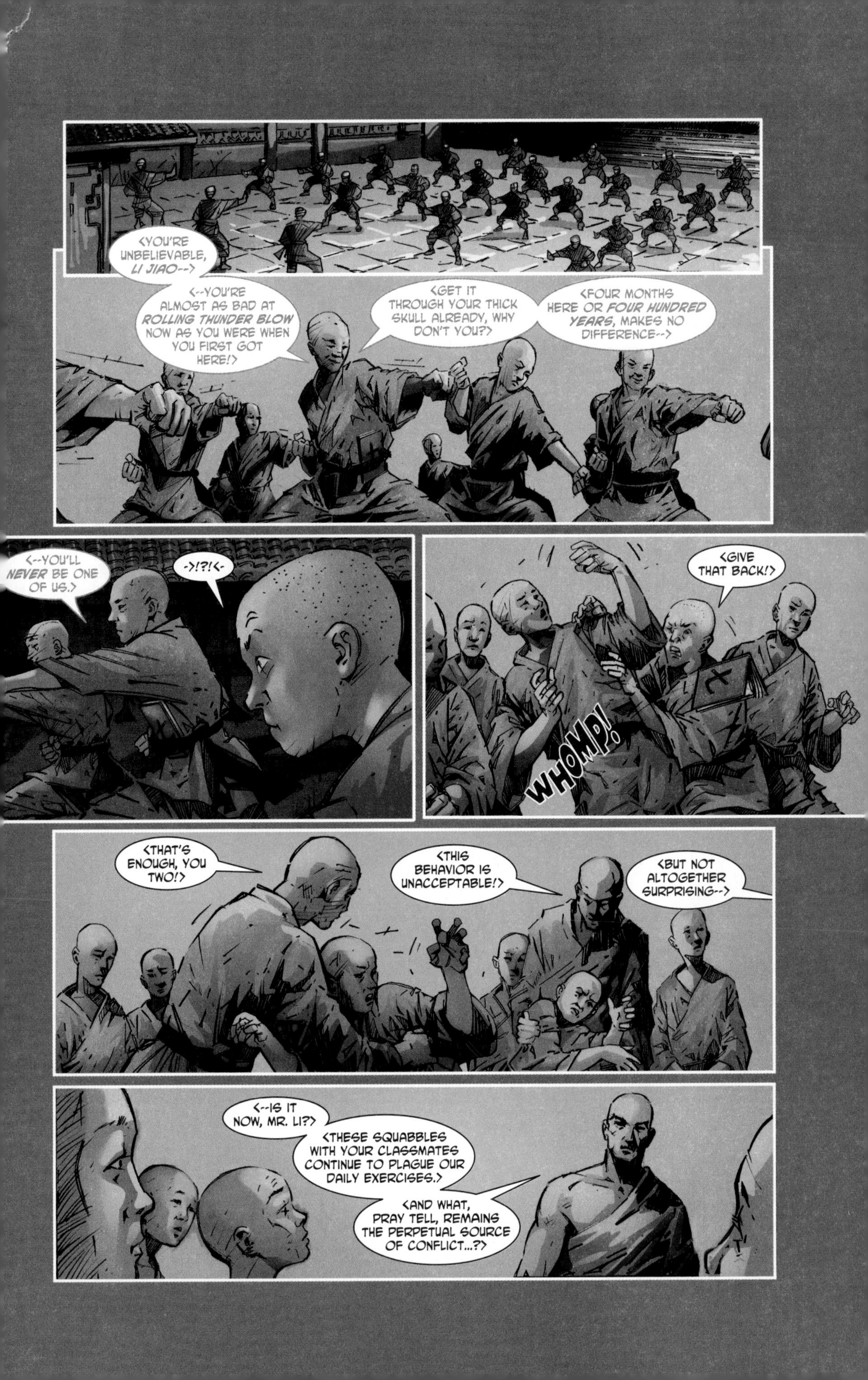
<YOU'RE UNBELIEVABLE, *LI JIAO*-->
<--YOU'RE ALMOST AS BAD AT *ROLLING THUNDER BLOW* NOW AS YOU WERE WHEN YOU FIRST GOT HERE!>
<GET IT THROUGH YOUR THICK SKULL ALREADY, WHY DON'T YOU?>
<FOUR MONTHS HERE OR *FOUR HUNDRED YEARS*, MAKES NO DIFFERENCE-->
<--YOU'LL *NEVER* BE ONE OF US.>
->!?!<-
<GIVE THAT BACK!>
WHOMP!
<THAT'S ENOUGH, YOU TWO!>
<THIS BEHAVIOR IS UNACCEPTABLE!>
<BUT NOT ALTOGETHER SURPRISING-->
<--IS IT NOW, MR. LI?>
<THESE SQUABBLES WITH YOUR CLASSMATES CONTINUE TO PLAGUE OUR DAILY EXERCISES.>
<AND WHAT, PRAY TELL, REMAINS THE PERPETUAL SOURCE OF CONFLICT...?>

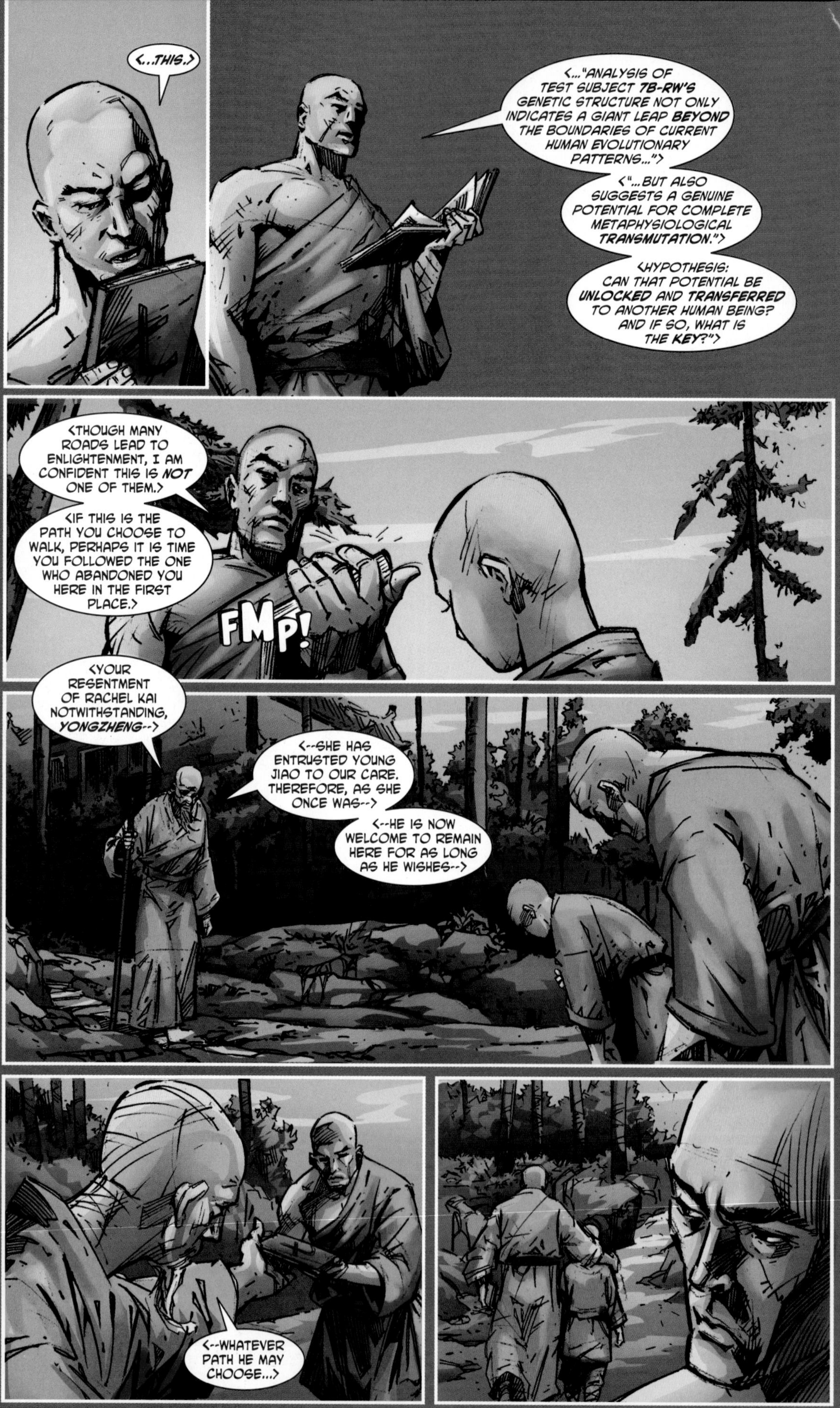

<...THIS.>
<..."ANALYSIS OF TEST SUBJECT 7B-RW'S GENETIC STRUCTURE NOT ONLY INDICATES A GIANT LEAP BEYOND THE BOUNDARIES OF CURRENT HUMAN EVOLUTIONARY PATTERNS...">
<"...BUT ALSO SUGGESTS A GENUINE POTENTIAL FOR COMPLETE METAPHYSIOLOGICAL TRANSMUTATION.">
<HYPOTHESIS: CAN THAT POTENTIAL BE UNLOCKED AND TRANSFERRED TO ANOTHER HUMAN BEING? AND IF SO, WHAT IS THE KEY?">
<THOUGH MANY ROADS LEAD TO ENLIGHTENMENT, I AM CONFIDENT THIS IS NOT ONE OF THEM.>
<IF THIS IS THE PATH YOU CHOOSE TO WALK, PERHAPS IT IS TIME YOU FOLLOWED THE ONE WHO ABANDONED YOU HERE IN THE FIRST PLACE.>
FMP!
<YOUR RESENTMENT OF RACHEL KAI NOTWITHSTANDING, YONGZHENG-->
<--SHE HAS ENTRUSTED YOUNG JIAO TO OUR CARE. THEREFORE, AS SHE ONCE WAS-->
<--HE IS NOW WELCOME TO REMAIN HERE FOR AS LONG AS HE WISHES-->
<--WHATEVER PATH HE MAY CHOOSE...>

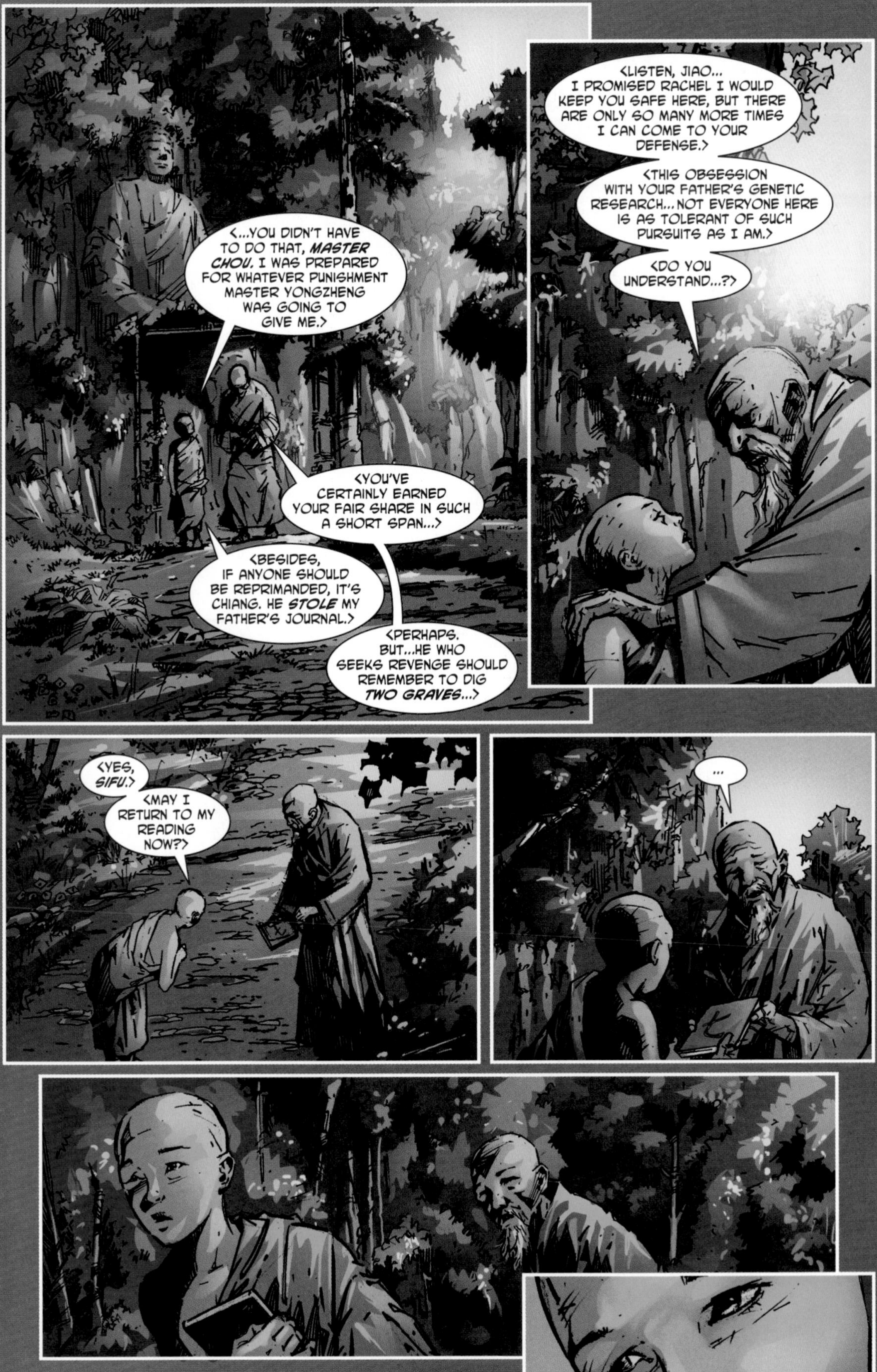
<...YOU DIDN'T HAVE TO DO THAT, MASTER CHOU. I WAS PREPARED FOR WHATEVER PUNISHMENT MASTER YONGZHENG WAS GOING TO GIVE ME.>
<YOU'VE CERTAINLY EARNED YOUR FAIR SHARE IN SUCH A SHORT SPAN...>
<BESIDES, IF ANYONE SHOULD BE REPRIMANDED, IT'S CHIANG. HE STOLE MY FATHER'S JOURNAL.>
<PERHAPS. BUT...HE WHO SEEKS REVENGE SHOULD REMEMBER TO DIG TWO GRAVES...>
<LISTEN, JIAO... I PROMISED RACHEL I WOULD KEEP YOU SAFE HERE, BUT THERE ARE ONLY SO MANY MORE TIMES I CAN COME TO YOUR DEFENSE.>
<THIS OBSESSION WITH YOUR FATHER'S GENETIC RESEARCH...NOT EVERYONE HERE IS AS TOLERANT OF SUCH PURSUITS AS I AM.>
<DO YOU UNDERSTAND...?>
<YES, SIFU.>
<MAY I RETURN TO MY READING NOW?>
...

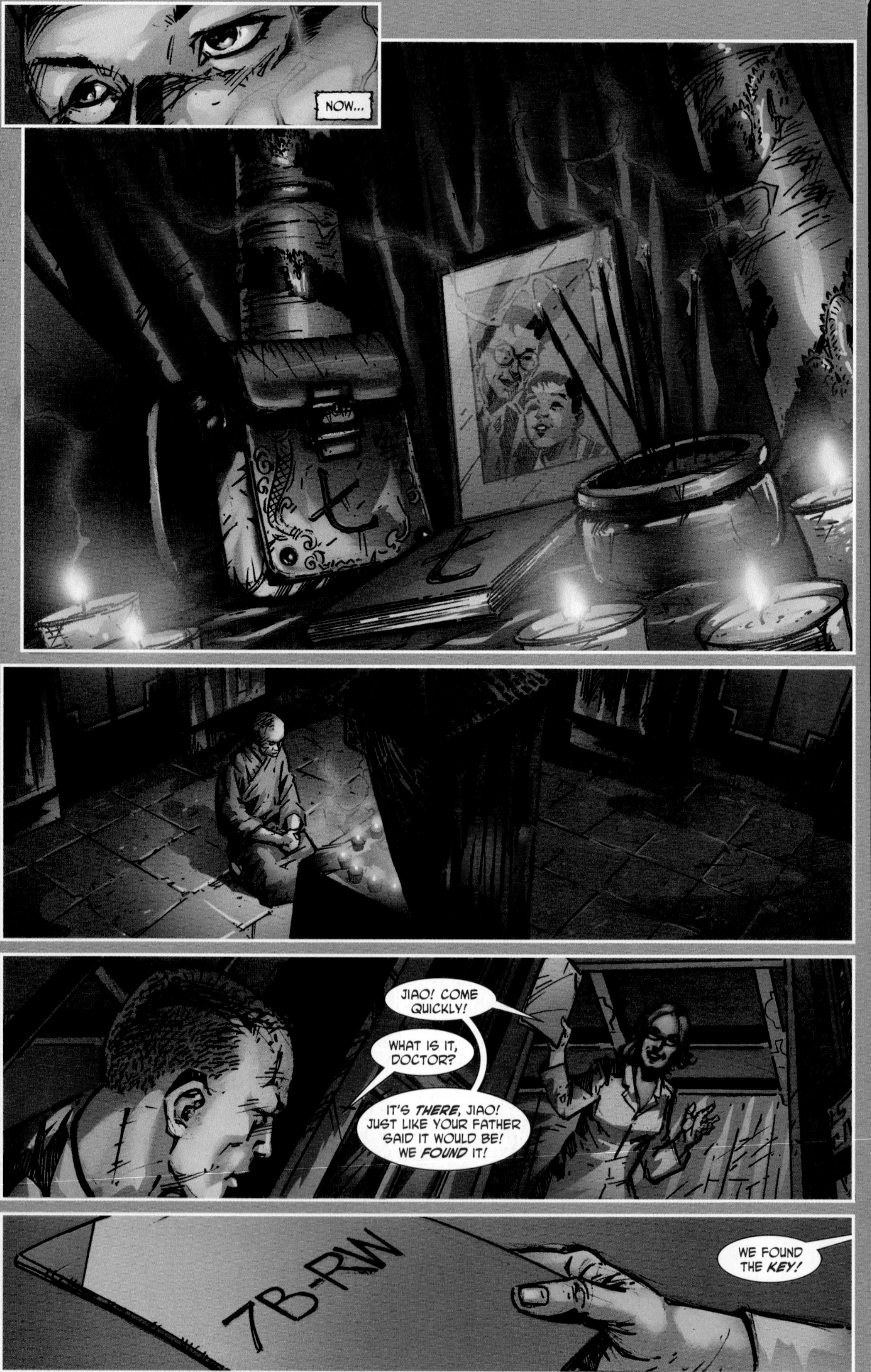
NOW...
JIAO! COME QUICKLY!
WHAT IS IT, DOCTOR?
IT'S **THERE**, JIAO! JUST LIKE YOUR FATHER SAID IT WOULD BE! WE **FOUND** IT!
7B-RW
WE FOUND THE **KEY!**

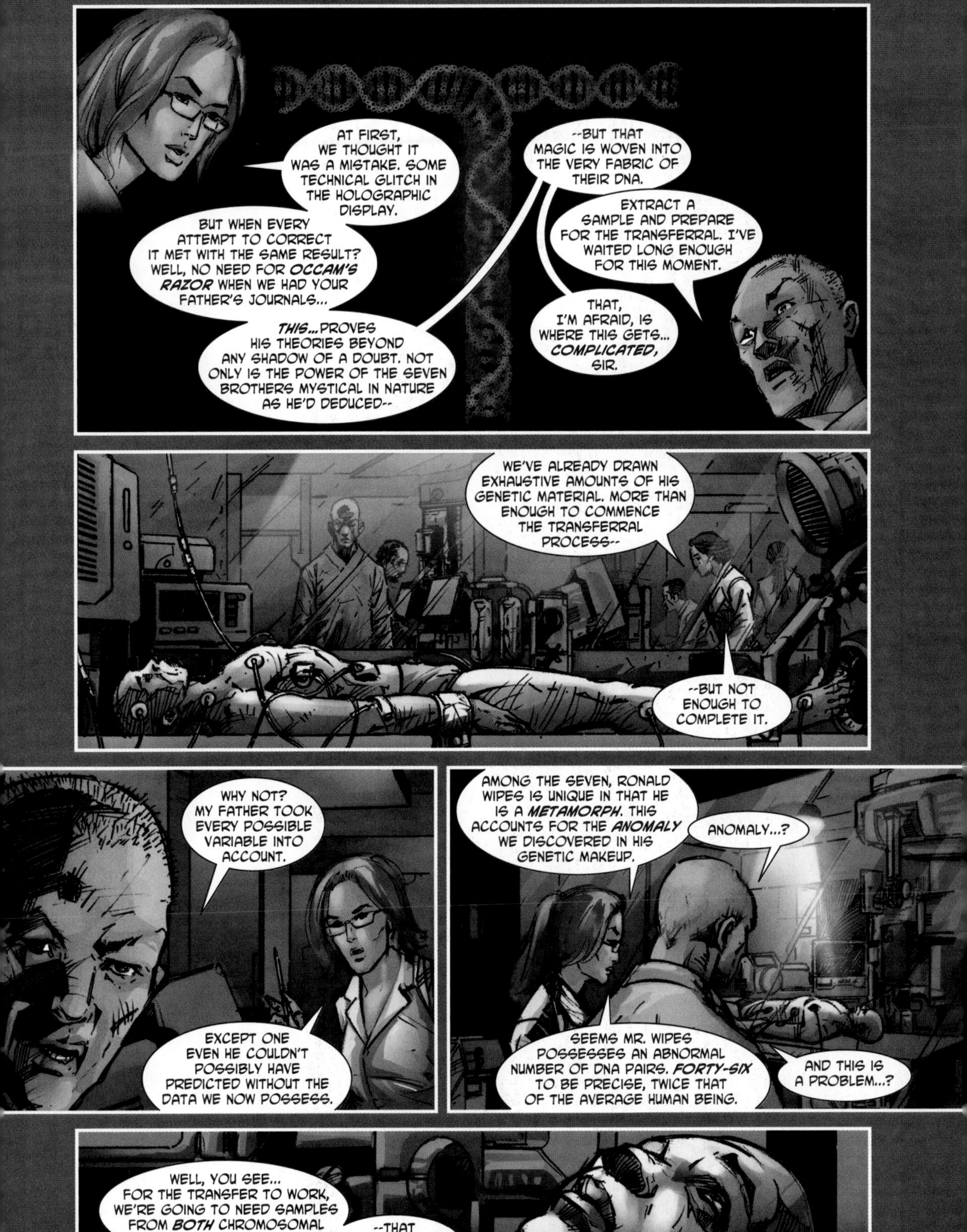
AT FIRST, WE THOUGHT IT WAS A MISTAKE. SOME TECHNICAL GLITCH IN THE HOLOGRAPHIC DISPLAY.
BUT WHEN EVERY ATTEMPT TO CORRECT IT MET WITH THE SAME RESULT? WELL, NO NEED FOR OCCAM'S RAZOR WHEN WE HAD YOUR FATHER'S JOURNALS...
THIS... PROVES HIS THEORIES BEYOND ANY SHADOW OF A DOUBT. NOT ONLY IS THE POWER OF THE SEVEN BROTHERS MYSTICAL IN NATURE AS HE'D DEDUCED--
--BUT THAT MAGIC IS WOVEN INTO THE VERY FABRIC OF THEIR DNA.
EXTRACT A SAMPLE AND PREPARE FOR THE TRANSFERRAL. I'VE WAITED LONG ENOUGH FOR THIS MOMENT.
THAT, I'M AFRAID, IS WHERE THIS GETS... COMPLICATED, SIR.
WE'VE ALREADY DRAWN EXHAUSTIVE AMOUNTS OF HIS GENETIC MATERIAL. MORE THAN ENOUGH TO COMMENCE THE TRANSFERRAL PROCESS--
--BUT NOT ENOUGH TO COMPLETE IT.
WHY NOT? MY FATHER TOOK EVERY POSSIBLE VARIABLE INTO ACCOUNT.
EXCEPT ONE EVEN HE COULDN'T POSSIBLY HAVE PREDICTED WITHOUT THE DATA WE NOW POSSESS.
AMONG THE SEVEN, RONALD WIPES IS UNIQUE IN THAT HE IS A METAMORPH. THIS ACCOUNTS FOR THE ANOMALY WE DISCOVERED IN HIS GENETIC MAKEUP.
ANOMALY...?
SEEMS MR. WIPES POSSESSES AN ABNORMAL NUMBER OF DNA PAIRS. FORTY-SIX TO BE PRECISE, TWICE THAT OF THE AVERAGE HUMAN BEING.
AND THIS IS A PROBLEM...?
WELL, YOU SEE... FOR THE TRANSFER TO WORK, WE'RE GOING TO NEED SAMPLES FROM BOTH CHROMOSOMAL SETS. UNFORTUNATELY--
--THAT EXTRA SET ISN'T HUMAN...

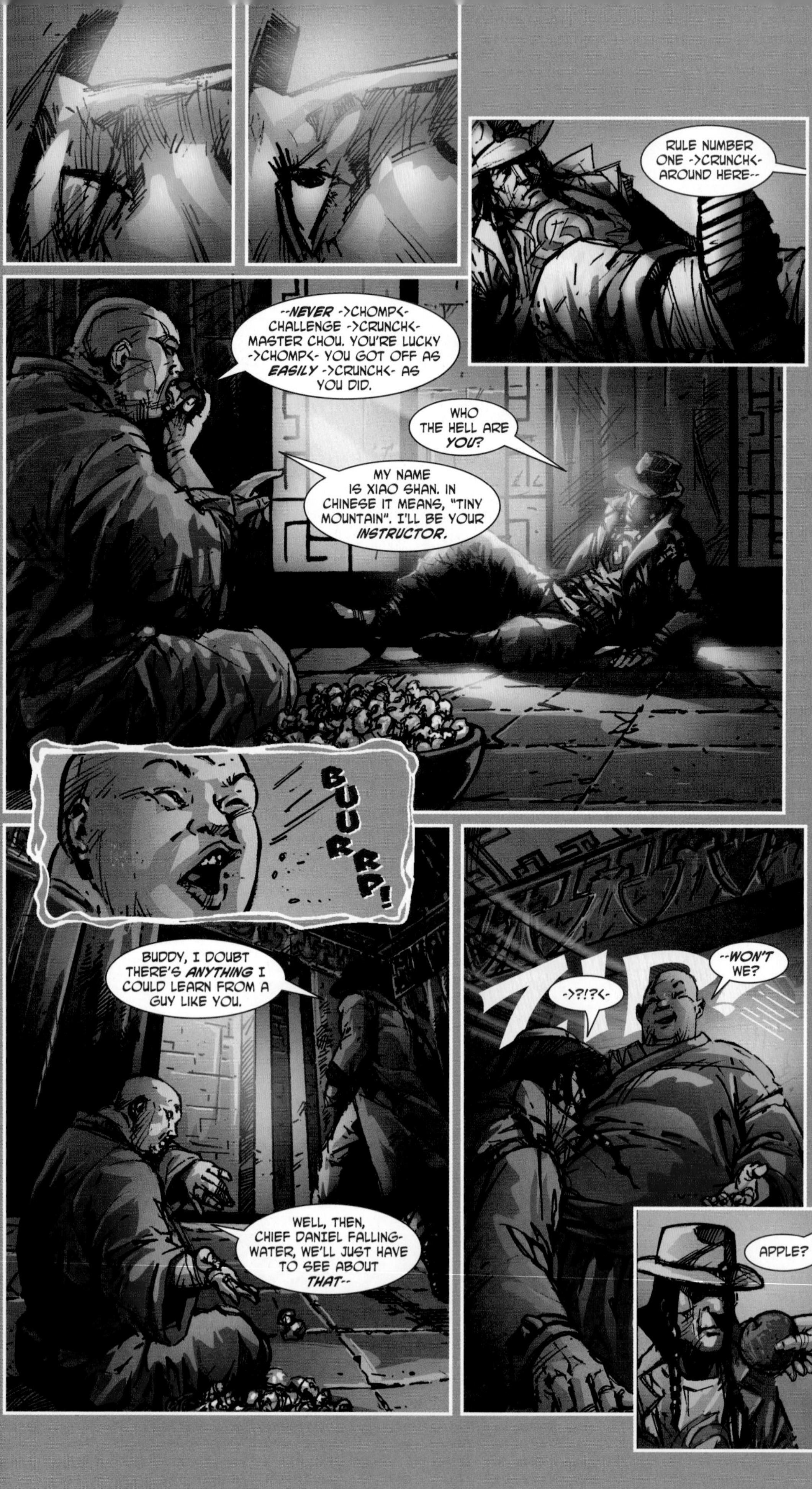
RULE NUMBER ONE ->CRUNCH<- AROUND HERE--
--NEVER ->CHOMP<- CHALLENGE ->CRUNCH<- MASTER CHOU. YOU'RE LUCKY ->CHOMP<- YOU GOT OFF AS EASILY ->CRUNCH<- AS YOU DID.
WHO THE HELL ARE YOU?
MY NAME IS XIAO SHAN. IN CHINESE IT MEANS, "TINY MOUNTAIN". I'LL BE YOUR INSTRUCTOR.
BUURP!
BUDDY, I DOUBT THERE'S ANYTHING I COULD LEARN FROM A GUY LIKE YOU.
WELL, THEN, CHIEF DANIEL FALLING-WATER, WE'LL JUST HAVE TO SEE ABOUT THAT--
ZIP!
->?!?<-
--WON'T WE?
APPLE?

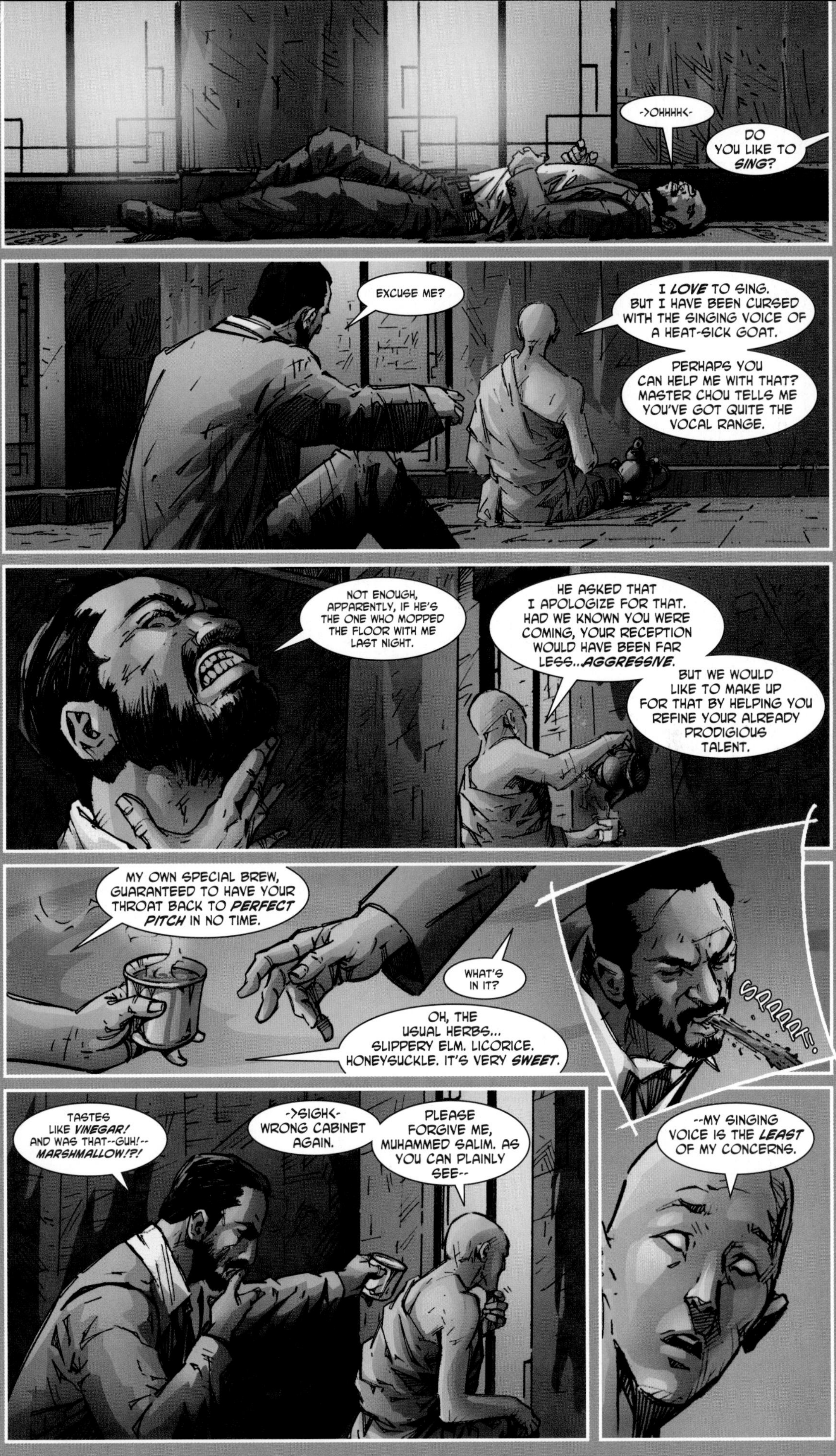

->OHHHH<-
DO YOU LIKE TO *SING?*
EXCUSE ME?
I *LOVE* TO SING. BUT I HAVE BEEN CURSED WITH THE SINGING VOICE OF A HEAT-SICK GOAT.
PERHAPS YOU CAN HELP ME WITH THAT? MASTER CHOU TELLS ME YOU'VE GOT QUITE THE VOCAL RANGE.
NOT ENOUGH, APPARENTLY, IF HE'S THE ONE WHO MOPPED THE FLOOR WITH ME LAST NIGHT.
HE ASKED THAT I APOLOGIZE FOR THAT. HAD WE KNOWN YOU WERE COMING, YOUR RECEPTION WOULD HAVE BEEN FAR LESS...*AGGRESSIVE*.
BUT WE WOULD LIKE TO MAKE UP FOR THAT BY HELPING YOU REFINE YOUR ALREADY PRODIGIOUS TALENT.
MY OWN SPECIAL BREW, GUARANTEED TO HAVE YOUR THROAT BACK TO *PERFECT PITCH* IN NO TIME.
WHAT'S IN IT?
OH, THE USUAL HERBS... SLIPPERY ELM. LICORICE. HONEYSUCKLE. IT'S VERY *SWEET*.
SPPPPT!
TASTES LIKE *VINEGAR!* AND WAS THAT--GUH!--*MARSHMALLOW!?!*
->SIGH<- WRONG CABINET AGAIN.
PLEASE FORGIVE ME, MUHAMMED SALIM. AS YOU CAN PLAINLY SEE--
--MY SINGING VOICE IS THE *LEAST* OF MY CONCERNS.

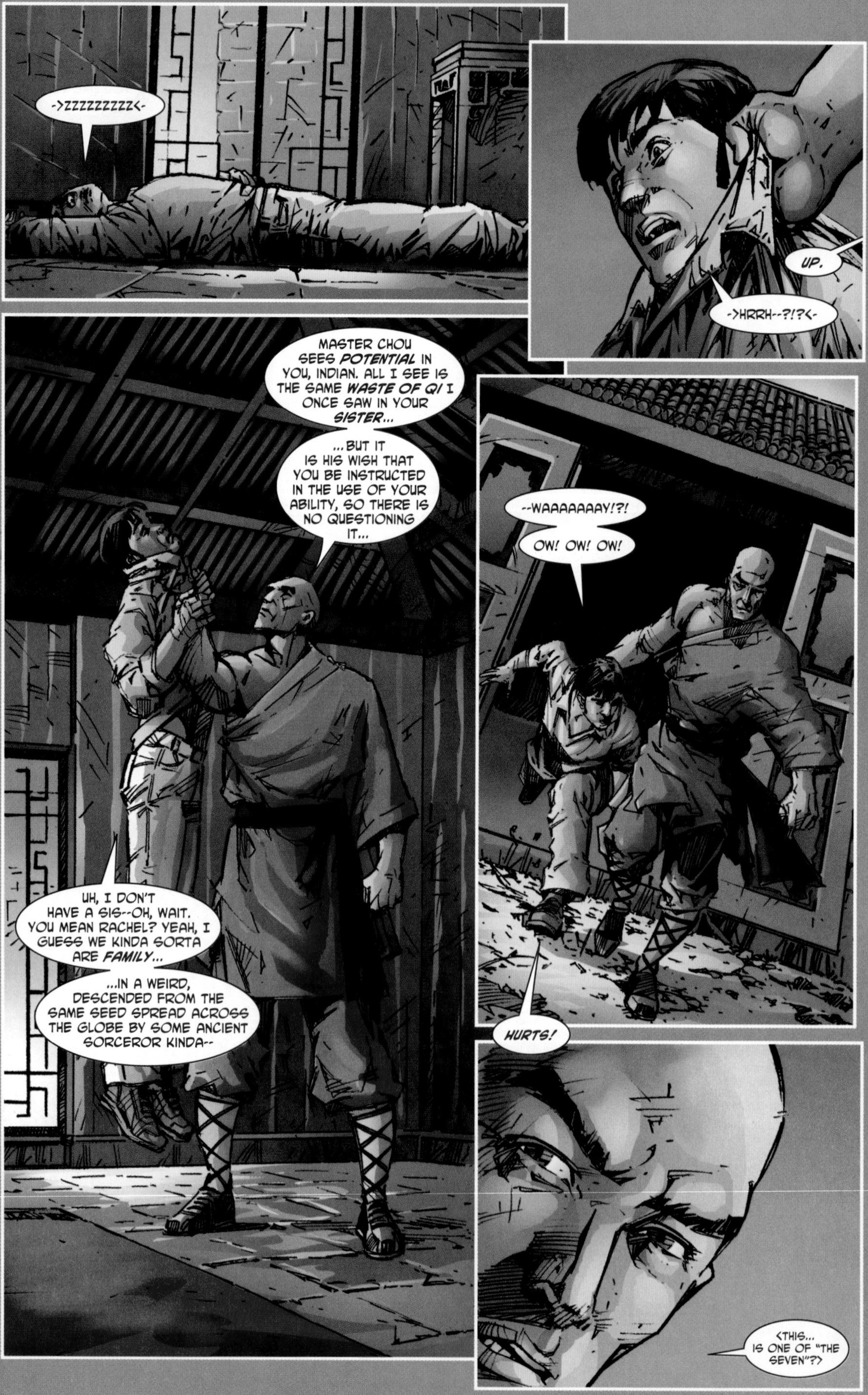
->ZZZZZZZZZ<-
UP.
->HRRH--?!?<-
MASTER CHOU SEES POTENTIAL IN YOU, INDIAN. ALL I SEE IS THE SAME WASTE OF QI I ONCE SAW IN YOUR SISTER...
...BUT IT IS HIS WISH THAT YOU BE INSTRUCTED IN THE USE OF YOUR ABILITY, SO THERE IS NO QUESTIONING IT...
UH, I DON'T HAVE A SIS--OH, WAIT. YOU MEAN RACHEL? YEAH, I GUESS WE KINDA SORTA ARE FAMILY...
...IN A WEIRD, DESCENDED FROM THE SAME SEED SPREAD ACROSS THE GLOBE BY SOME ANCIENT SORCEROR KINDA--
--WAAAAAAAY!?!
OW! OW! OW!
HURTS!
<THIS... IS ONE OF "THE SEVEN"?>

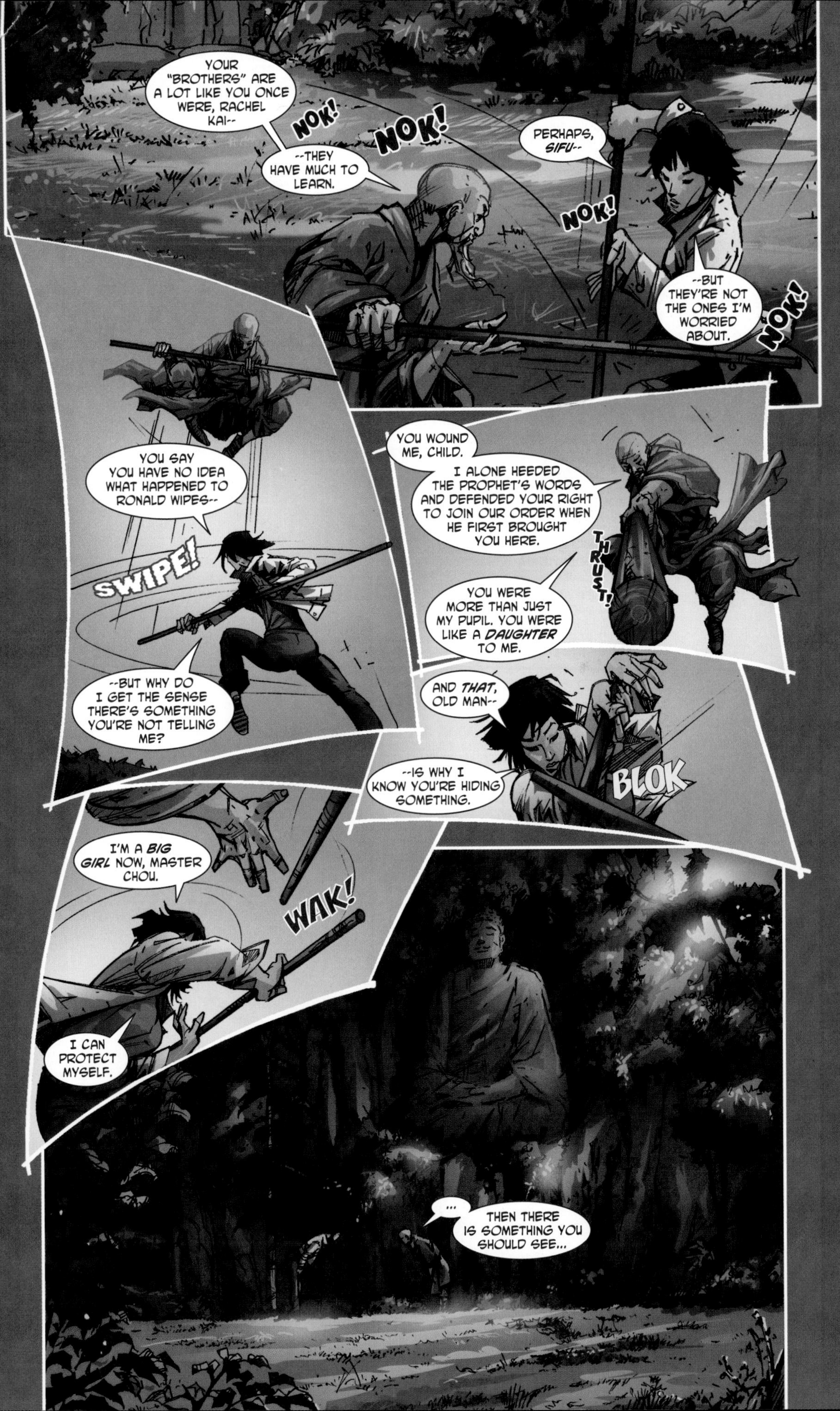
YOUR "BROTHERS" ARE A LOT LIKE YOU ONCE WERE, RACHEL KAI--
NOK!
NOK!
--THEY HAVE MUCH TO LEARN.
PERHAPS, SIFU--
NOK!
--BUT THEY'RE NOT THE ONES I'M WORRIED ABOUT.
NOK!
YOU SAY YOU HAVE NO IDEA WHAT HAPPENED TO RONALD WIPES--
SWIPE!
--BUT WHY DO I GET THE SENSE THERE'S SOMETHING YOU'RE NOT TELLING ME?
YOU WOUND ME, CHILD.
I ALONE HEEDED THE PROPHET'S WORDS AND DEFENDED YOUR RIGHT TO JOIN OUR ORDER WHEN HE FIRST BROUGHT YOU HERE.
THRUST!
YOU WERE MORE THAN JUST MY PUPIL. YOU WERE LIKE A DAUGHTER TO ME.
AND THAT, OLD MAN--
--IS WHY I KNOW YOU'RE HIDING SOMETHING.
BLOK
I'M A BIG GIRL NOW, MASTER CHOU.
WAK!
I CAN PROTECT MYSELF.
...
THEN THERE IS SOMETHING YOU SHOULD SEE...

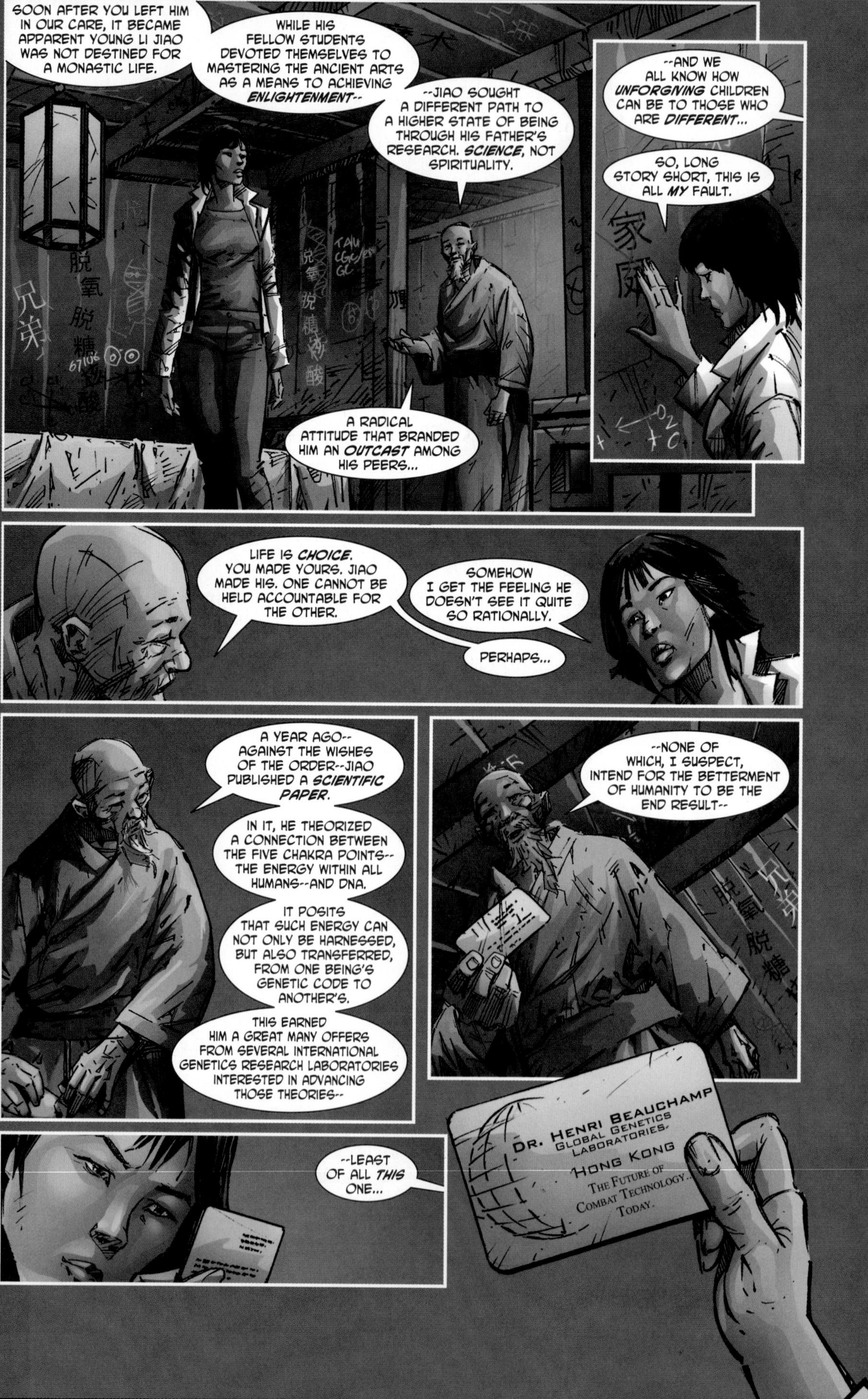
SOON AFTER YOU LEFT HIM IN OUR CARE, IT BECAME APPARENT YOUNG LI JIAO WAS NOT DESTINED FOR A MONASTIC LIFE.
WHILE HIS FELLOW STUDENTS DEVOTED THEMSELVES TO MASTERING THE ANCIENT ARTS AS A MEANS TO ACHIEVING ENLIGHTENMENT--
--JIAO SOUGHT A DIFFERENT PATH TO A HIGHER STATE OF BEING THROUGH HIS FATHER'S RESEARCH. SCIENCE, NOT SPIRITUALITY.
A RADICAL ATTITUDE THAT BRANDED HIM AN OUTCAST AMONG HIS PEERS...
--AND WE ALL KNOW HOW UNFORGIVING CHILDREN CAN BE TO THOSE WHO ARE DIFFERENT...
SO, LONG STORY SHORT, THIS IS ALL MY FAULT.
LIFE IS CHOICE. YOU MADE YOURS. JIAO MADE HIS. ONE CANNOT BE HELD ACCOUNTABLE FOR THE OTHER.
SOMEHOW I GET THE FEELING HE DOESN'T SEE IT QUITE SO RATIONALLY.
PERHAPS...
A YEAR AGO--AGAINST THE WISHES OF THE ORDER--JIAO PUBLISHED A SCIENTIFIC PAPER.
IN IT, HE THEORIZED A CONNECTION BETWEEN THE FIVE CHAKRA POINTS--THE ENERGY WITHIN ALL HUMANS--AND DNA.
IT POSITS THAT SUCH ENERGY CAN NOT ONLY BE HARNESSED, BUT ALSO TRANSFERRED, FROM ONE BEING'S GENETIC CODE TO ANOTHER'S.
THIS EARNED HIM A GREAT MANY OFFERS FROM SEVERAL INTERNATIONAL GENETICS RESEARCH LABORATORIES INTERESTED IN ADVANCING THOSE THEORIES--
--NONE OF WHICH, I SUSPECT, INTEND FOR THE BETTERMENT OF HUMANITY TO BE THE END RESULT--
--LEAST OF ALL THIS ONE...
DR. HENRI BEAUCHAMP
GLOBAL GENETICS LABORATORIES
HONG KONG
THE FUTURE OF COMBAT TECHNOLOGY... TODAY.

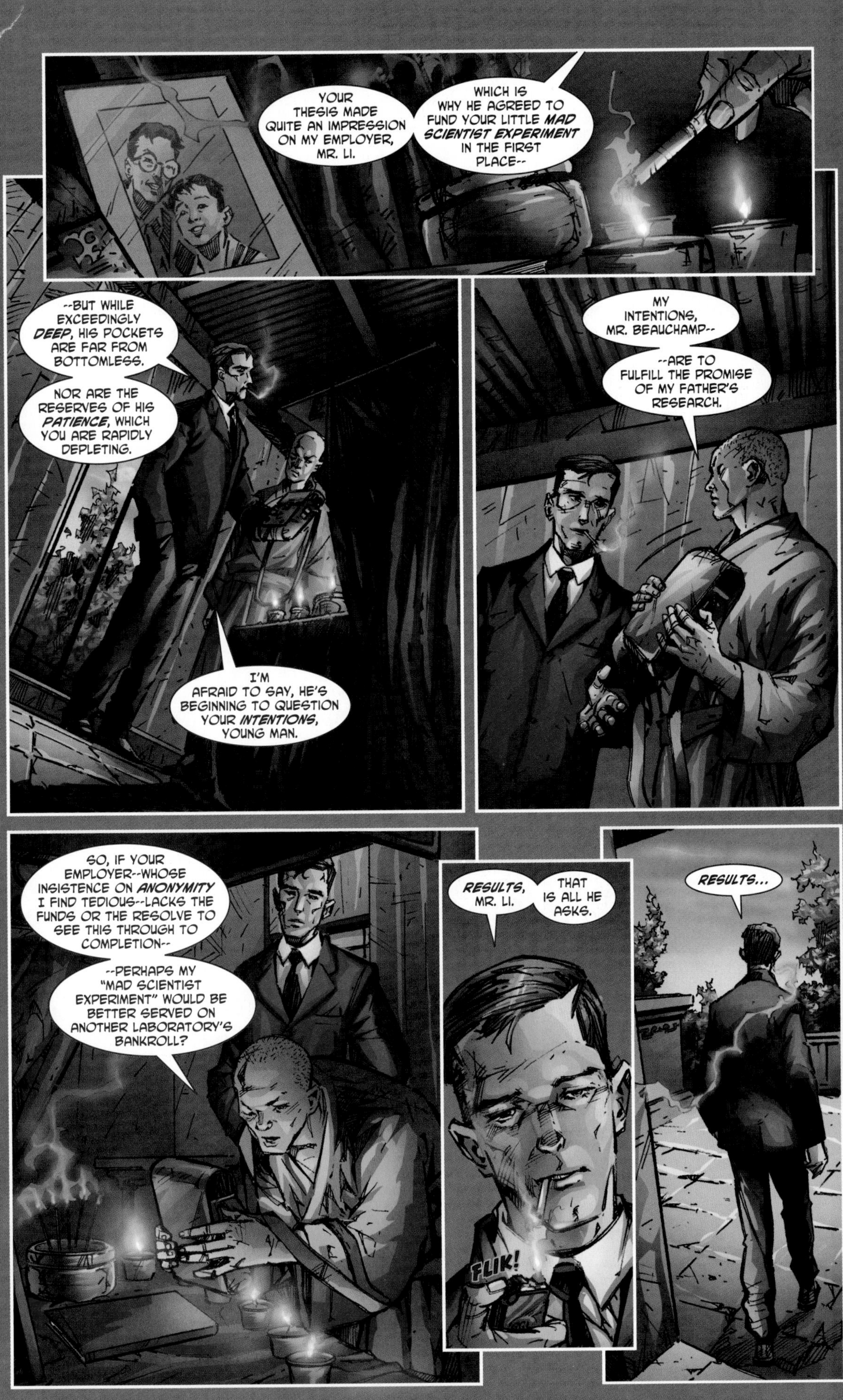
YOUR THESIS MADE QUITE AN IMPRESSION ON MY EMPLOYER, MR. LI.
WHICH IS WHY HE AGREED TO FUND YOUR LITTLE *MAD SCIENTIST EXPERIMENT* IN THE FIRST PLACE--
--BUT WHILE EXCEEDINGLY *DEEP*, HIS POCKETS ARE FAR FROM BOTTOMLESS.
NOR ARE THE RESERVES OF HIS *PATIENCE*, WHICH YOU ARE RAPIDLY DEPLETING.
I'M AFRAID TO SAY, HE'S BEGINNING TO QUESTION YOUR *INTENTIONS*, YOUNG MAN.
MY INTENTIONS, MR. BEAUCHAMP--
--ARE TO FULFILL THE PROMISE OF MY FATHER'S RESEARCH.
SO, IF YOUR EMPLOYER--WHOSE INSISTENCE ON *ANONYMITY* I FIND TEDIOUS--LACKS THE FUNDS OR THE RESOLVE TO SEE THIS THROUGH TO COMPLETION--
--PERHAPS MY "MAD SCIENTIST EXPERIMENT" WOULD BE BETTER SERVED ON ANOTHER LABORATORY'S BANKROLL?
RESULTS, MR. LI.
THAT IS ALL HE ASKS.
FLIK!
RESULTS...

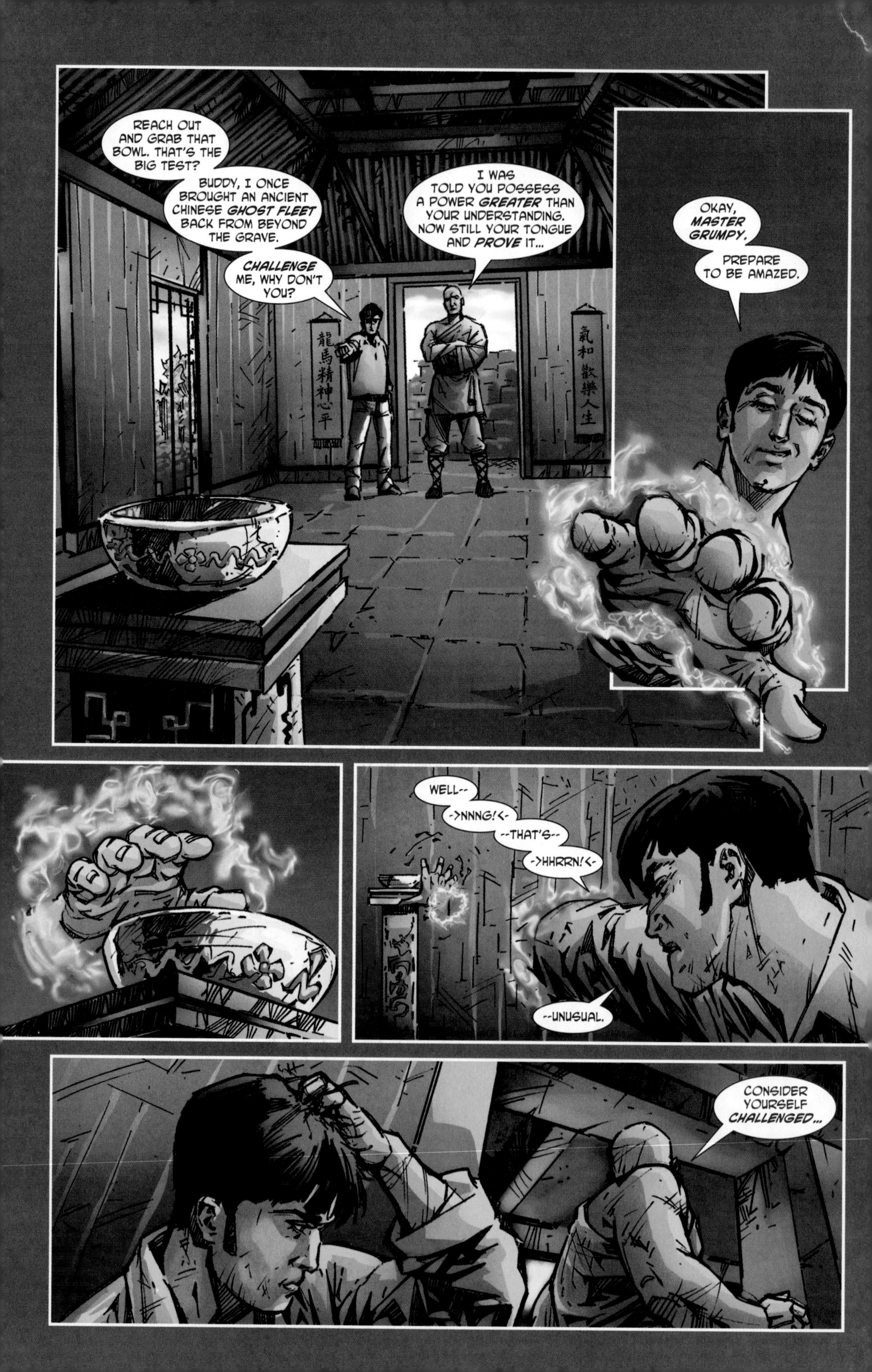

REACH OUT AND GRAB THAT BOWL. THAT'S THE BIG TEST?
BUDDY, I ONCE BROUGHT AN ANCIENT CHINESE GHOST FLEET BACK FROM BEYOND THE GRAVE.
CHALLENGE ME, WHY DON'T YOU?
I WAS TOLD YOU POSSESS A POWER GREATER THAN YOUR UNDERSTANDING. NOW STILL YOUR TONGUE AND PROVE IT...
OKAY, MASTER GRUMPY.
PREPARE TO BE AMAZED.
WELL--
->NNNG!<-
--THAT'S--
->HHRRN!<-
--UNUSUAL.
CONSIDER YOURSELF CHALLENGED...

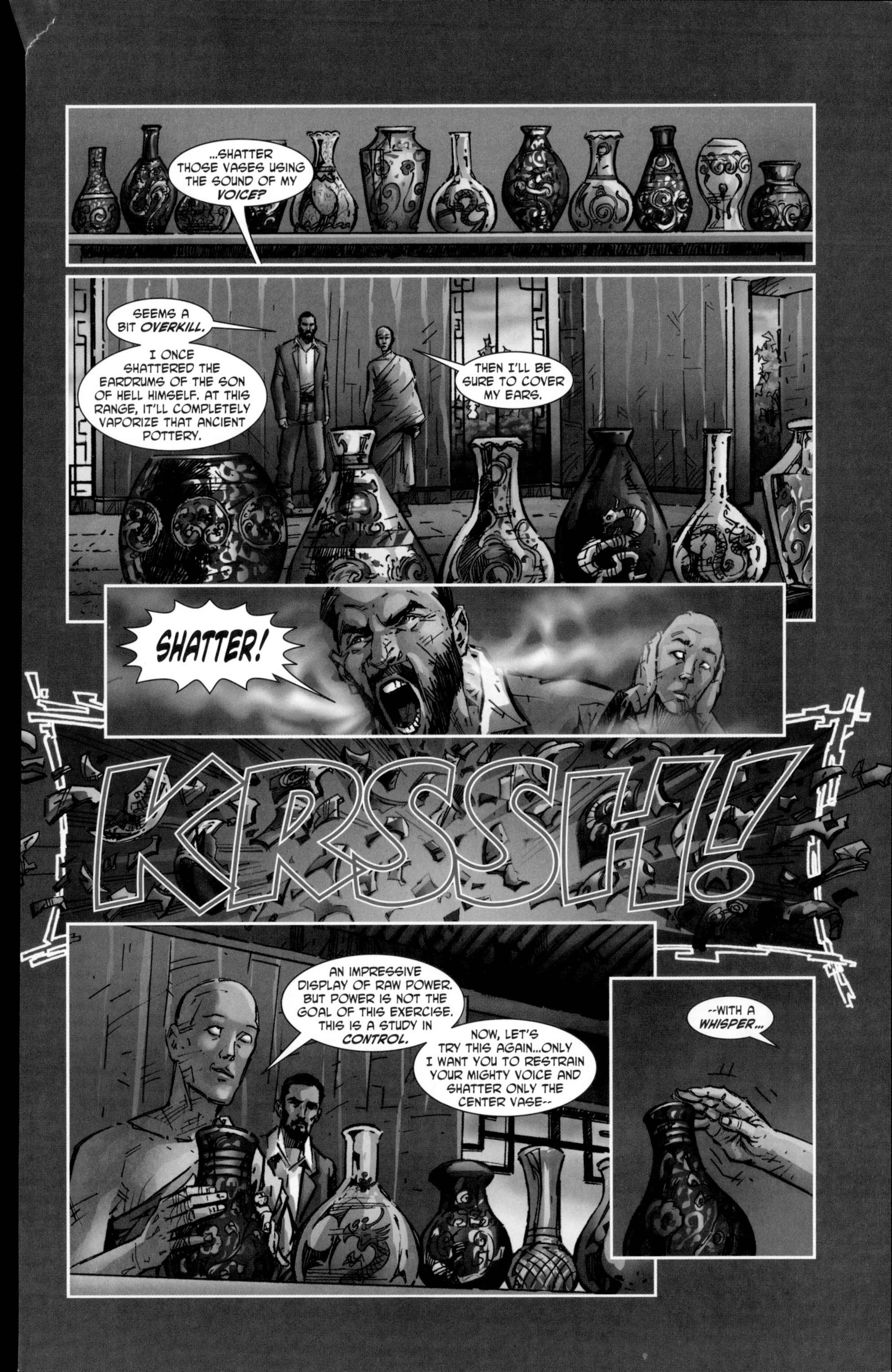
...SHATTER THOSE VASES USING THE SOUND OF MY VOICE?
SEEMS A BIT OVERKILL.
I ONCE SHATTERED THE EARDRUMS OF THE SON OF HELL HIMSELF. AT THIS RANGE, IT'LL COMPLETELY VAPORIZE THAT ANCIENT POTTERY.
THEN I'LL BE SURE TO COVER MY EARS.
SHATTER!
KRSSSH!
AN IMPRESSIVE DISPLAY OF RAW POWER. BUT POWER IS NOT THE GOAL OF THIS EXERCISE. THIS IS A STUDY IN CONTROL.
NOW, LET'S TRY THIS AGAIN...ONLY I WANT YOU TO RESTRAIN YOUR MIGHTY VOICE AND SHATTER ONLY THE CENTER VASE--
--WITH A WHISPER...

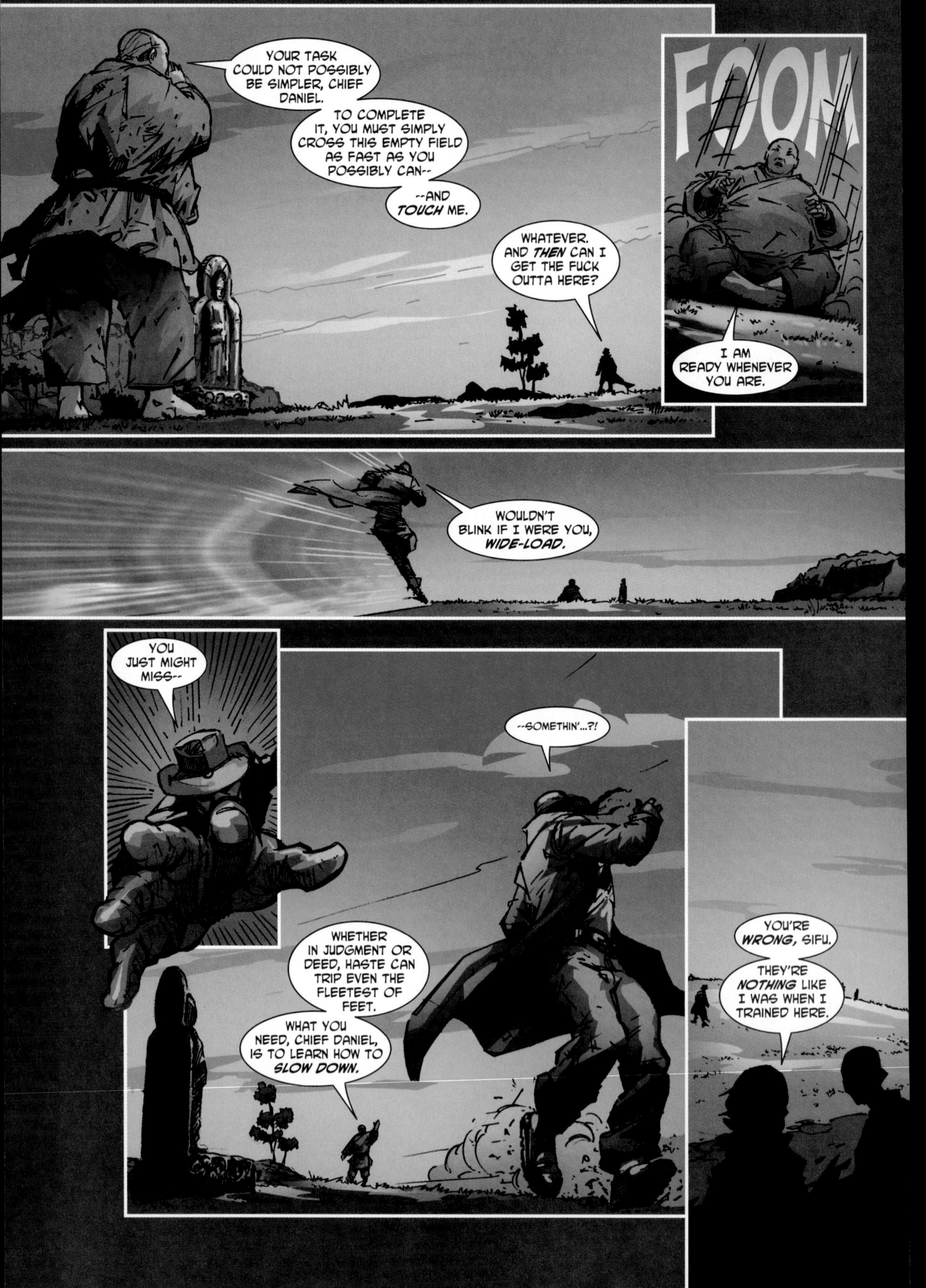
YOUR TASK COULD NOT POSSIBLY BE SIMPLER, CHIEF DANIEL.
TO COMPLETE IT, YOU MUST SIMPLY CROSS THIS EMPTY FIELD AS FAST AS YOU POSSIBLY CAN--
--AND *TOUCH* ME.
WHATEVER. AND *THEN* CAN I GET THE FUCK OUTTA HERE?
FOOM
I AM READY WHENEVER YOU ARE.
WOULDN'T BLINK IF I WERE YOU, *WIDE-LOAD.*
YOU JUST MIGHT MISS--
--SOMETHIN'...?!
WHETHER IN JUDGMENT OR DEED, HASTE CAN TRIP EVEN THE FLEETEST OF FEET.
WHAT YOU NEED, CHIEF DANIEL, IS TO LEARN HOW TO *SLOW DOWN.*
YOU'RE *WRONG,* SIFU.
THEY'RE *NOTHING* LIKE I WAS WHEN I TRAINED HERE.

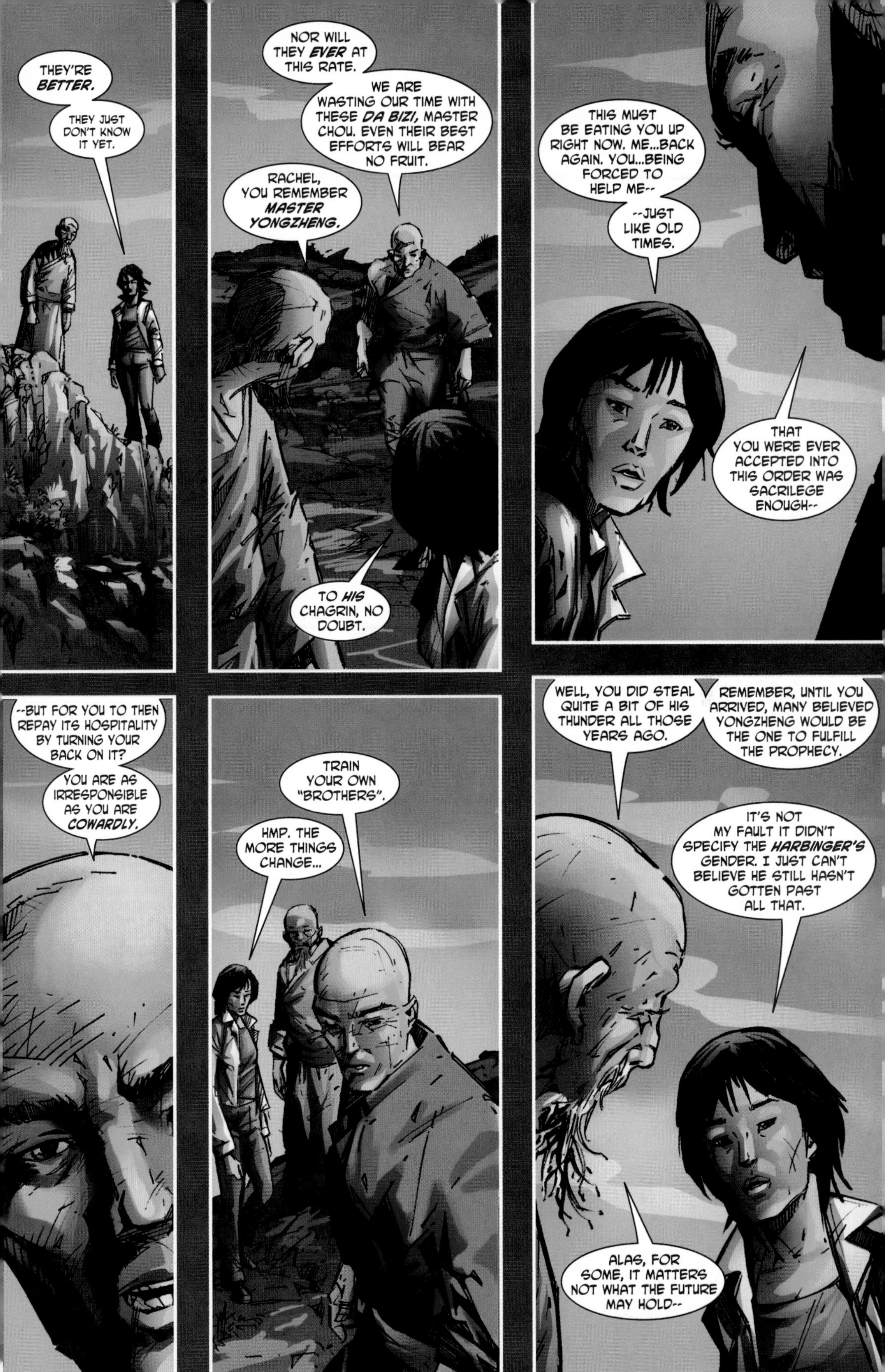
THEY'RE *BETTER.*
THEY JUST DON'T KNOW IT YET.
NOR WILL THEY *EVER* AT THIS RATE.
WE ARE WASTING OUR TIME WITH THESE *DA BIZI,* MASTER CHOU. EVEN THEIR BEST EFFORTS WILL BEAR NO FRUIT.
RACHEL, YOU REMEMBER *MASTER YONGZHENG.*
TO *HIS* CHAGRIN, NO DOUBT.
THIS MUST BE EATING YOU UP RIGHT NOW. ME...BACK AGAIN. YOU...BEING FORCED TO HELP ME--
--JUST LIKE OLD TIMES.
THAT YOU WERE EVER ACCEPTED INTO THIS ORDER WAS SACRILEGE ENOUGH--
--BUT FOR YOU TO THEN REPAY ITS HOSPITALITY BY TURNING YOUR BACK ON IT?
YOU ARE AS IRRESPONSIBLE AS YOU ARE *COWARDLY.*
TRAIN YOUR OWN "BROTHERS".
HMP. THE MORE THINGS CHANGE...
WELL, YOU DID STEAL QUITE A BIT OF HIS THUNDER ALL THOSE YEARS AGO.
REMEMBER, UNTIL YOU ARRIVED, MANY BELIEVED YONGZHENG WOULD BE THE ONE TO FULFILL THE PROPHECY.
IT'S NOT MY FAULT IT DIDN'T SPECIFY THE *HARBINGER'S* GENDER. I JUST CAN'T BELIEVE HE STILL HASN'T GOTTEN PAST ALL THAT.
ALAS, FOR SOME, IT MATTERS NOT WHAT THE FUTURE MAY HOLD--

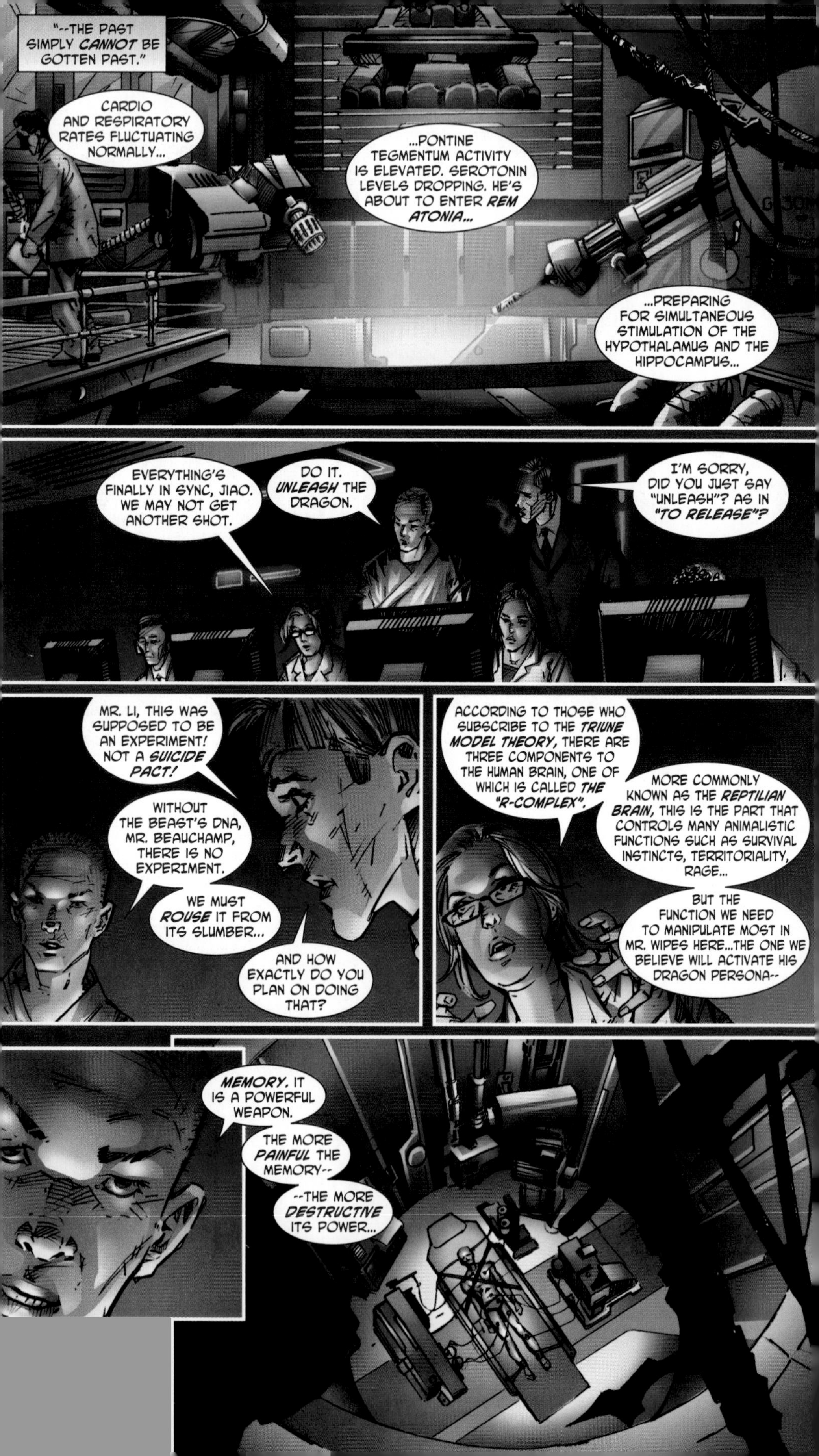
"--THE PAST SIMPLY CANNOT BE GOTTEN PAST."
CARDIO AND RESPIRATORY RATES FLUCTUATING NORMALLY...
...PONTINE TEGMENTUM ACTIVITY IS ELEVATED. SEROTONIN LEVELS DROPPING. HE'S ABOUT TO ENTER REM ATONIA...
...PREPARING FOR SIMULTANEOUS STIMULATION OF THE HYPOTHALAMUS AND THE HIPPOCAMPUS...
EVERYTHING'S FINALLY IN SYNC, JIAO. WE MAY NOT GET ANOTHER SHOT.
DO IT. UNLEASH THE DRAGON.
I'M SORRY, DID YOU JUST SAY "UNLEASH"? AS IN "TO RELEASE"?
MR. LI, THIS WAS SUPPOSED TO BE AN EXPERIMENT! NOT A SUICIDE PACT!
WITHOUT THE BEAST'S DNA, MR. BEAUCHAMP, THERE IS NO EXPERIMENT.
WE MUST ROUSE IT FROM ITS SLUMBER...
AND HOW EXACTLY DO YOU PLAN ON DOING THAT?
ACCORDING TO THOSE WHO SUBSCRIBE TO THE TRIUNE MODEL THEORY, THERE ARE THREE COMPONENTS TO THE HUMAN BRAIN, ONE OF WHICH IS CALLED THE "R-COMPLEX".
MORE COMMONLY KNOWN AS THE REPTILIAN BRAIN, THIS IS THE PART THAT CONTROLS MANY ANIMALISTIC FUNCTIONS SUCH AS SURVIVAL INSTINCTS, TERRITORIALITY, RAGE...
BUT THE FUNCTION WE NEED TO MANIPULATE MOST IN MR. WIPES HERE...THE ONE WE BELIEVE WILL ACTIVATE HIS DRAGON PERSONA--
MEMORY. IT IS A POWERFUL WEAPON.
THE MORE PAINFUL THE MEMORY--
--THE MORE DESTRUCTIVE ITS POWER...

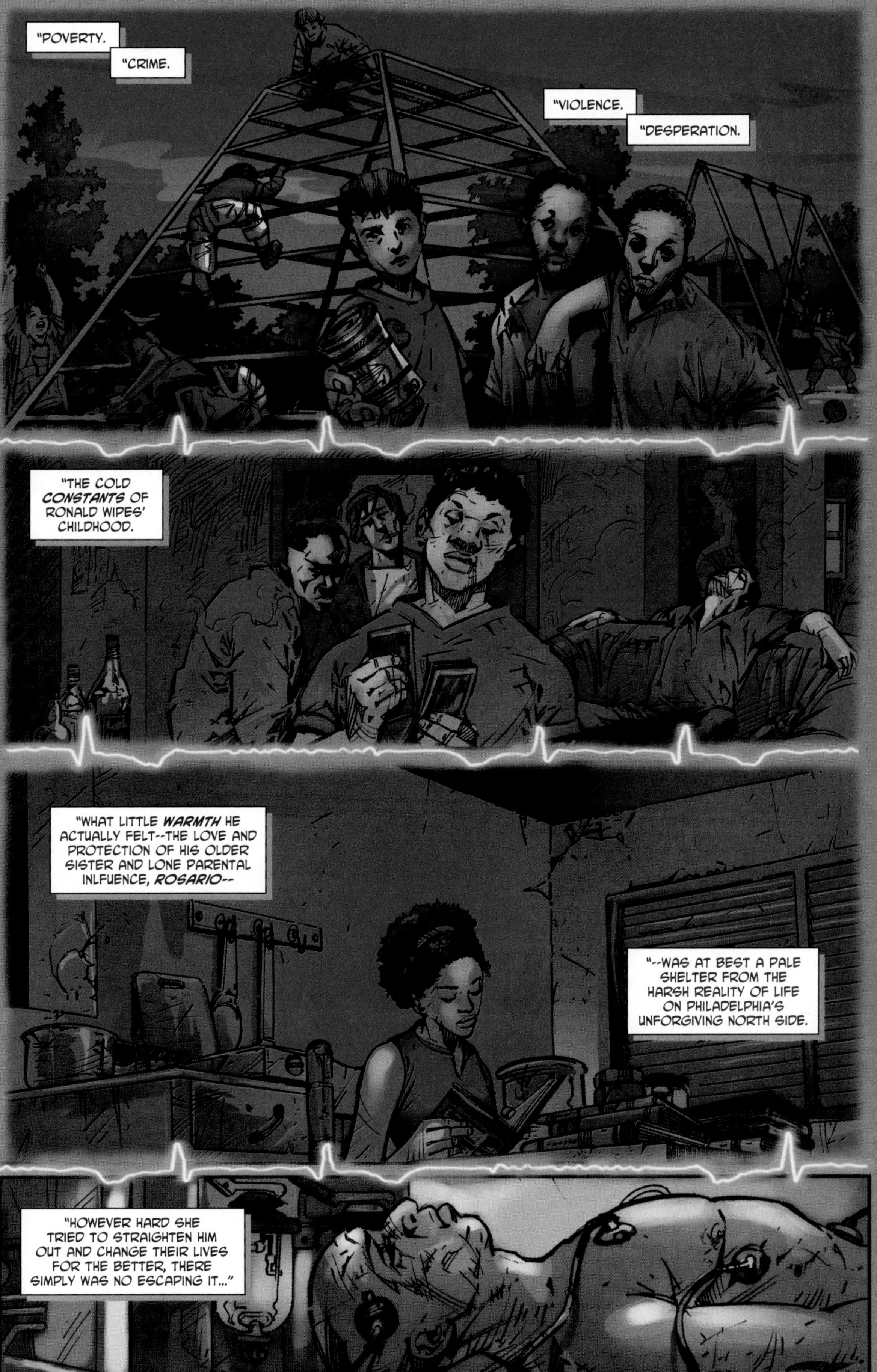
"POVERTY.
"CRIME.
"VIOLENCE.
"DESPERATION.
"THE COLD CONSTANTS OF RONALD WIPES' CHILDHOOD.
"WHAT LITTLE WARMTH HE ACTUALLY FELT--THE LOVE AND PROTECTION OF HIS OLDER SISTER AND LONE PARENTAL INLFUENCE, ROSARIO--
"--WAS AT BEST A PALE SHELTER FROM THE HARSH REALITY OF LIFE ON PHILADELPHIA'S UNFORGIVING NORTH SIDE.
"HOWEVER HARD SHE TRIED TO STRAIGHTEN HIM OUT AND CHANGE THEIR LIVES FOR THE BETTER, THERE SIMPLY WAS NO ESCAPING IT..."

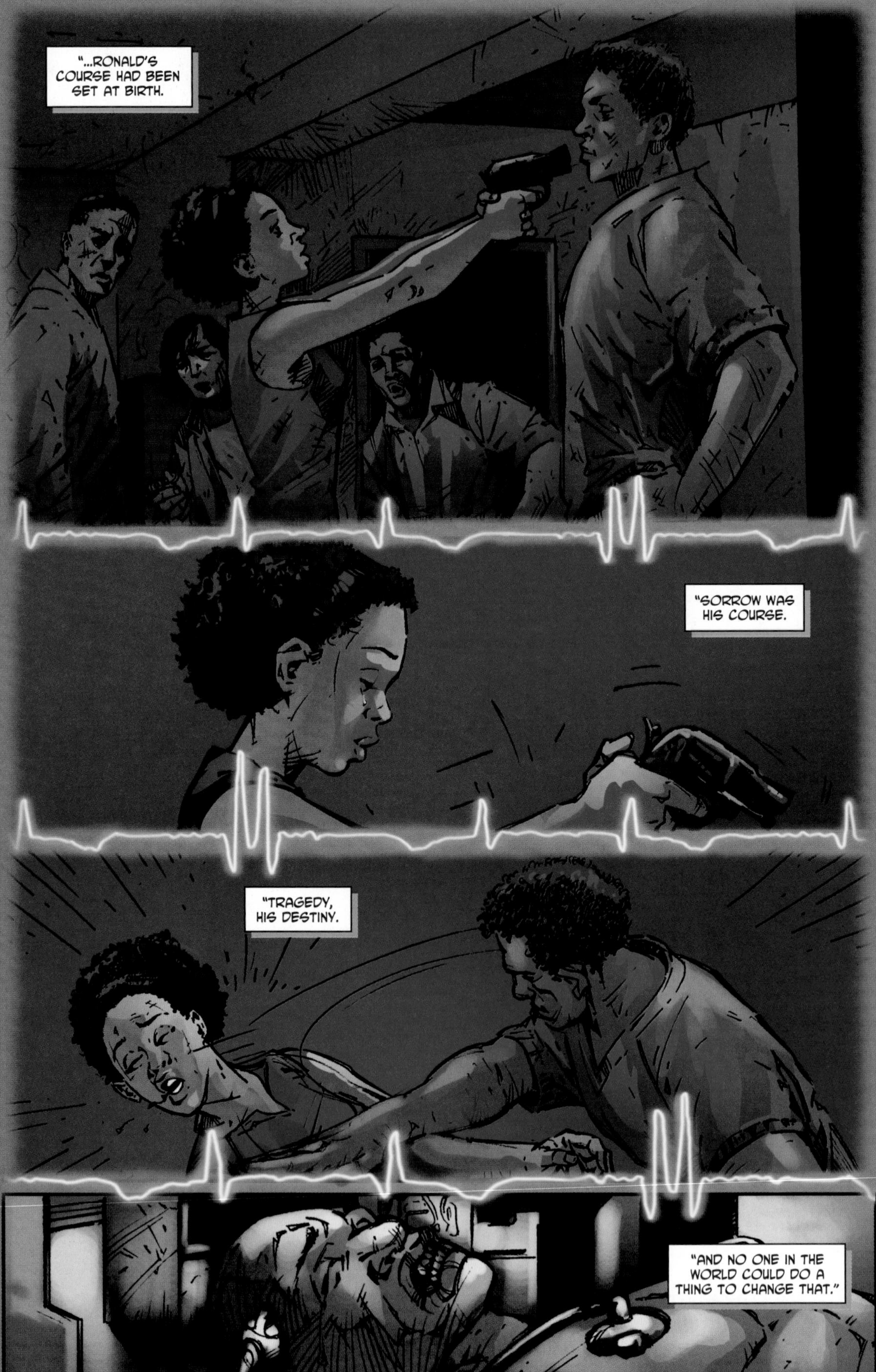
"...RONALD'S COURSE HAD BEEN SET AT BIRTH.
"SORROW WAS HIS COURSE.
"TRAGEDY, HIS DESTINY.
"AND NO ONE IN THE WORLD COULD DO A THING TO CHANGE THAT."

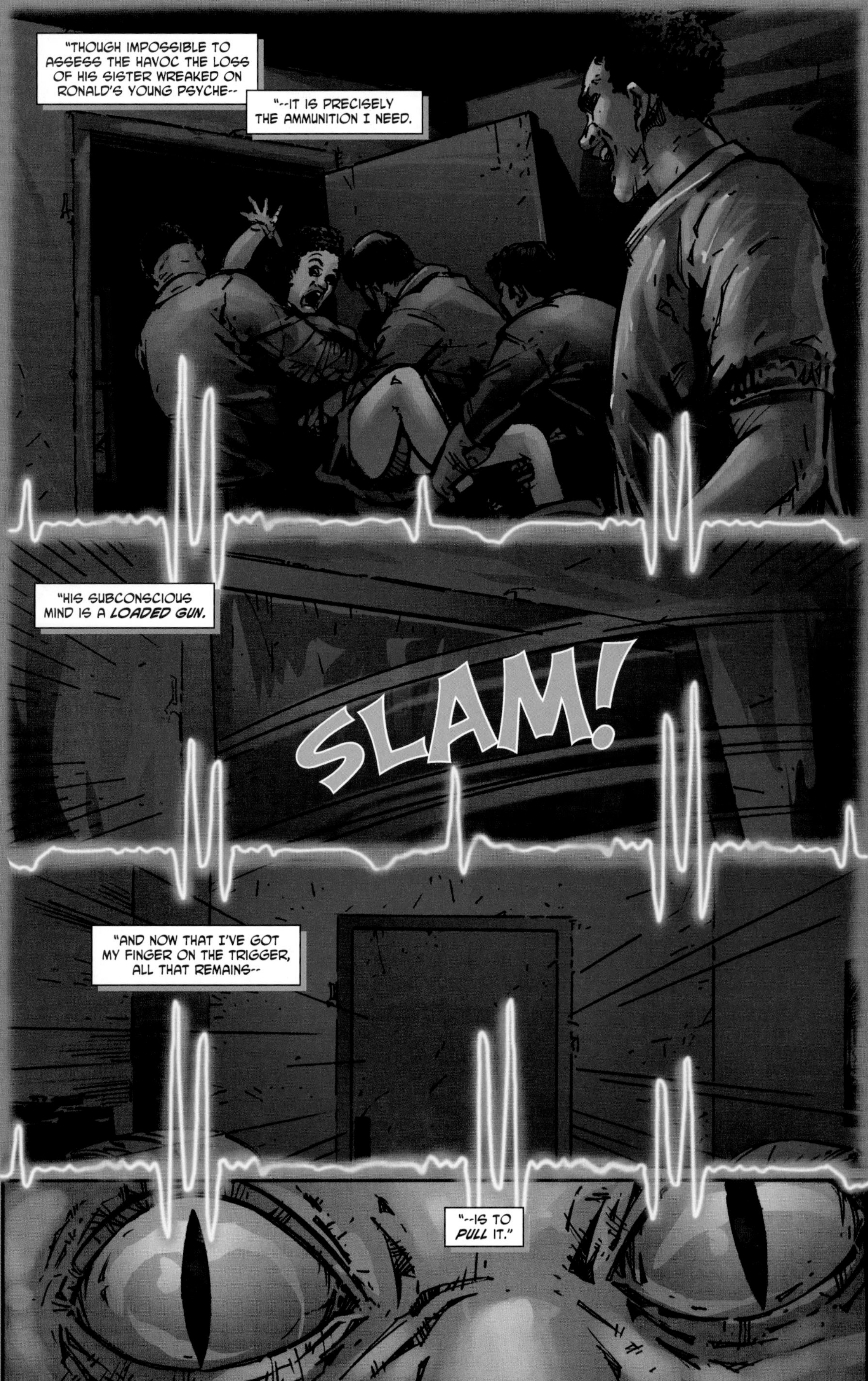
"THOUGH IMPOSSIBLE TO ASSESS THE HAVOC THE LOSS OF HIS SISTER WREAKED ON RONALD'S YOUNG PSYCHE--
"--IT IS PRECISELY THE AMMUNITION I NEED.
"HIS SUBCONSCIOUS MIND IS A *LOADED GUN.*
SLAM!
"AND NOW THAT I'VE GOT MY FINGER ON THE TRIGGER, ALL THAT REMAINS--
"--IS TO *PULL* IT."

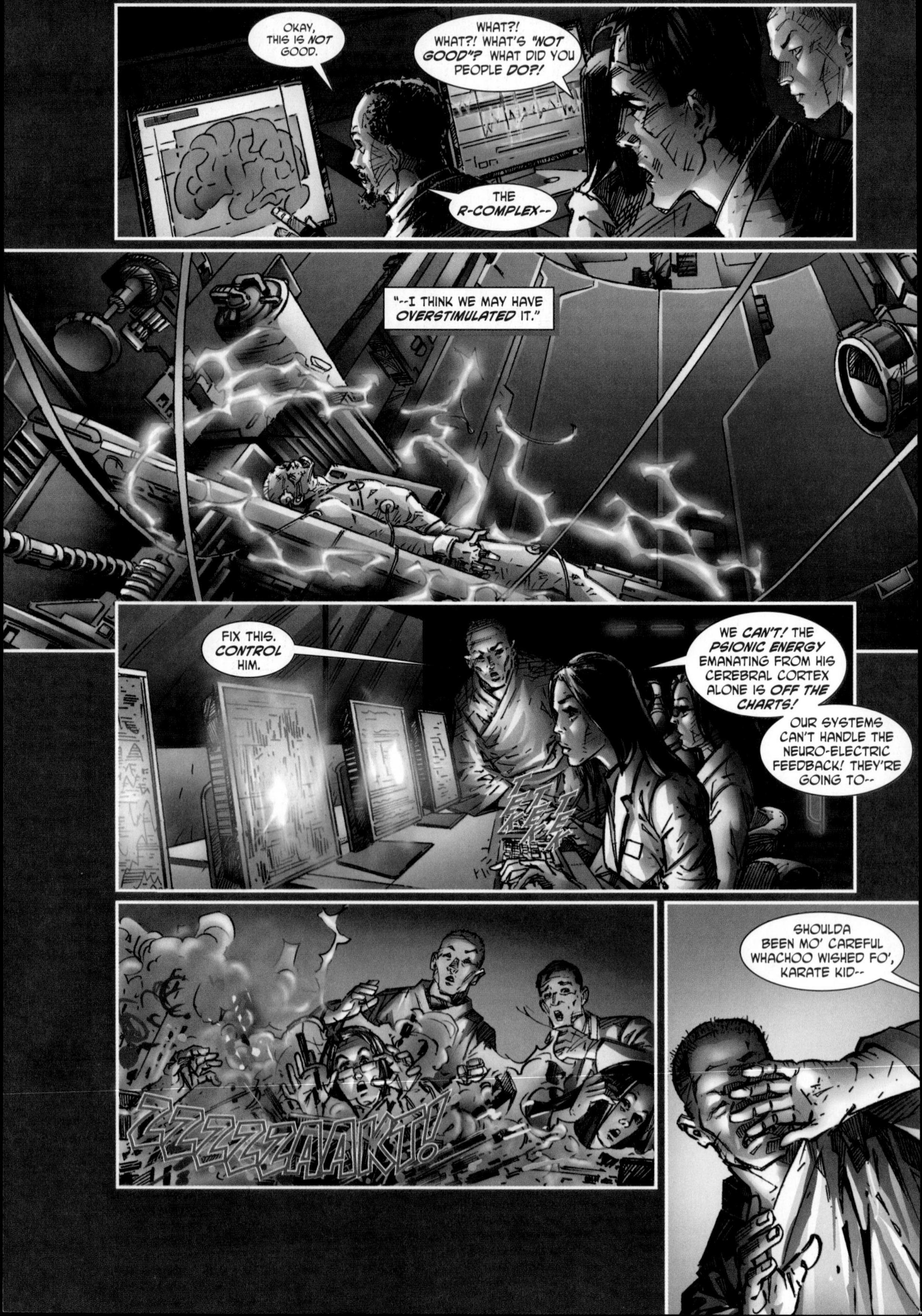
OKAY, THIS IS NOT GOOD.
WHAT?! WHAT?! WHAT'S "NOT GOOD"? WHAT DID YOU PEOPLE DO?!
THE R-COMPLEX--
"--I THINK WE MAY HAVE OVERSTIMULATED IT."
FIX THIS. CONTROL HIM.
WE CAN'T! THE PSIONIC ENERGY EMANATING FROM HIS CEREBRAL CORTEX ALONE IS OFF THE CHARTS!
OUR SYSTEMS CAN'T HANDLE THE NEURO-ELECTRIC FEEDBACK! THEY'RE GOING TO--
ZZZZZAAKT!
SHOULDA BEEN MO' CAREFUL WHACHOO WISHED FO', KARATE KID--

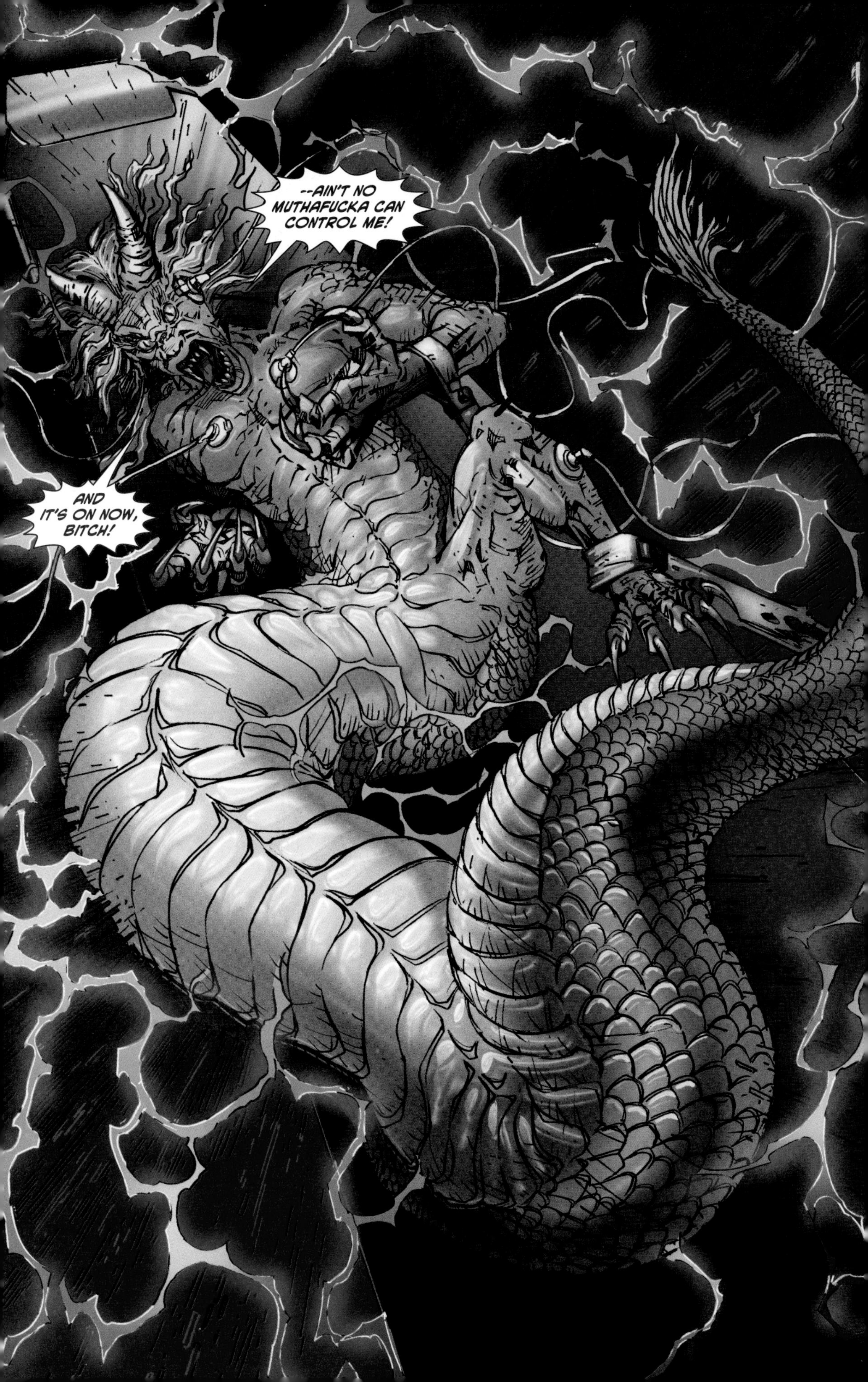
--AIN'T NO MUTHAFUCKA CAN CONTROL ME!
AND IT'S ON NOW, BITCH!

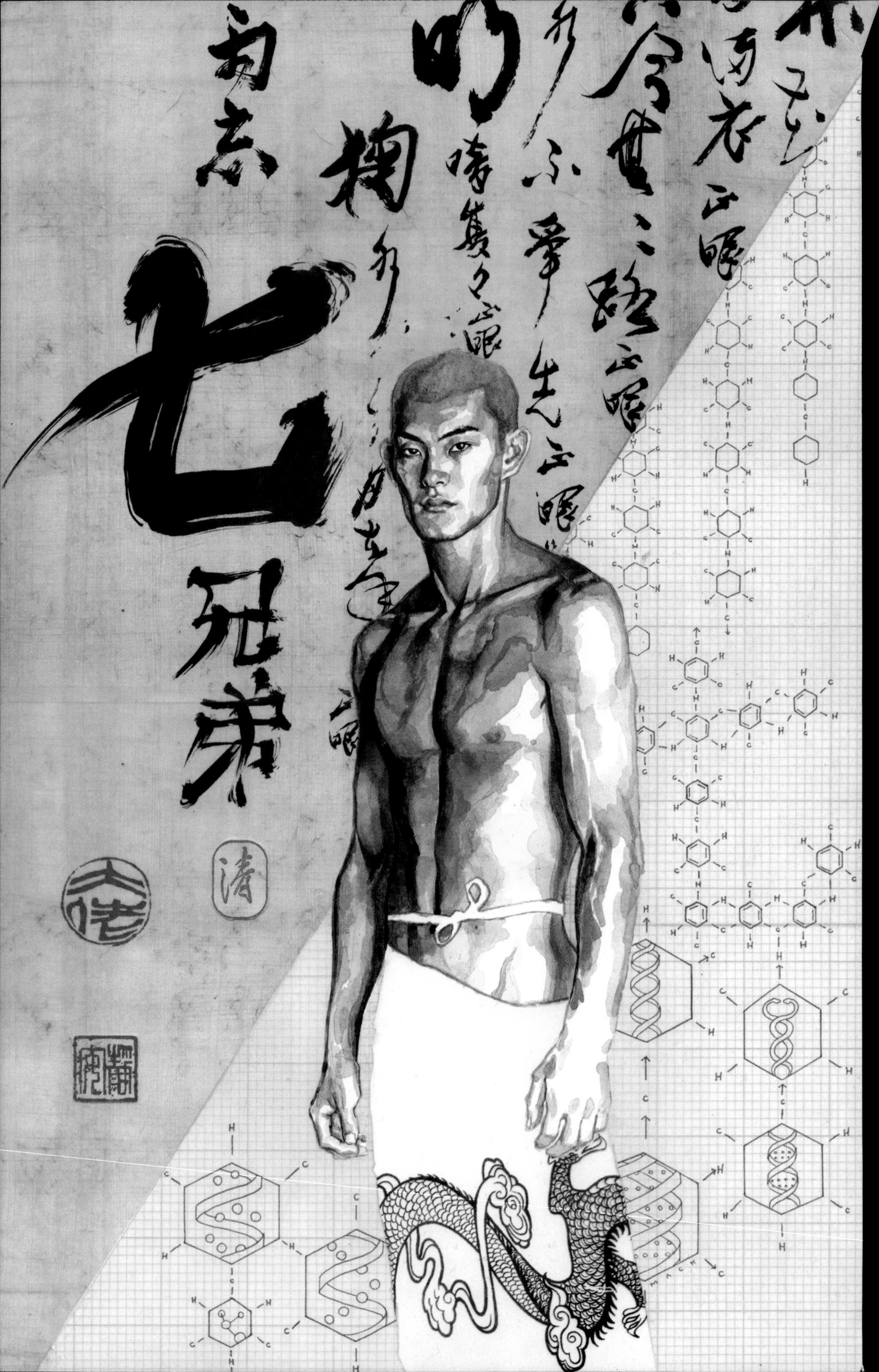
七
兄弟
清
MACK

"Oh for fuck's sake, Gandhi!
When did you become
such a pussy?"
— Chief Daniel Fallingwater

Chapter - 4

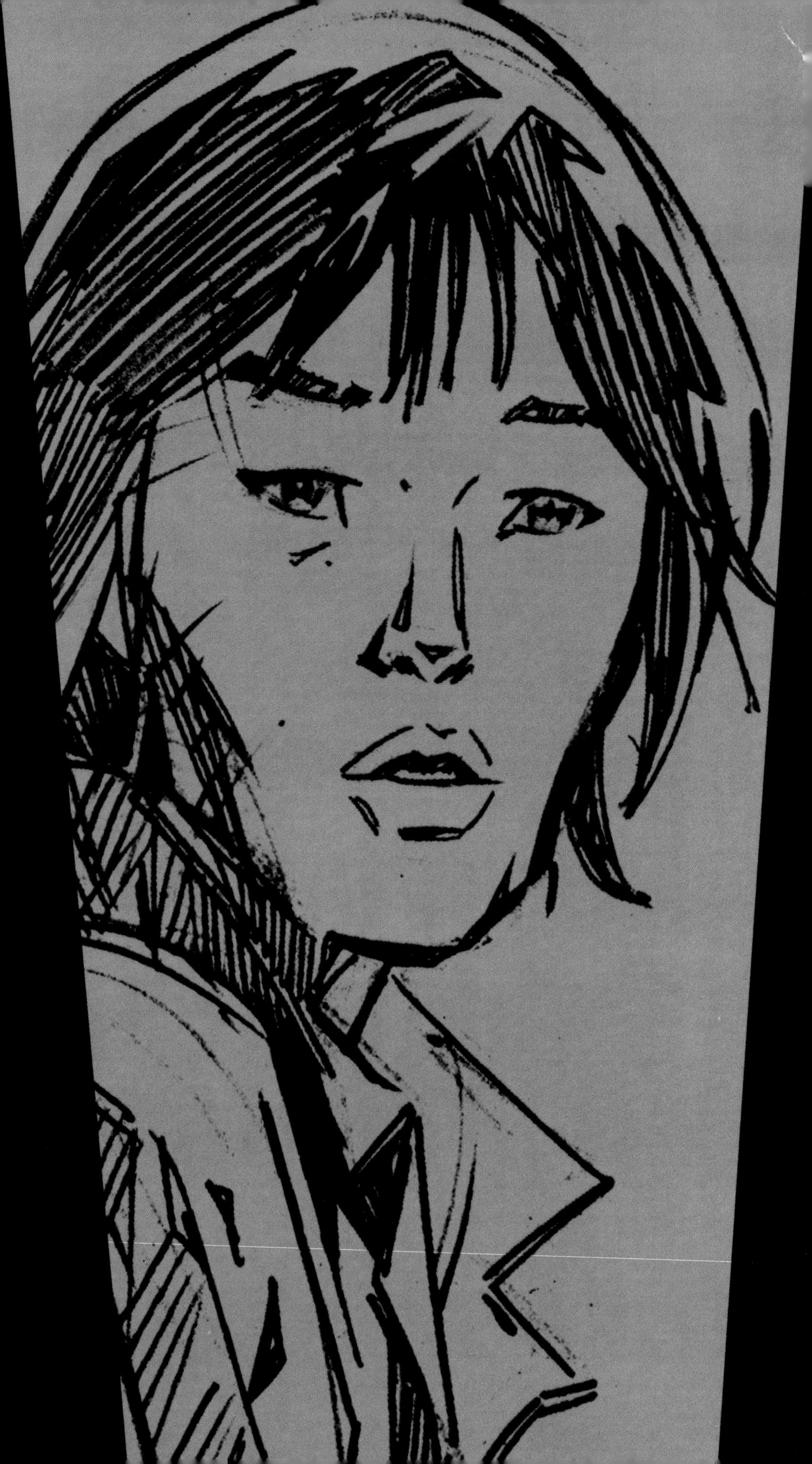

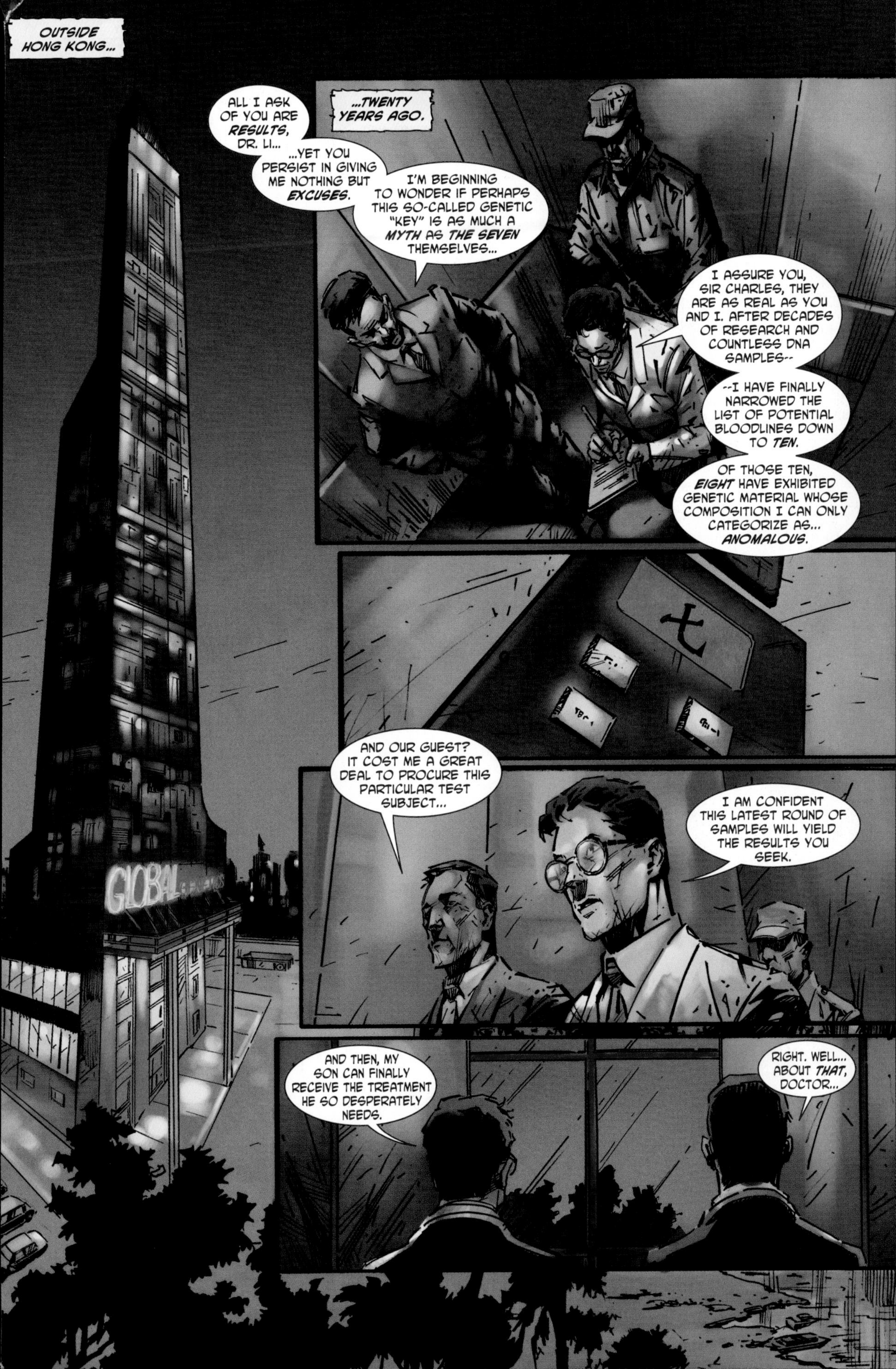
OUTSIDE HONG KONG...
...TWENTY YEARS AGO.
ALL I ASK OF YOU ARE RESULTS, DR. LI...
...YET YOU PERSIST IN GIVING ME NOTHING BUT EXCUSES.
I'M BEGINNING TO WONDER IF PERHAPS THIS SO-CALLED GENETIC "KEY" IS AS MUCH A MYTH AS THE SEVEN THEMSELVES...
I ASSURE YOU, SIR CHARLES, THEY ARE AS REAL AS YOU AND I. AFTER DECADES OF RESEARCH AND COUNTLESS DNA SAMPLES--
--I HAVE FINALLY NARROWED THE LIST OF POTENTIAL BLOODLINES DOWN TO TEN.
OF THOSE TEN, EIGHT HAVE EXHIBITED GENETIC MATERIAL WHOSE COMPOSITION I CAN ONLY CATEGORIZE AS... ANOMALOUS.
GLOBAL
AND OUR GUEST? IT COST ME A GREAT DEAL TO PROCURE THIS PARTICULAR TEST SUBJECT...
I AM CONFIDENT THIS LATEST ROUND OF SAMPLES WILL YIELD THE RESULTS YOU SEEK.
AND THEN, MY SON CAN FINALLY RECEIVE THE TREATMENT HE SO DESPERATELY NEEDS.
RIGHT. WELL... ABOUT THAT, DOCTOR...

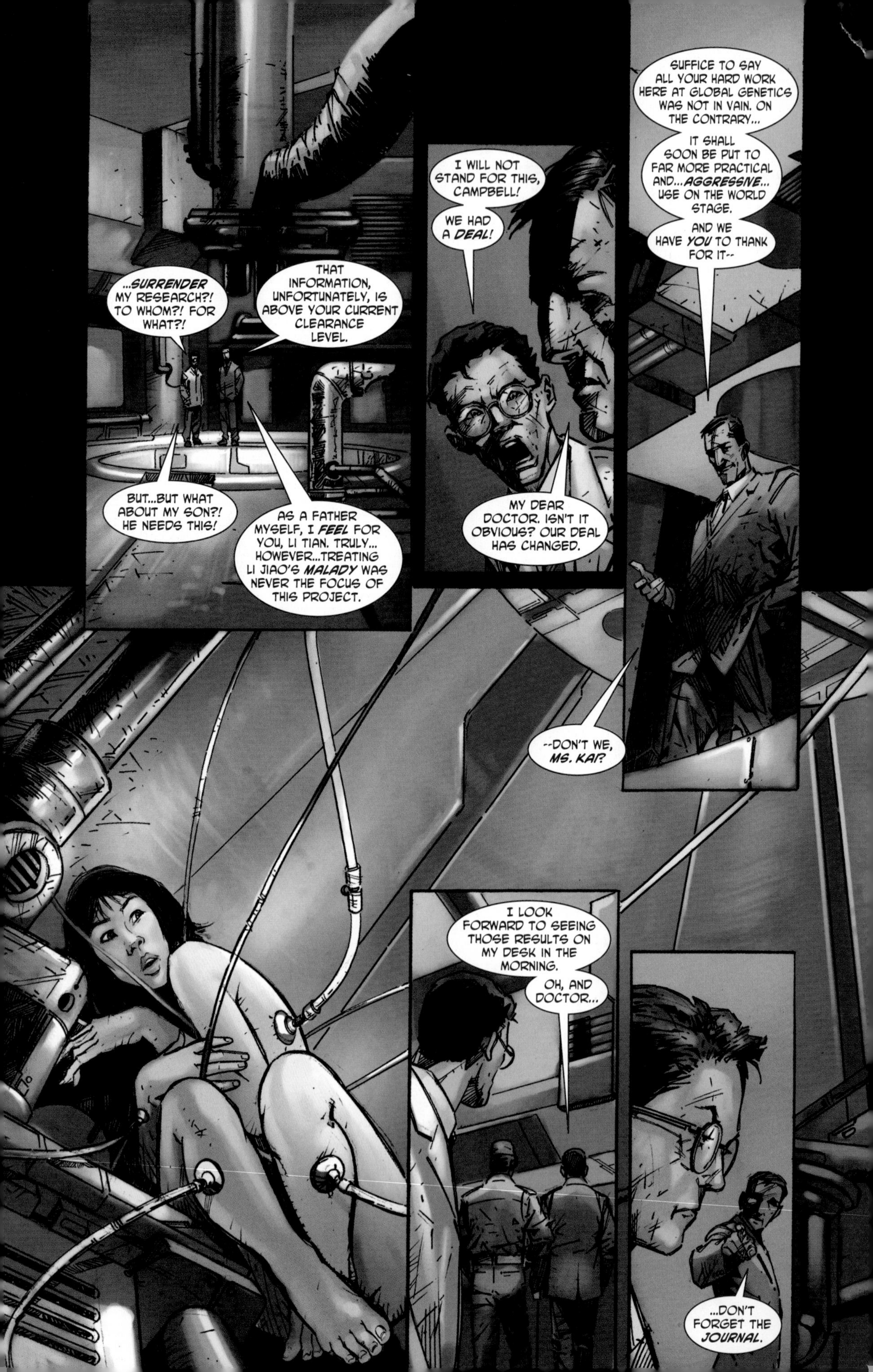
...SURRENDER MY RESEARCH?! TO WHOM?! FOR WHAT?!
THAT INFORMATION, UNFORTUNATELY, IS ABOVE YOUR CURRENT CLEARANCE LEVEL.
BUT...BUT WHAT ABOUT MY SON?! HE NEEDS THIS!
AS A FATHER MYSELF, I FEEL FOR YOU, LI TIAN. TRULY... HOWEVER...TREATING LI JIAO'S MALADY WAS NEVER THE FOCUS OF THIS PROJECT.
I WILL NOT STAND FOR THIS, CAMPBELL!
WE HAD A DEAL!
MY DEAR DOCTOR. ISN'T IT OBVIOUS? OUR DEAL HAS CHANGED.
SUFFICE TO SAY ALL YOUR HARD WORK HERE AT GLOBAL GENETICS WAS NOT IN VAIN. ON THE CONTRARY...
IT SHALL SOON BE PUT TO FAR MORE PRACTICAL AND...AGGRESSIVE... USE ON THE WORLD STAGE.
AND WE HAVE YOU TO THANK FOR IT--
--DON'T WE, MS. KAI?
I LOOK FORWARD TO SEEING THOSE RESULTS ON MY DESK IN THE MORNING.
OH, AND DOCTOR...
...DON'T FORGET THE JOURNAL.

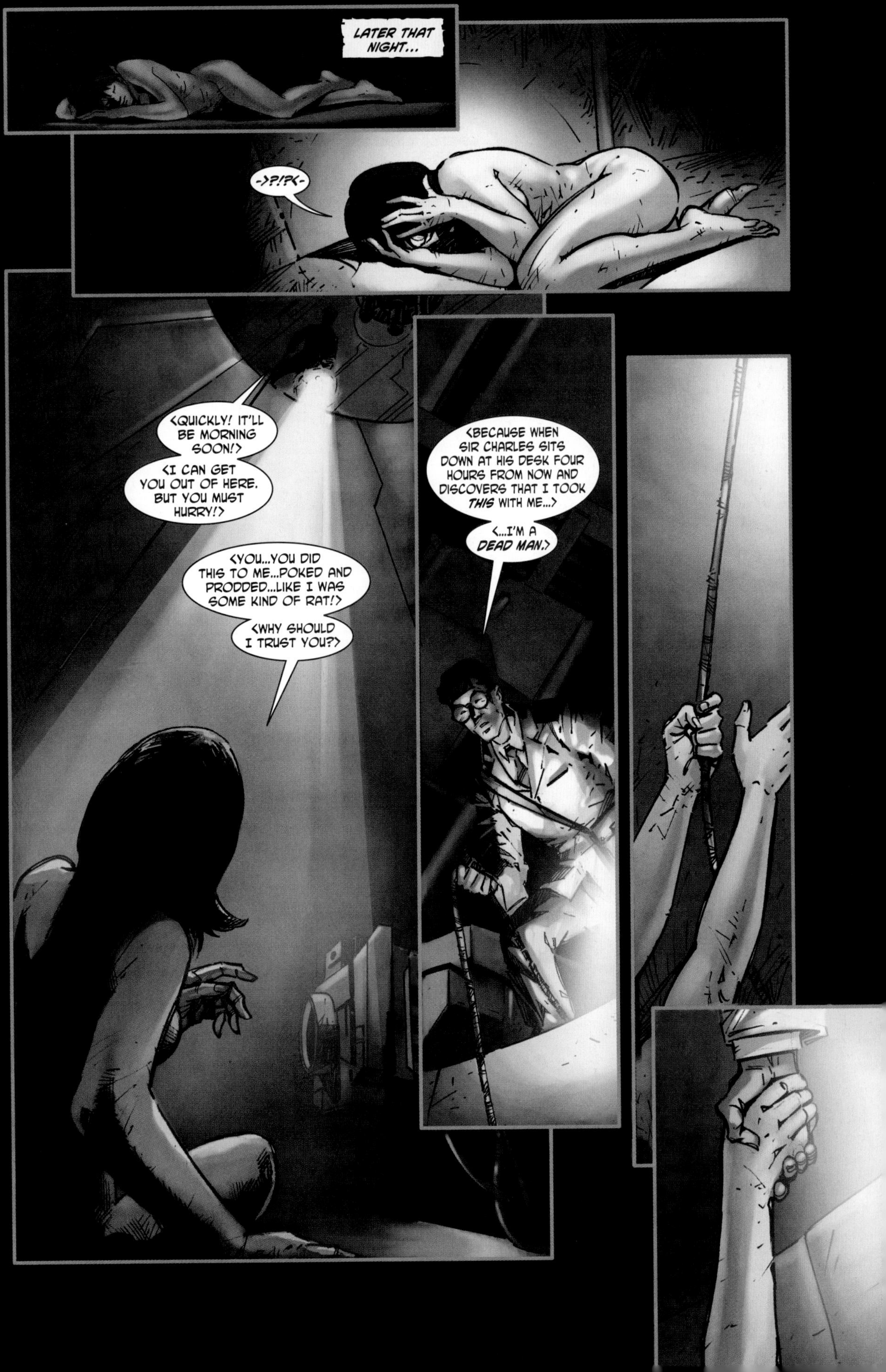
LATER THAT NIGHT...
->?!?<-
<QUICKLY! IT'LL BE MORNING SOON!>
<I CAN GET YOU OUT OF HERE. BUT YOU MUST HURRY!>
<YOU...YOU DID THIS TO ME...POKED AND PRODDED...LIKE I WAS SOME KIND OF RAT!>
<WHY SHOULD I TRUST YOU?>
<BECAUSE WHEN SIR CHARLES SITS DOWN AT HIS DESK FOUR HOURS FROM NOW AND DISCOVERS THAT I TOOK THIS WITH ME...>
<...I'M A DEAD MAN.>

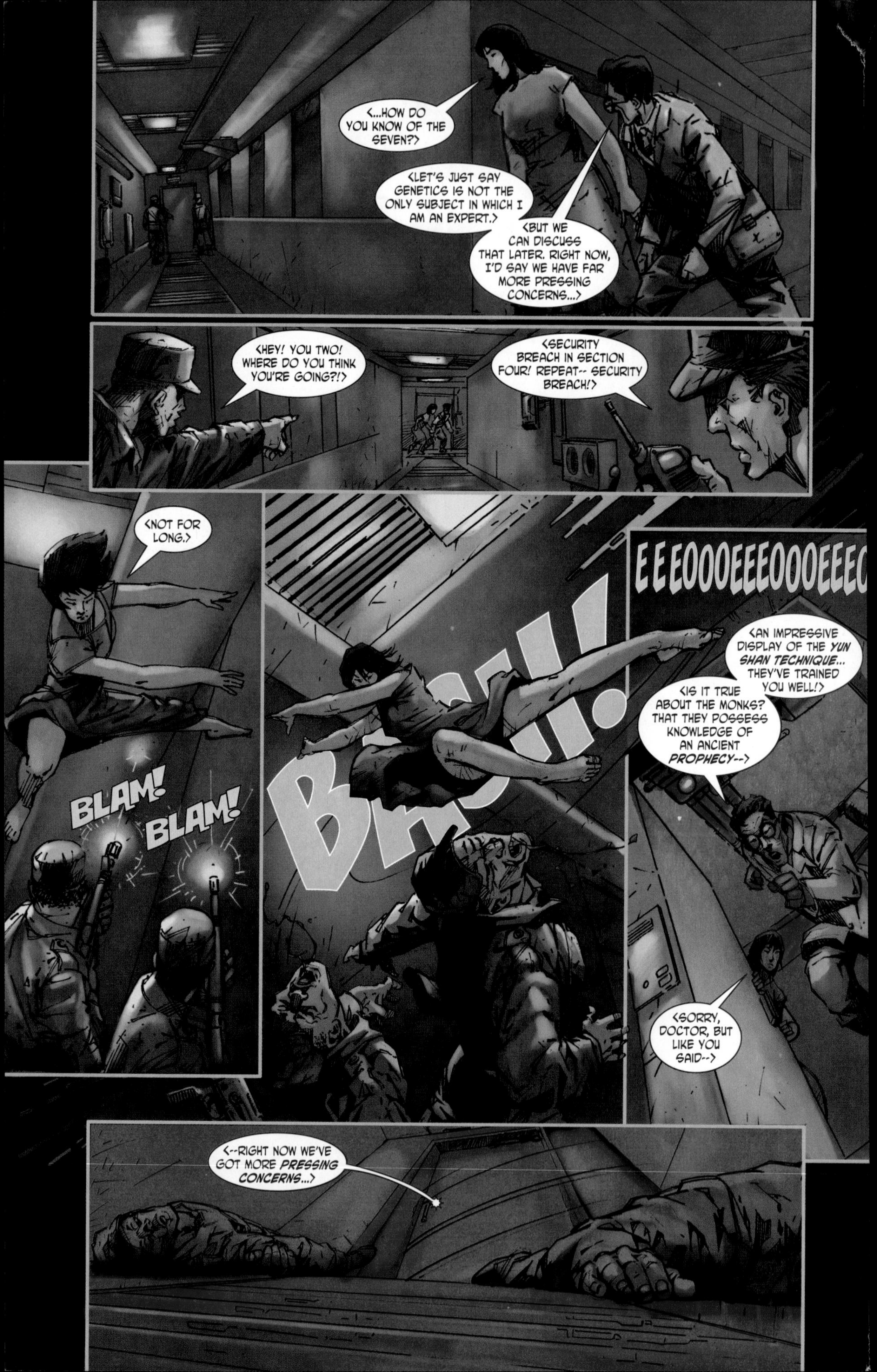

<...HOW DO YOU KNOW OF THE SEVEN?>
<LET'S JUST SAY GENETICS IS NOT THE ONLY SUBJECT IN WHICH I AM AN EXPERT.>
<BUT WE CAN DISCUSS THAT LATER. RIGHT NOW, I'D SAY WE HAVE FAR MORE PRESSING CONCERNS...>
<HEY! YOU TWO! WHERE DO YOU THINK YOU'RE GOING?!>
<SECURITY BREACH IN SECTION FOUR! REPEAT-- SECURITY BREACH!>
<NOT FOR LONG.>
BLAM!
BLAM!
E E EOOOEEEOOOEEEO
<AN IMPRESSIVE DISPLAY OF THE *YUN SHAN TECHNIQUE*... THEY'VE TRAINED YOU WELL!>
<IS IT TRUE ABOUT THE MONKS? THAT THEY POSSESS KNOWLEDGE OF AN ANCIENT *PROPHECY*-->
<SORRY, DOCTOR, BUT LIKE YOU SAID-->
<--RIGHT NOW WE'VE GOT MORE *PRESSING CONCERNS*...>

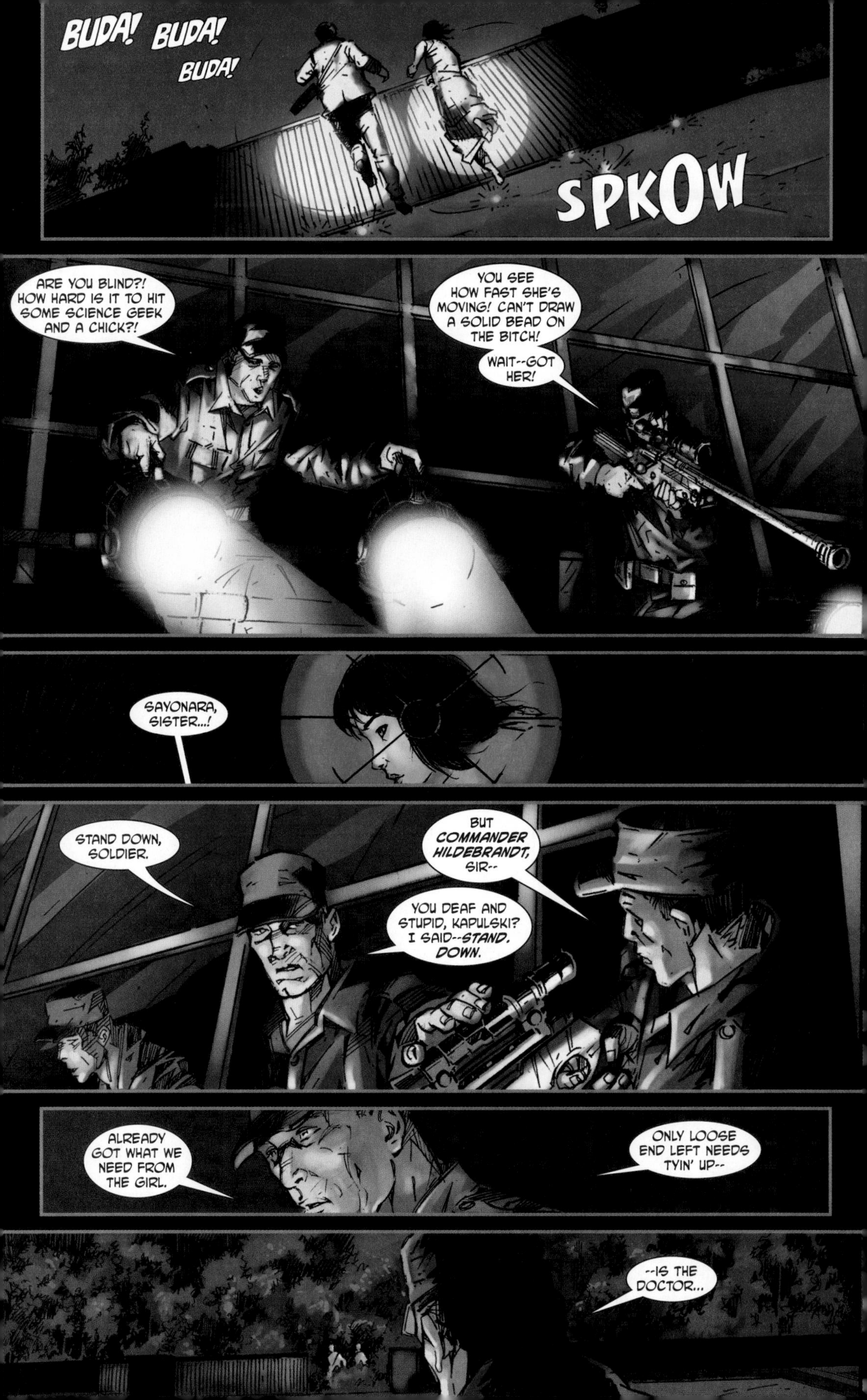
BUDA! BUDA!
BUDA!
SPKOW
ARE YOU BLIND?! HOW HARD IS IT TO HIT SOME SCIENCE GEEK AND A CHICK?!
YOU SEE HOW FAST SHE'S MOVING! CAN'T DRAW A SOLID BEAD ON THE BITCH!
WAIT--GOT HER!
SAYONARA, SISTER...!
STAND DOWN, SOLDIER.
BUT COMMANDER HILDEBRANDT, SIR--
YOU DEAF AND STUPID, KAPULSKI? I SAID--STAND. DOWN.
ALREADY GOT WHAT WE NEED FROM THE GIRL.
ONLY LOOSE END LEFT NEEDS TYIN' UP--
--IS THE DOCTOR...

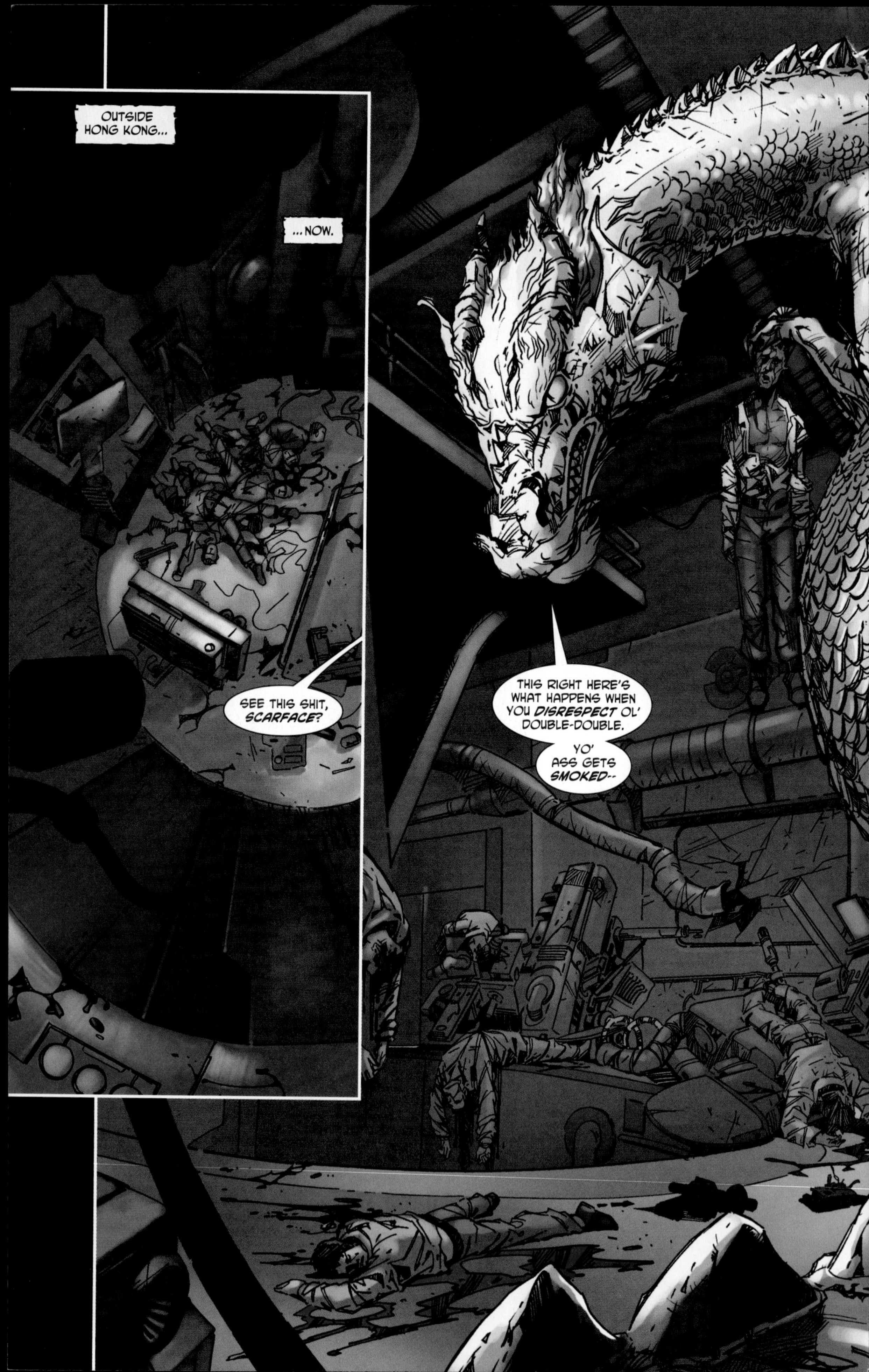
OUTSIDE HONG KONG...
...NOW.
SEE THIS SHIT, SCARFACE?
THIS RIGHT HERE'S WHAT HAPPENS WHEN YOU DISRESPECT OL' DOUBLE-DOUBLE.
YO' ASS GETS SMOKED--

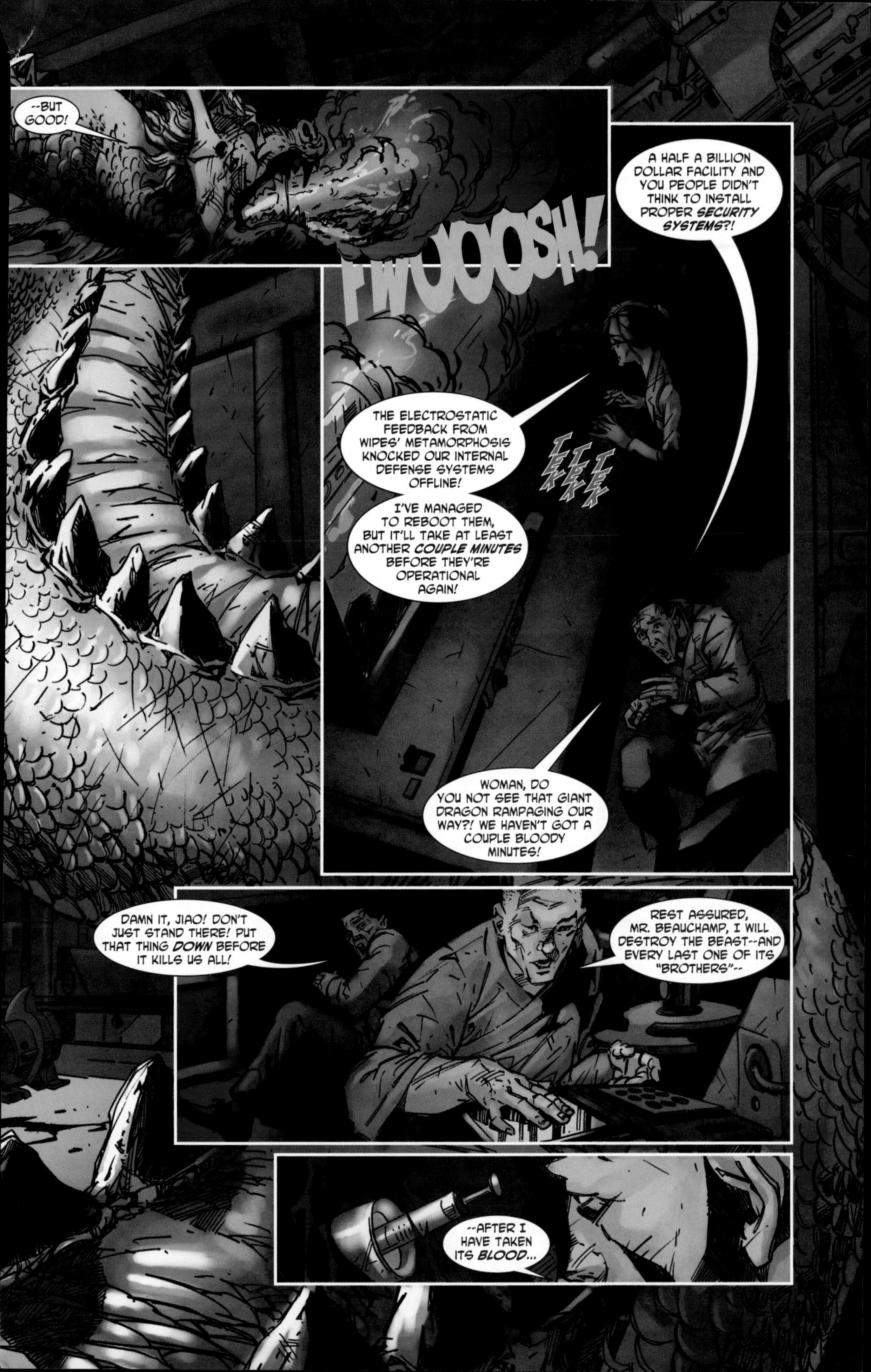
--BUT GOOD!
FWOOOSH!
A HALF A BILLION DOLLAR FACILITY AND YOU PEOPLE DIDN'T THINK TO INSTALL PROPER *SECURITY SYSTEMS?!*
THE ELECTROSTATIC FEEDBACK FROM WIPES' METAMORPHOSIS KNOCKED OUR INTERNAL DEFENSE SYSTEMS OFFLINE!
I'VE MANAGED TO REBOOT THEM, BUT IT'LL TAKE AT LEAST ANOTHER *COUPLE MINUTES* BEFORE THEY'RE OPERATIONAL AGAIN!
TEKK TEKK TEKK
WOMAN, DO YOU NOT SEE THAT GIANT DRAGON RAMPAGING OUR WAY?! WE HAVEN'T GOT A COUPLE BLOODY MINUTES!
DAMN IT, JIAO! DON'T JUST STAND THERE! PUT THAT THING *DOWN* BEFORE IT KILLS US ALL!
REST ASSURED, MR. BEAUCHAMP, I WILL DESTROY THE BEAST--AND EVERY LAST ONE OF ITS "BROTHERS"--
--AFTER I HAVE TAKEN ITS *BLOOD*...

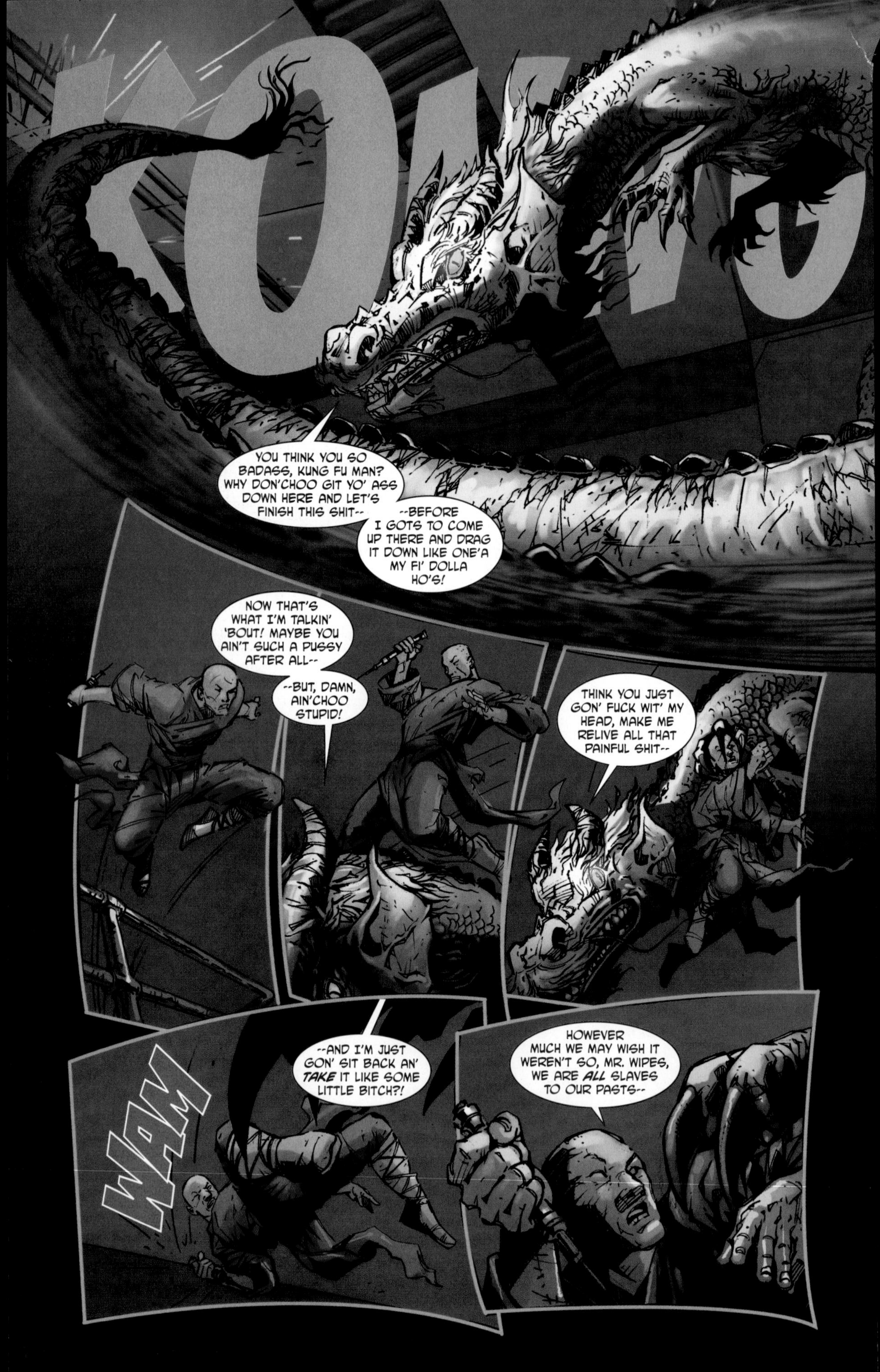
KOWHO
YOU THINK YOU SO BADASS, KUNG FU MAN? WHY DON'CHOO GIT YO' ASS DOWN HERE AND LET'S FINISH THIS SHIT--
--BEFORE I GOTS TO COME UP THERE AND DRAG IT DOWN LIKE ONE'A MY FI' DOLLA HO'S!
NOW THAT'S WHAT I'M TALKIN' 'BOUT! MAYBE YOU AIN'T SUCH A PUSSY AFTER ALL--
--BUT, DAMN, AIN'CHOO STUPID!
THINK YOU JUST GON' FUCK WIT' MY HEAD, MAKE ME RELIVE ALL THAT PAINFUL SHIT--
WAM
--AND I'M JUST GON' SIT BACK AN' *TAKE* IT LIKE SOME LITTLE BITCH?!
HOWEVER MUCH WE MAY WISH IT WEREN'T SO, MR. WIPES, WE ARE *ALL* SLAVES TO OUR PASTS--

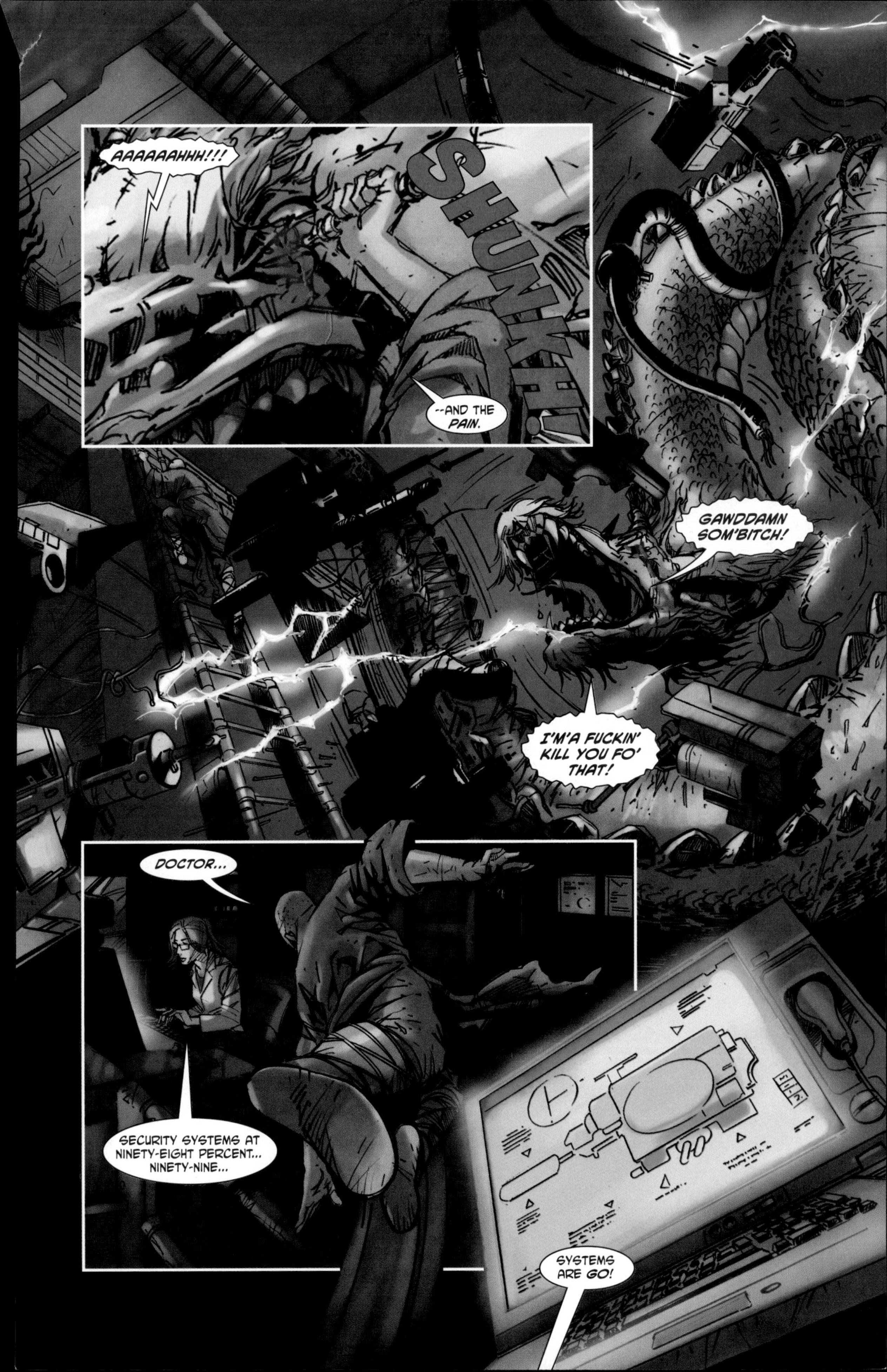
AAAAAAHHH!!!
SHUNKH!
--AND THE PAIN.
GAWDDAMN SOM'BITCH!
I'M'A FUCKIN' KILL YOU FO' THAT!
DOCTOR...
SECURITY SYSTEMS AT NINETY-EIGHT PERCENT... NINETY-NINE...
SYSTEMS ARE GO!

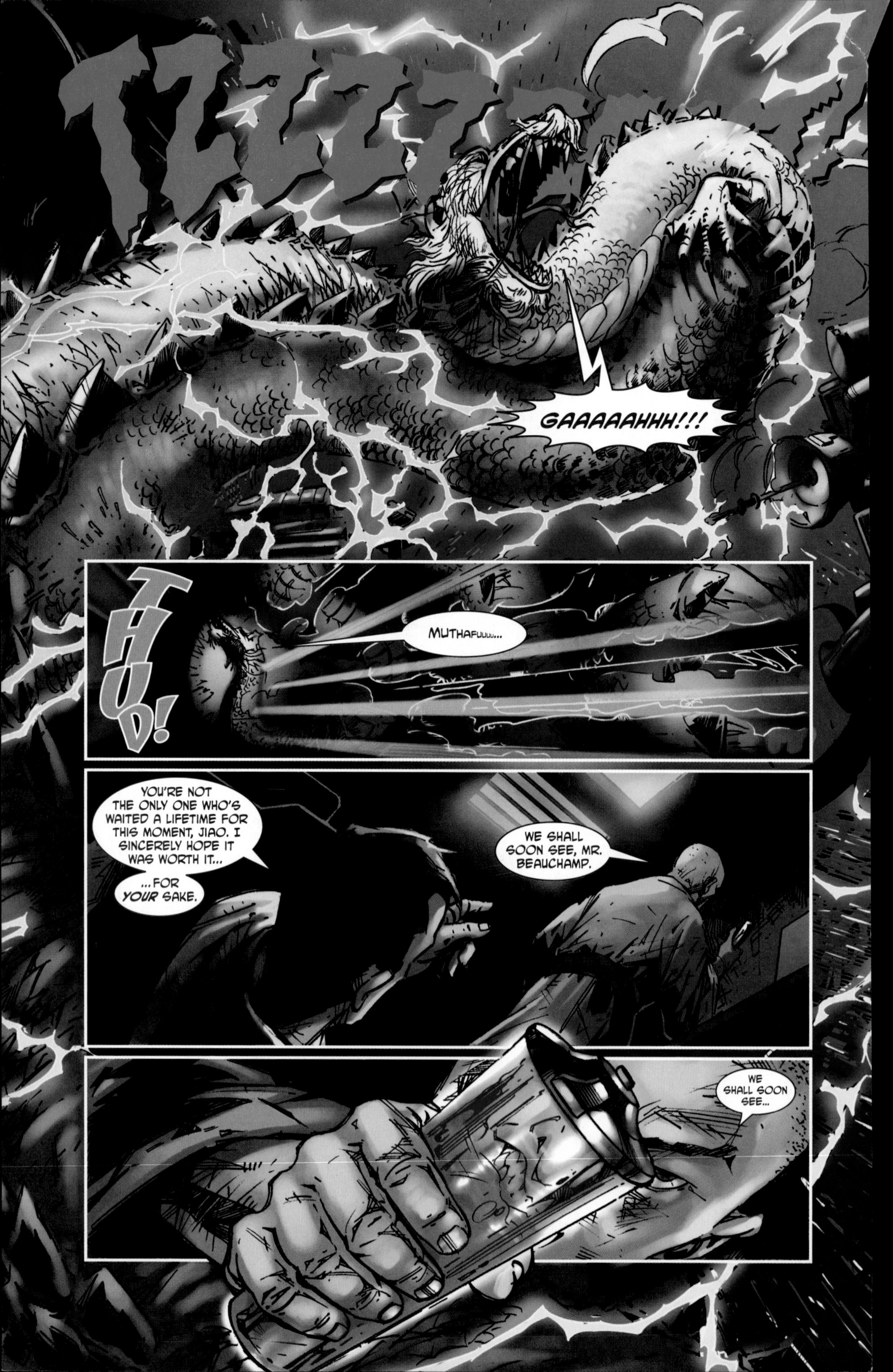
TZZZZ
GAAAAAHHH!!!
THUD!
MUTHAFUUUU...
YOU'RE NOT THE ONLY ONE WHO'S WAITED A LIFETIME FOR THIS MOMENT, JIAO. I SINCERELY HOPE IT WAS WORTH IT...
...FOR *YOUR* SAKE.
WE SHALL SOON SEE, MR. BEAUCHAMP.
WE SHALL SOON SEE...

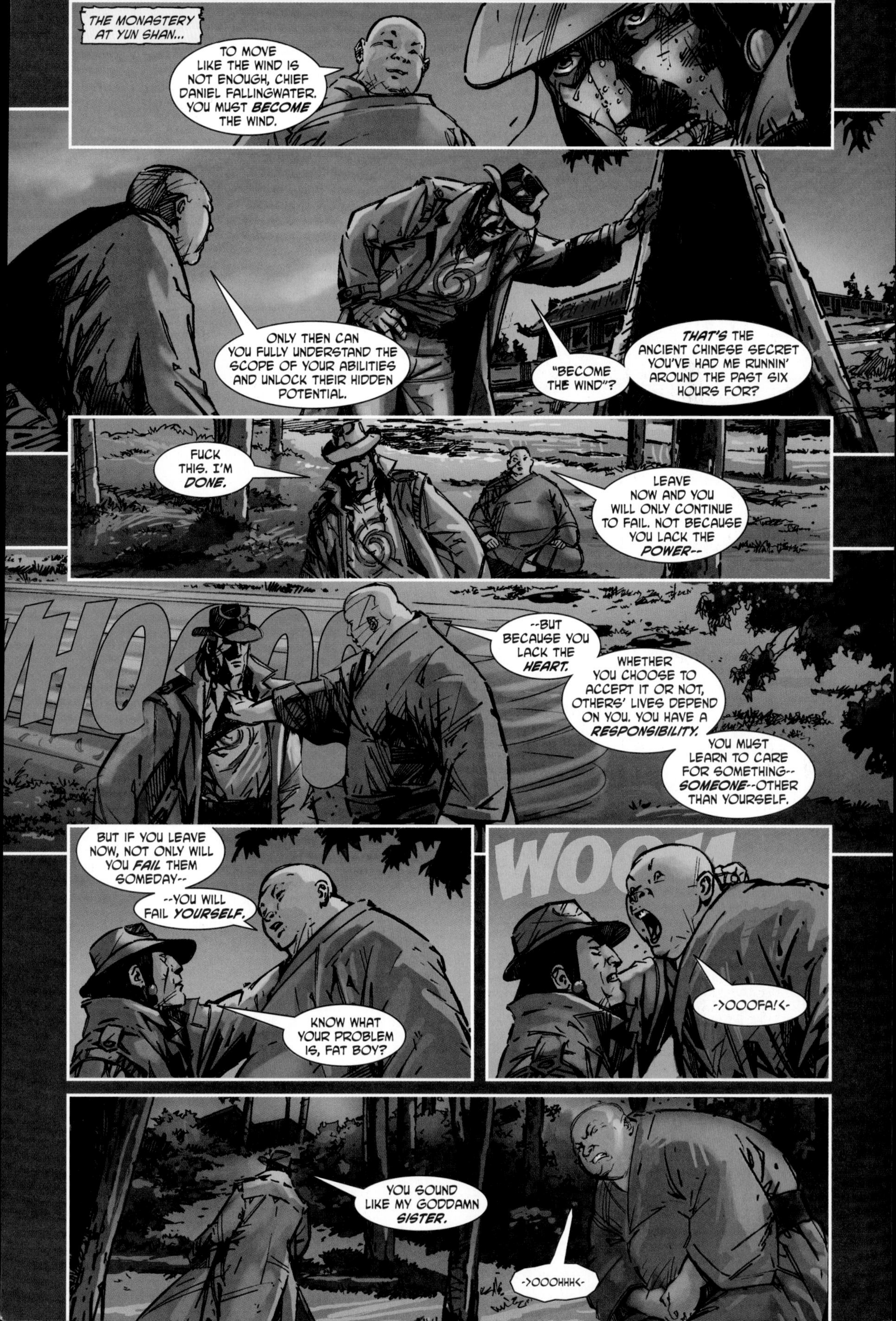
THE MONASTERY AT YUN SHAN...
TO MOVE LIKE THE WIND IS NOT ENOUGH, CHIEF DANIEL FALLINGWATER. YOU MUST BECOME THE WIND.
ONLY THEN CAN YOU FULLY UNDERSTAND THE SCOPE OF YOUR ABILITIES AND UNLOCK THEIR HIDDEN POTENTIAL.
"BECOME THE WIND"?
THAT'S THE ANCIENT CHINESE SECRET YOU'VE HAD ME RUNNIN' AROUND THE PAST SIX HOURS FOR?
FUCK THIS. I'M DONE.
LEAVE NOW AND YOU WILL ONLY CONTINUE TO FAIL. NOT BECAUSE YOU LACK THE POWER--
--BUT BECAUSE YOU LACK THE HEART.
WHETHER YOU CHOOSE TO ACCEPT IT OR NOT, OTHERS' LIVES DEPEND ON YOU. YOU HAVE A RESPONSIBILITY.
YOU MUST LEARN TO CARE FOR SOMETHING-- SOMEONE--OTHER THAN YOURSELF.
BUT IF YOU LEAVE NOW, NOT ONLY WILL YOU FAIL THEM SOMEDAY--
--YOU WILL FAIL YOURSELF.
KNOW WHAT YOUR PROBLEM IS, FAT BOY?
WOOF!!
->OOOFA!<-
YOU SOUND LIKE MY GODDAMN SISTER.
->OOOHHH<-

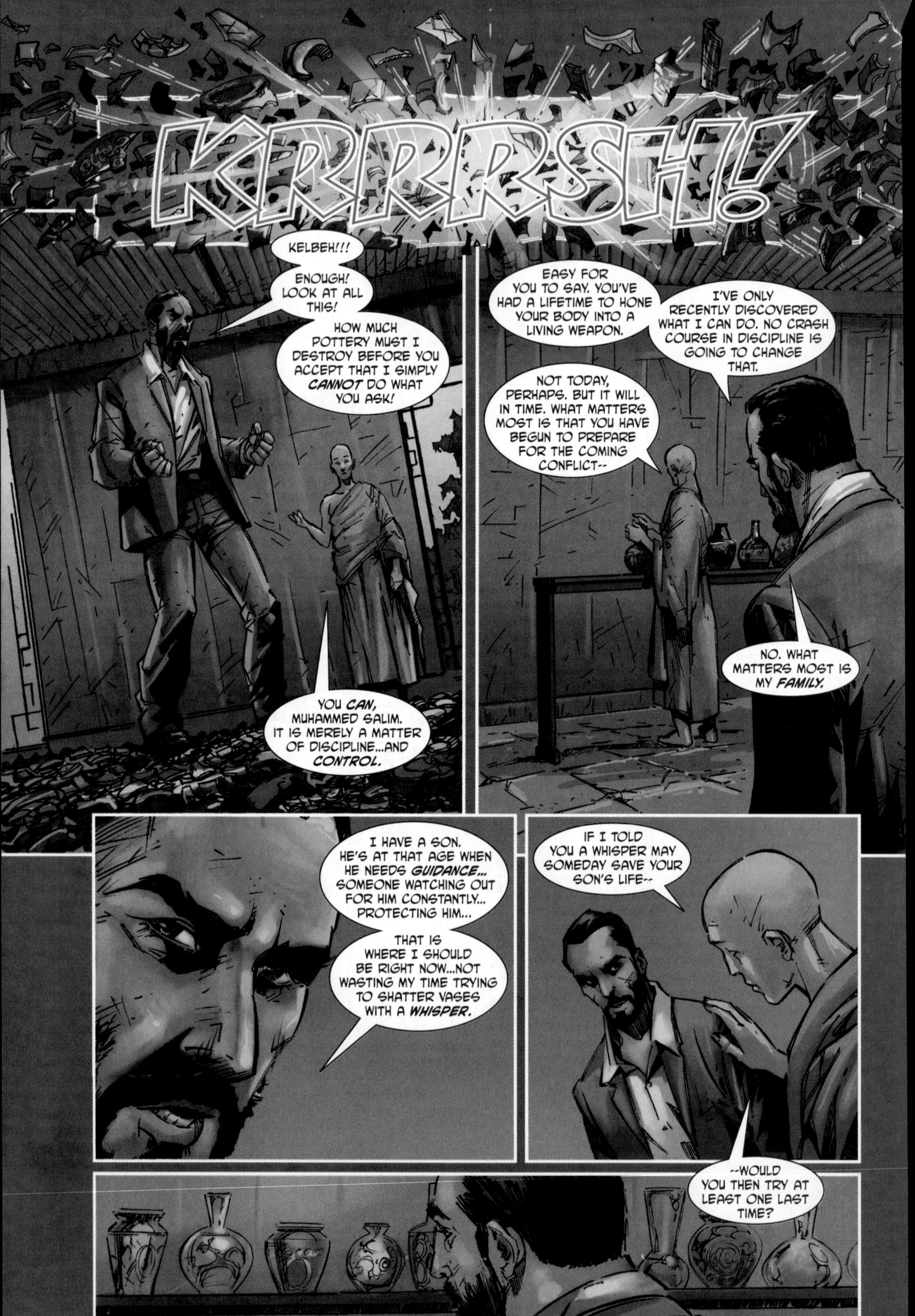
KRRRRSH!!
KELBEH!!!
ENOUGH! LOOK AT ALL THIS!
HOW MUCH POTTERY MUST I DESTROY BEFORE YOU ACCEPT THAT I SIMPLY *CANNOT* DO WHAT YOU ASK!
YOU *CAN,* MUHAMMED SALIM. IT IS MERELY A MATTER OF DISCIPLINE...AND *CONTROL.*
EASY FOR YOU TO SAY. YOU'VE HAD A LIFETIME TO HONE YOUR BODY INTO A LIVING WEAPON.
I'VE ONLY RECENTLY DISCOVERED WHAT I CAN DO. NO CRASH COURSE IN DISCIPLINE IS GOING TO CHANGE THAT.
NOT TODAY, PERHAPS. BUT IT WILL IN TIME. WHAT MATTERS MOST IS THAT YOU HAVE BEGUN TO PREPARE FOR THE COMING CONFLICT--
NO. WHAT MATTERS MOST IS MY *FAMILY.*
I HAVE A SON. HE'S AT THAT AGE WHEN HE NEEDS *GUIDANCE...* SOMEONE WATCHING OUT FOR HIM CONSTANTLY... PROTECTING HIM...
THAT IS WHERE I SHOULD BE RIGHT NOW...NOT WASTING MY TIME TRYING TO SHATTER VASES WITH A *WHISPER.*
IF I TOLD YOU A WHISPER MAY SOMEDAY SAVE YOUR SON'S LIFE--
--WOULD YOU THEN TRY AT LEAST ONE LAST TIME?

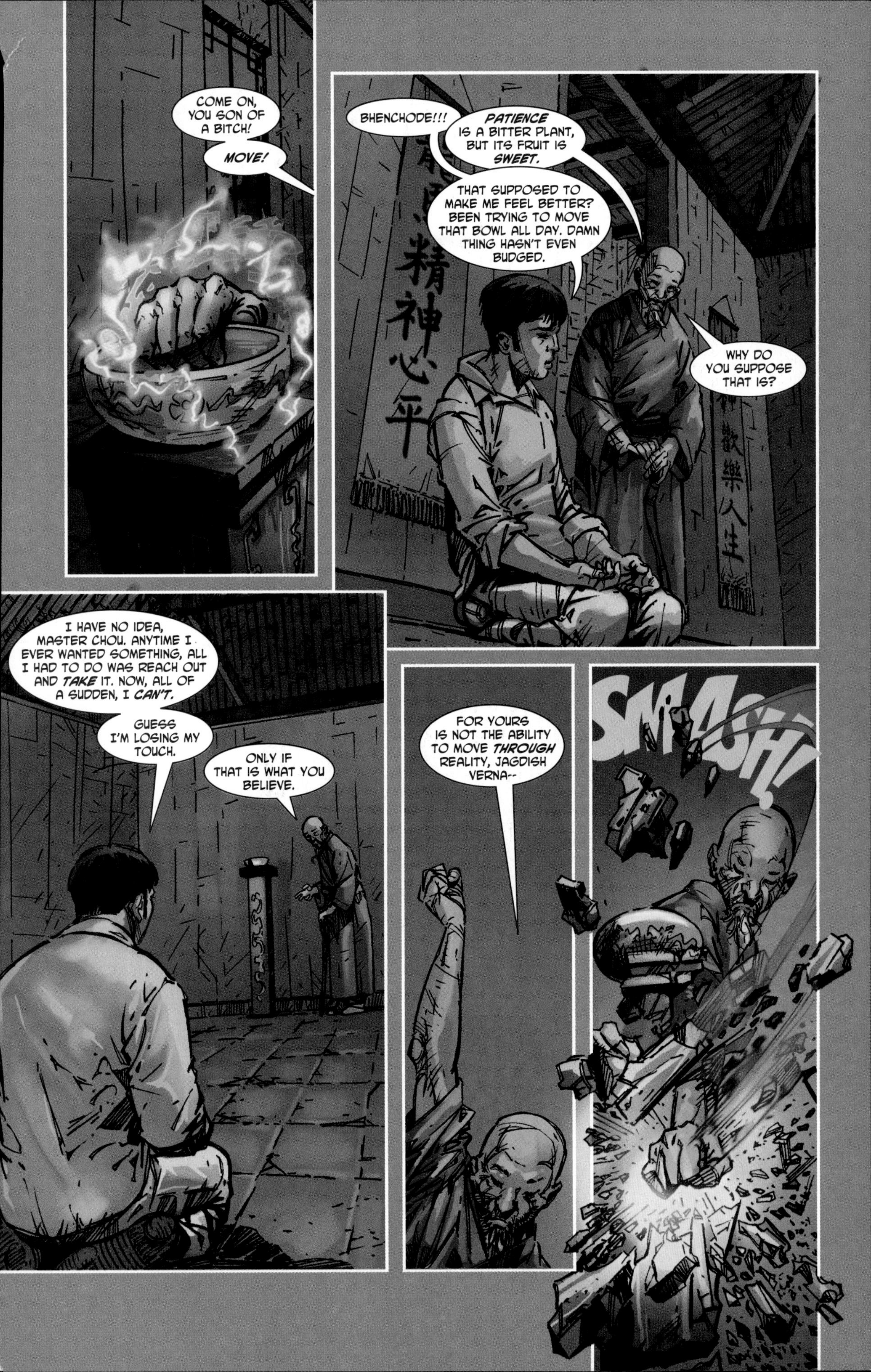
COME ON, YOU SON OF A BITCH!
MOVE!
BHENCHODE!!!
PATIENCE IS A BITTER PLANT, BUT ITS FRUIT IS SWEET.
THAT SUPPOSED TO MAKE ME FEEL BETTER? BEEN TRYING TO MOVE THAT BOWL ALL DAY. DAMN THING HASN'T EVEN BUDGED.
WHY DO YOU SUPPOSE THAT IS?
I HAVE NO IDEA, MASTER CHOU. ANYTIME I EVER WANTED SOMETHING, ALL I HAD TO DO WAS REACH OUT AND TAKE IT. NOW, ALL OF A SUDDEN, I CAN'T.
GUESS I'M LOSING MY TOUCH.
ONLY IF THAT IS WHAT YOU BELIEVE.
FOR YOURS IS NOT THE ABILITY TO MOVE THROUGH REALITY, JAGDISH VERNA--
SMASH!

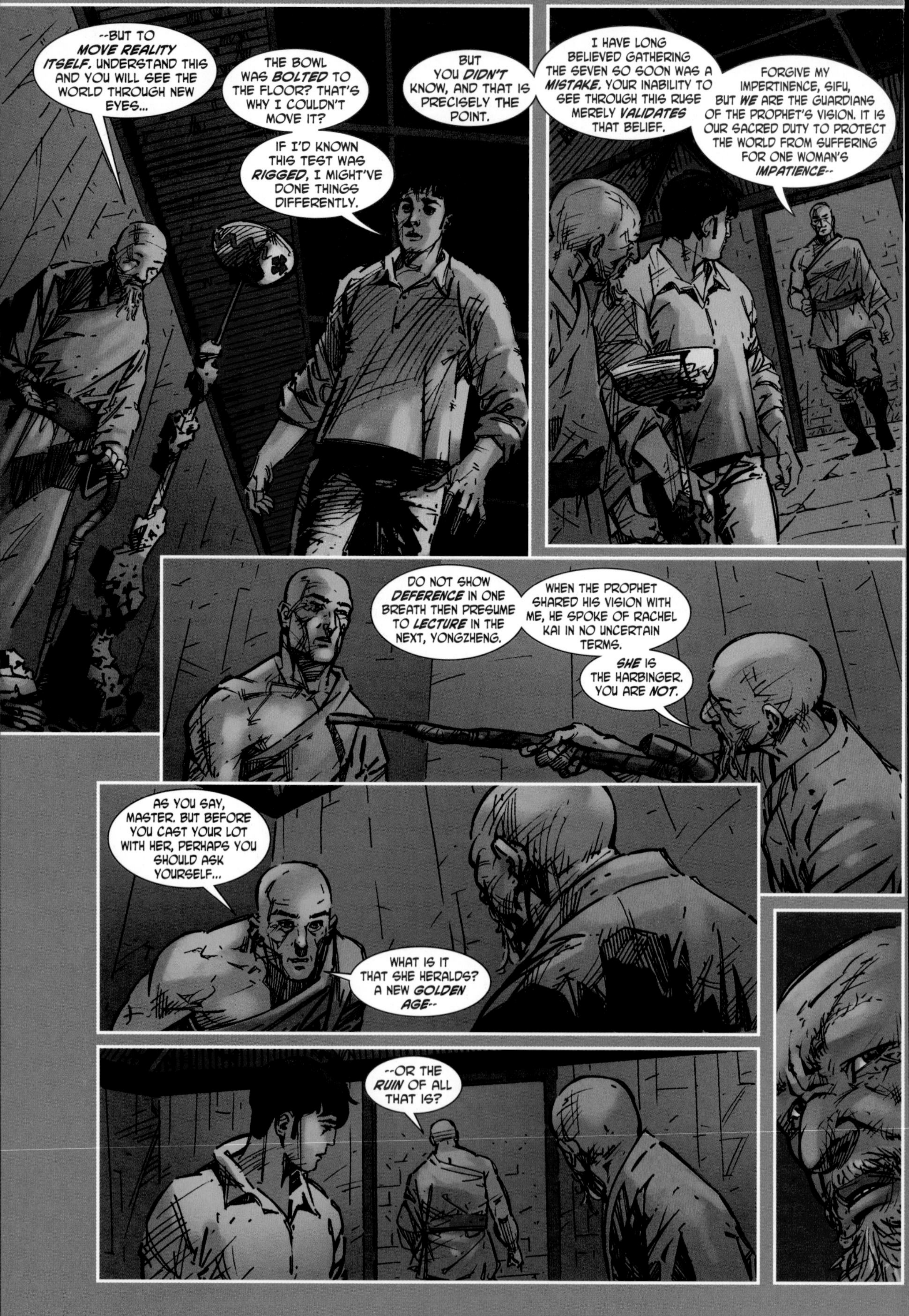
--BUT TO MOVE REALITY ITSELF. UNDERSTAND THIS AND YOU WILL SEE THE WORLD THROUGH NEW EYES...
THE BOWL WAS BOLTED TO THE FLOOR? THAT'S WHY I COULDN'T MOVE IT?
IF I'D KNOWN THIS TEST WAS RIGGED, I MIGHT'VE DONE THINGS DIFFERENTLY.
BUT YOU DIDN'T KNOW, AND THAT IS PRECISELY THE POINT.
I HAVE LONG BELIEVED GATHERING THE SEVEN SO SOON WAS A MISTAKE. YOUR INABILITY TO SEE THROUGH THIS RUSE MERELY VALIDATES THAT BELIEF.
FORGIVE MY IMPERTINENCE, SIFU, BUT WE ARE THE GUARDIANS OF THE PROPHET'S VISION. IT IS OUR SACRED DUTY TO PROTECT THE WORLD FROM SUFFERING FOR ONE WOMAN'S IMPATIENCE--
DO NOT SHOW DEFERENCE IN ONE BREATH THEN PRESUME TO LECTURE IN THE NEXT, YONGZHENG.
WHEN THE PROPHET SHARED HIS VISION WITH ME, HE SPOKE OF RACHEL KAI IN NO UNCERTAIN TERMS.
SHE IS THE HARBINGER. YOU ARE NOT.
AS YOU SAY, MASTER. BUT BEFORE YOU CAST YOUR LOT WITH HER, PERHAPS YOU SHOULD ASK YOURSELF...
WHAT IS IT THAT SHE HERALDS? A NEW GOLDEN AGE--
--OR THE RUIN OF ALL THAT IS?

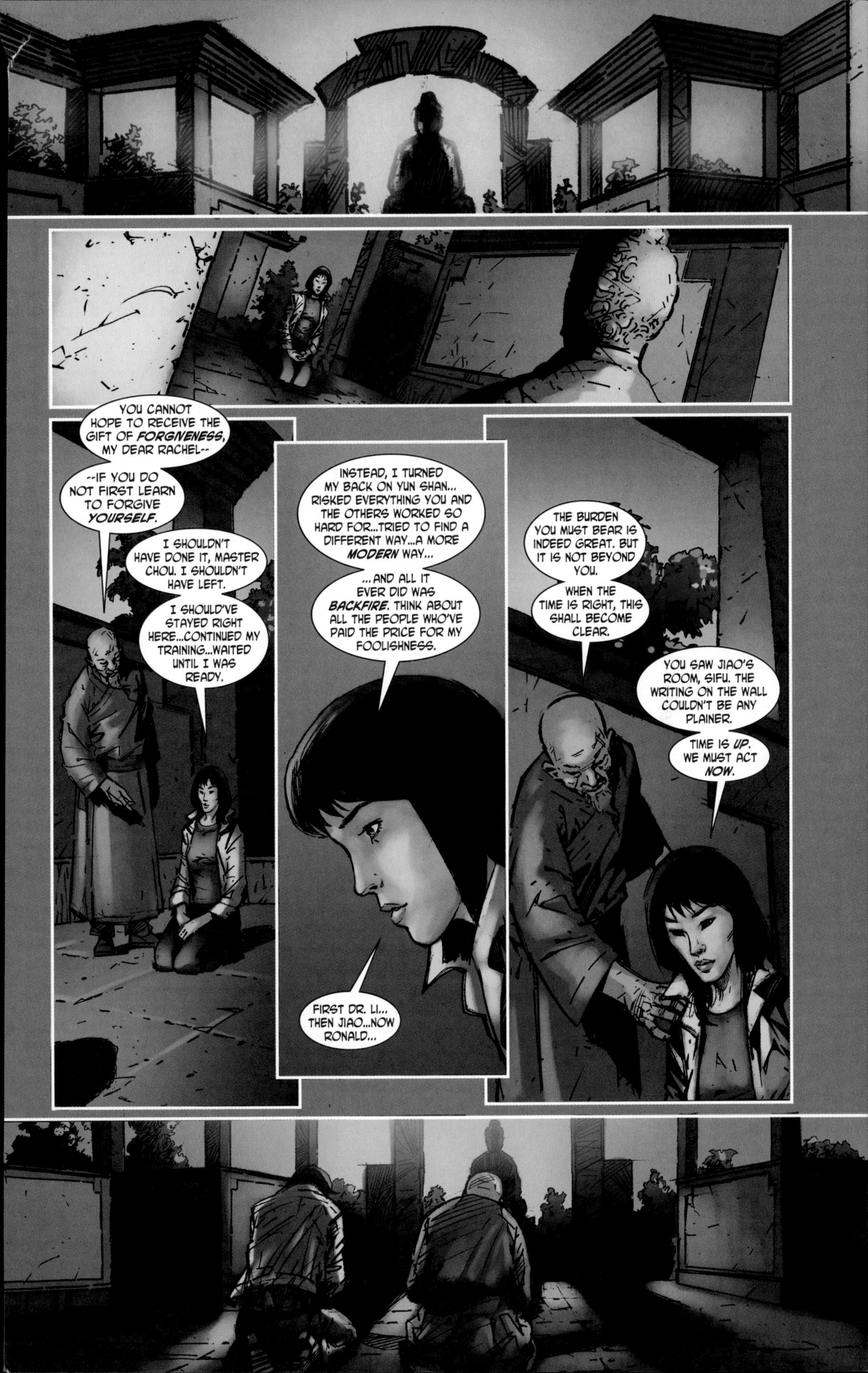
YOU CANNOT HOPE TO RECEIVE THE GIFT OF FORGIVENESS, MY DEAR RACHEL--
--IF YOU DO NOT FIRST LEARN TO FORGIVE YOURSELF.
I SHOULDN'T HAVE DONE IT, MASTER CHOU. I SHOULDN'T HAVE LEFT.
I SHOULD'VE STAYED RIGHT HERE...CONTINUED MY TRAINING...WAITED UNTIL I WAS READY.
INSTEAD, I TURNED MY BACK ON YUN SHAN... RISKED EVERYTHING YOU AND THE OTHERS WORKED SO HARD FOR...TRIED TO FIND A DIFFERENT WAY...A MORE MODERN WAY...
...AND ALL IT EVER DID WAS BACKFIRE. THINK ABOUT ALL THE PEOPLE WHO'VE PAID THE PRICE FOR MY FOOLISHNESS.
FIRST DR. LI... THEN JIAO...NOW RONALD...
THE BURDEN YOU MUST BEAR IS INDEED GREAT. BUT IT IS NOT BEYOND YOU.
WHEN THE TIME IS RIGHT, THIS SHALL BECOME CLEAR.
YOU SAW JIAO'S ROOM, SIFU. THE WRITING ON THE WALL COULDN'T BE ANY PLAINER.
TIME IS UP. WE MUST ACT NOW.

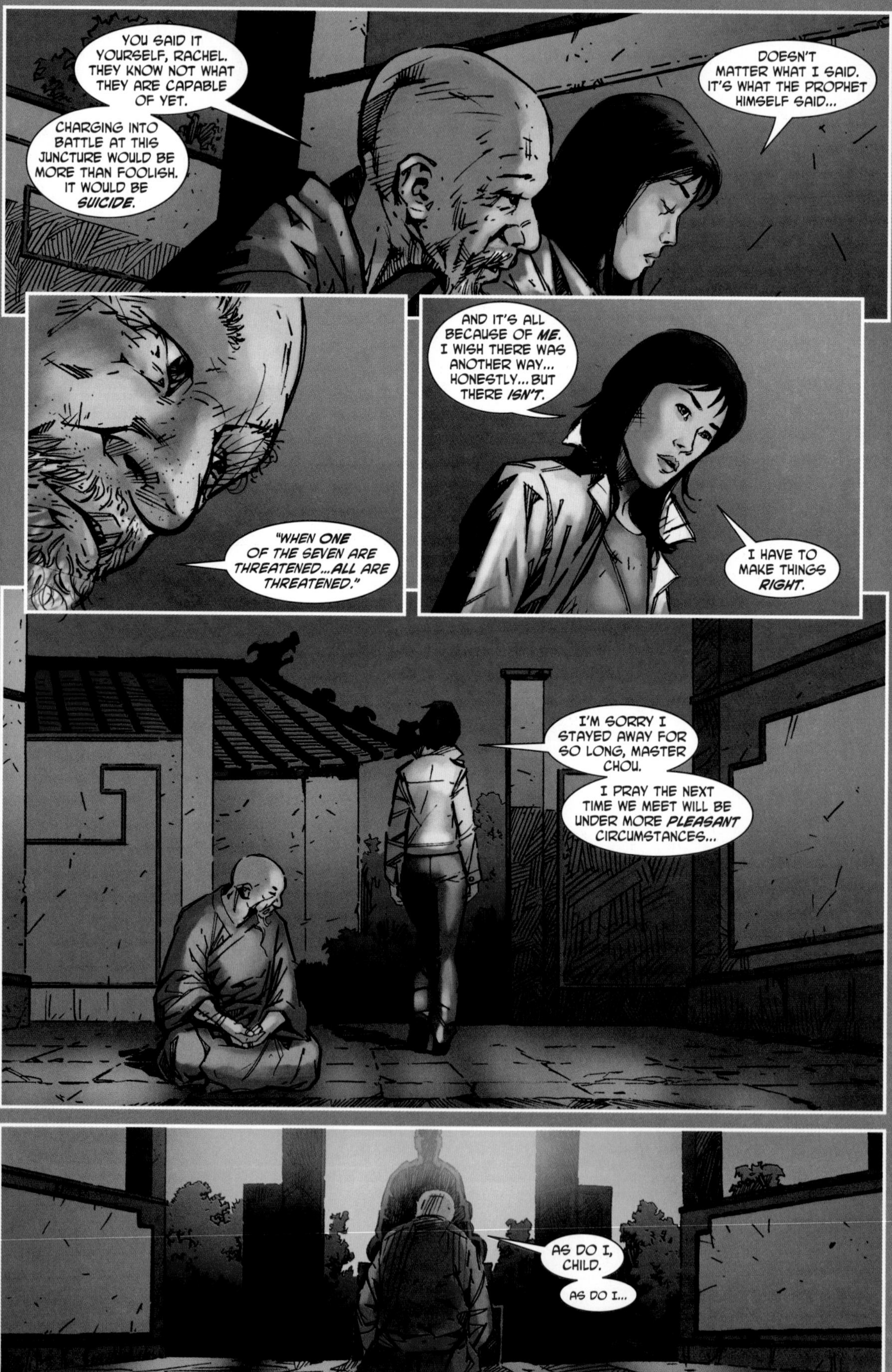
YOU SAID IT YOURSELF, RACHEL. THEY KNOW NOT WHAT THEY ARE CAPABLE OF YET.
CHARGING INTO BATTLE AT THIS JUNCTURE WOULD BE MORE THAN FOOLISH. IT WOULD BE SUICIDE.
DOESN'T MATTER WHAT I SAID. IT'S WHAT THE PROPHET HIMSELF SAID...
"WHEN ONE OF THE SEVEN ARE THREATENED...ALL ARE THREATENED."
AND IT'S ALL BECAUSE OF ME. I WISH THERE WAS ANOTHER WAY... HONESTLY... BUT THERE ISN'T.
I HAVE TO MAKE THINGS RIGHT.
I'M SORRY I STAYED AWAY FOR SO LONG, MASTER CHOU.
I PRAY THE NEXT TIME WE MEET WILL BE UNDER MORE PLEASANT CIRCUMSTANCES...
AS DO I, CHILD.
AS DO I...

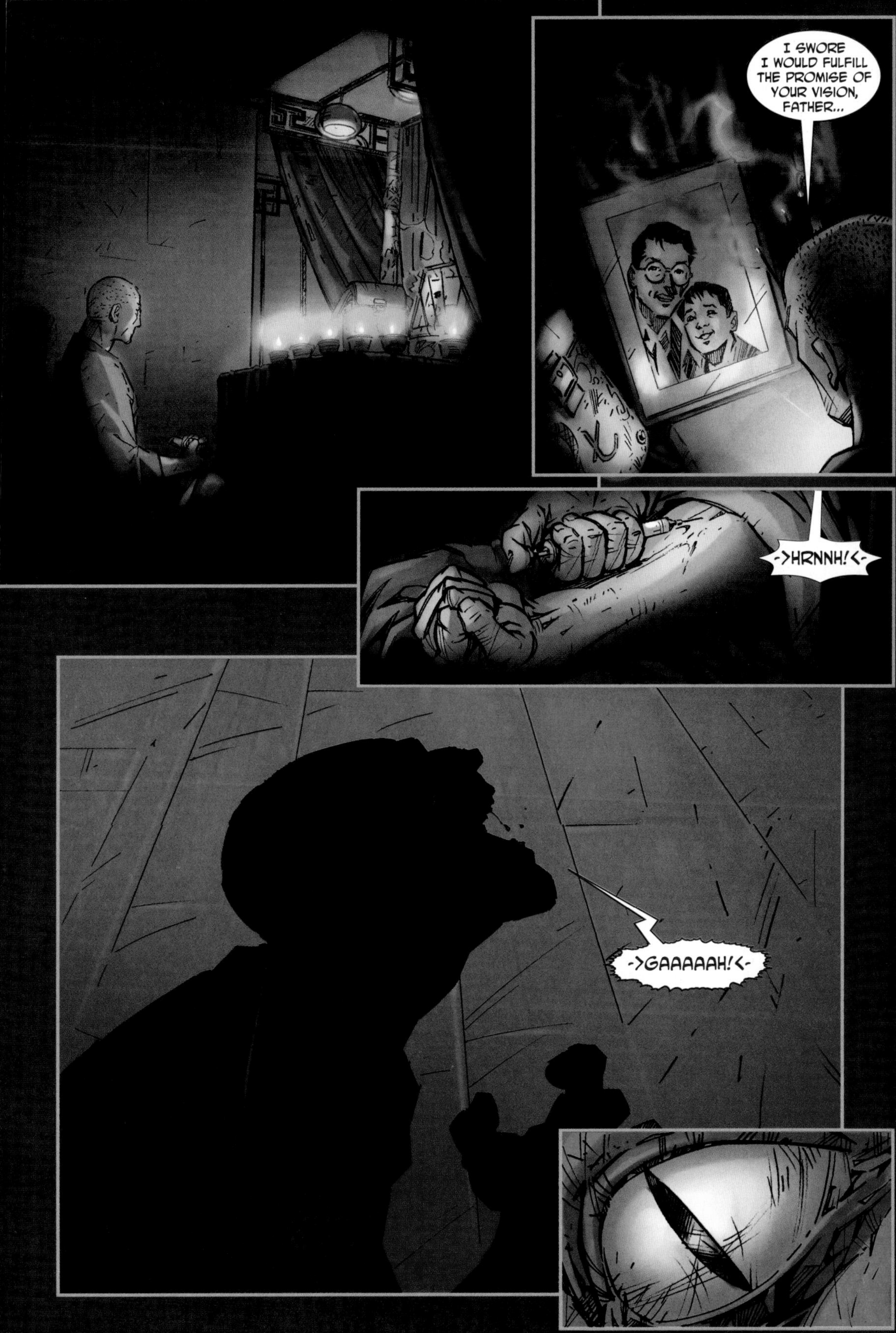

I SWORE I WOULD FULFILL THE PROMISE OF YOUR VISION, FATHER...
->HRNNH!<-
->GAAAAAH!<-

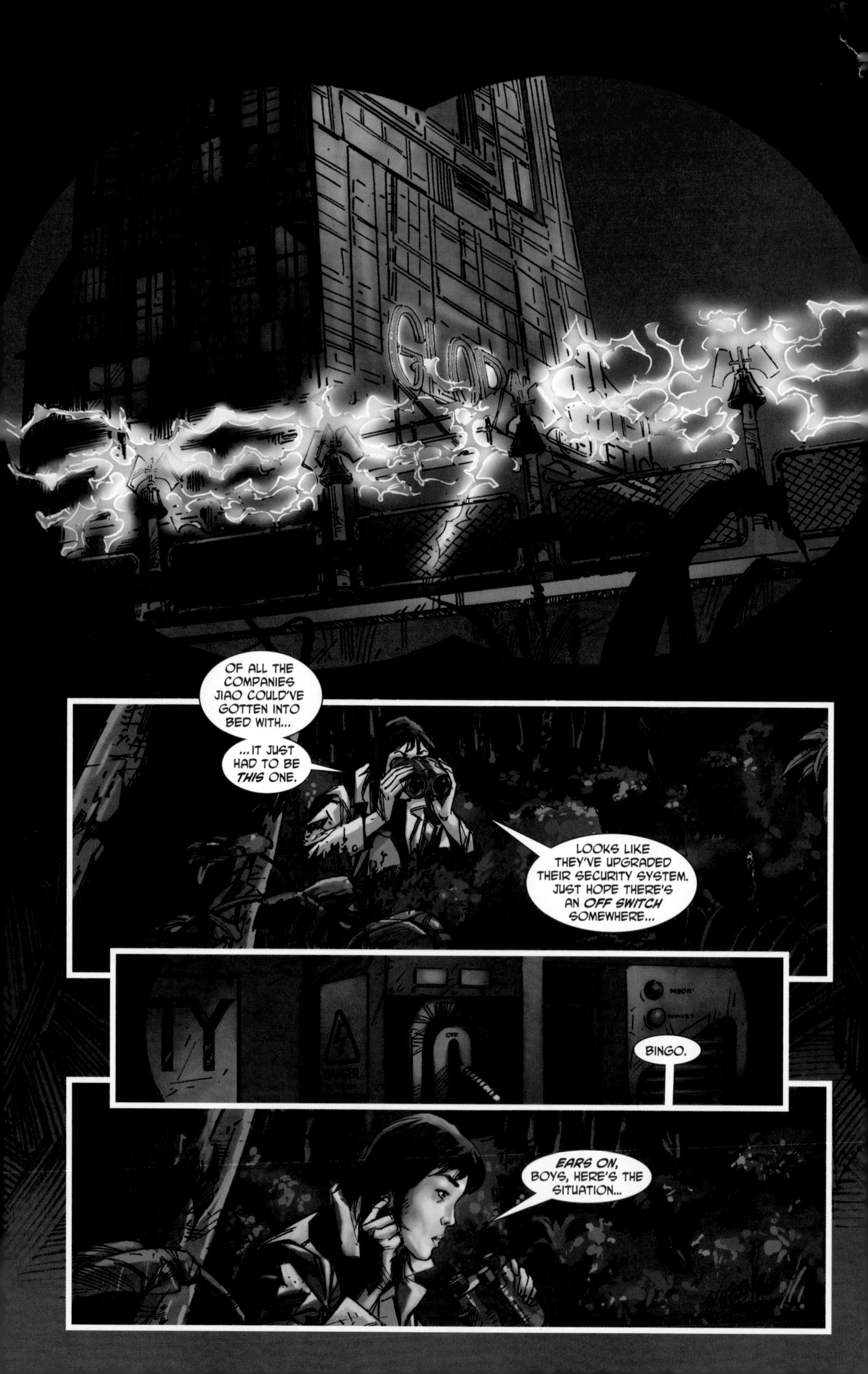

OF ALL THE COMPANIES JIAO COULD'VE GOTTEN INTO BED WITH...
...IT JUST HAD TO BE *THIS* ONE.
LOOKS LIKE THEY'VE UPGRADED THEIR SECURITY SYSTEM. JUST HOPE THERE'S AN *OFF SWITCH* SOMEWHERE...
BINGO.
EARS ON, BOYS, HERE'S THE SITUATION...

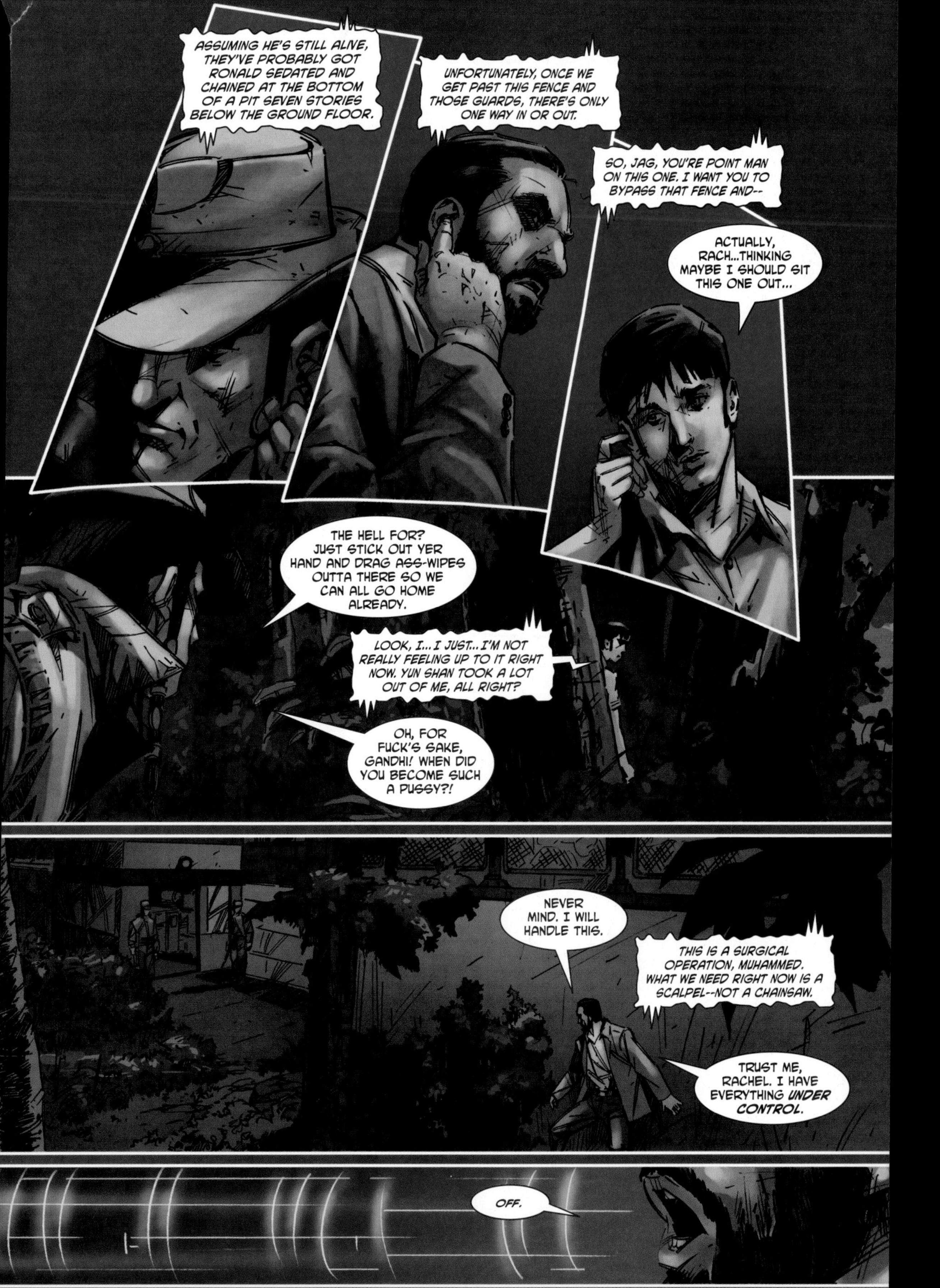

ASSUMING HE'S STILL ALIVE, THEY'VE PROBABLY GOT RONALD SEDATED AND CHAINED AT THE BOTTOM OF A PIT SEVEN STORIES BELOW THE GROUND FLOOR.
UNFORTUNATELY, ONCE WE GET PAST THIS FENCE AND THOSE GUARDS, THERE'S ONLY ONE WAY IN OR OUT.
SO, JAG, YOU'RE POINT MAN ON THIS ONE. I WANT YOU TO BYPASS THAT FENCE AND--
ACTUALLY, RACH...THINKING MAYBE I SHOULD SIT THIS ONE OUT...
THE HELL FOR? JUST STICK OUT YER HAND AND DRAG ASS-WIPES OUTTA THERE SO WE CAN ALL GO HOME ALREADY.
LOOK, I... I JUST... I'M NOT REALLY FEELING UP TO IT RIGHT NOW. YUN SHAN TOOK A LOT OUT OF ME, ALL RIGHT?
OH, FOR FUCK'S SAKE, GANDHI! WHEN DID YOU BECOME SUCH A PUSSY?!
NEVER MIND. I WILL HANDLE THIS.
THIS IS A SURGICAL OPERATION, MUHAMMED. WHAT WE NEED RIGHT NOW IS A SCALPEL--NOT A CHAINSAW.
TRUST ME, RACHEL. I HAVE EVERYTHING UNDER CONTROL.
OFF.

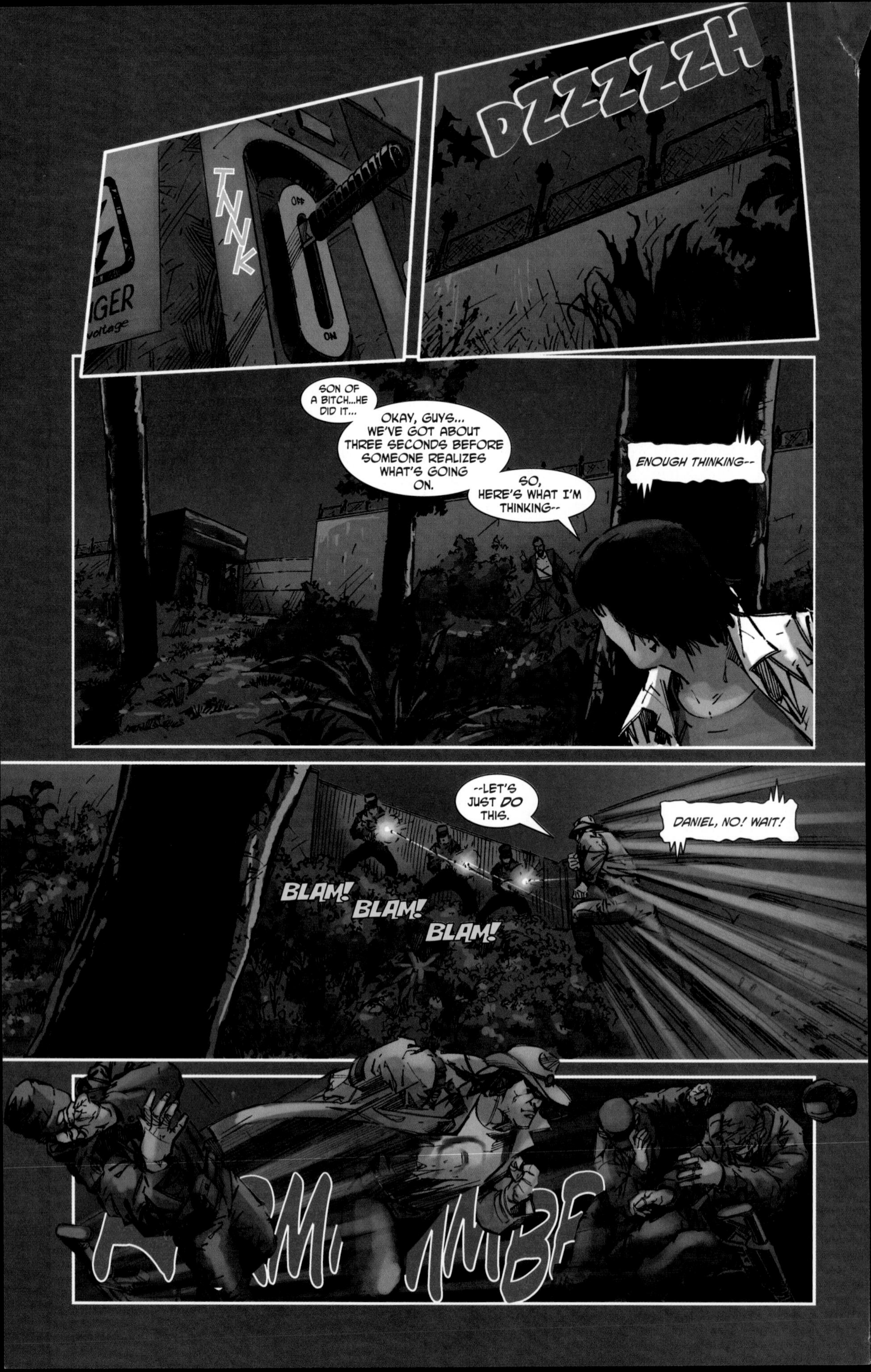

TNNK
IGER
voltage
OFF
ON
DZZZZZZH
SON OF A BITCH...HE DID IT...
OKAY, GUYS... WE'VE GOT ABOUT THREE SECONDS BEFORE SOMEONE REALIZES WHAT'S GOING ON.
SO, HERE'S WHAT I'M THINKING--
ENOUGH THINKING--
--LET'S JUST DO THIS.
DANIEL, NO! WAIT!
BLAM!
BLAM!
BLAM!

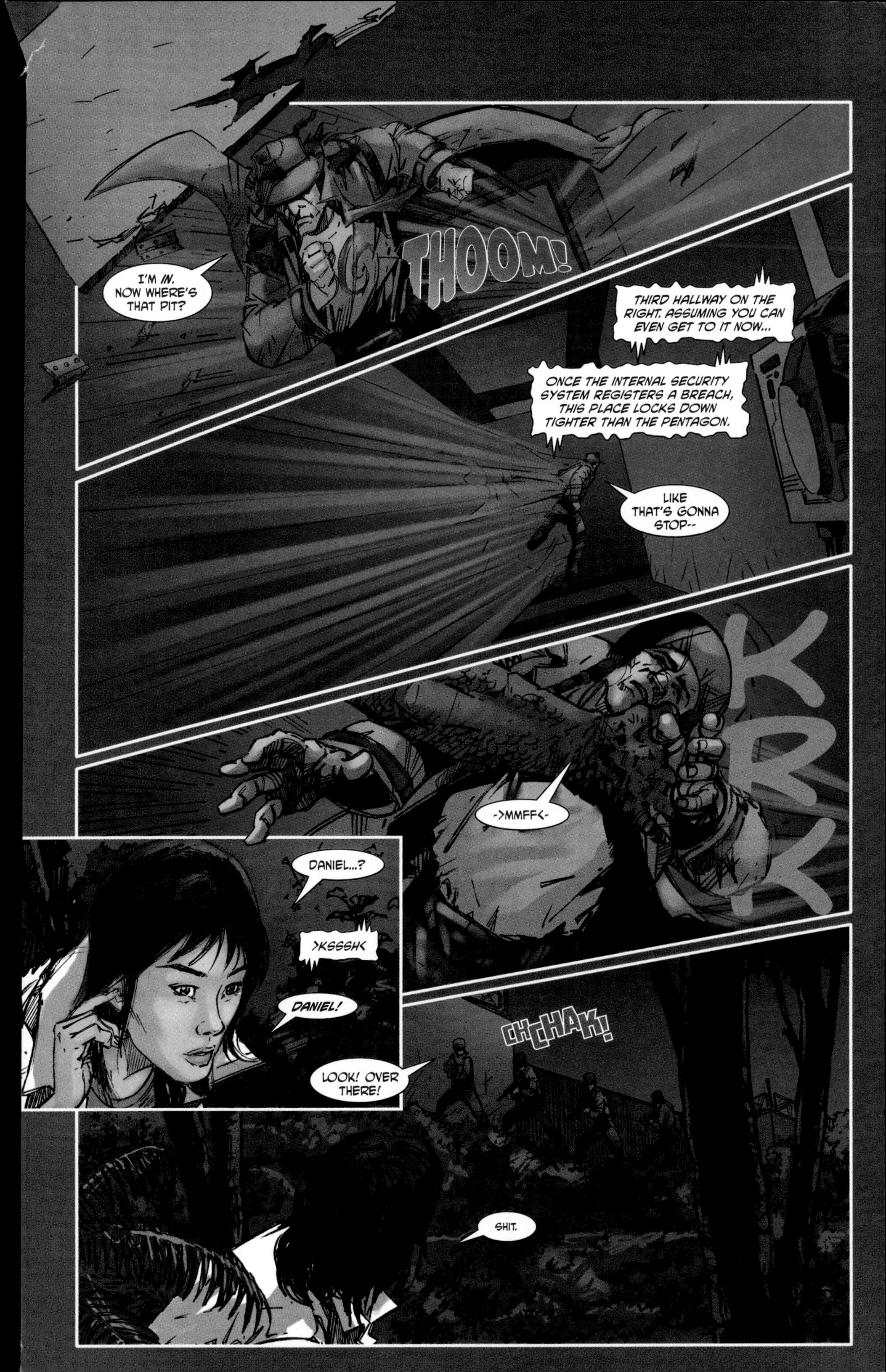
THOOM!
I'M *IN*. NOW WHERE'S THAT PIT?
THIRD HALLWAY ON THE RIGHT. ASSUMING YOU CAN EVEN GET TO IT NOW...
ONCE THE INTERNAL SECURITY SYSTEM REGISTERS A BREACH, THIS PLACE LOCKS DOWN TIGHTER THAN THE PENTAGON.
LIKE THAT'S GONNA STOP--
KRK
->MMFF<-
DANIEL...?
>KSSSH<
DANIEL!
CHCHAK!
LOOK! OVER THERE!
SHIT.

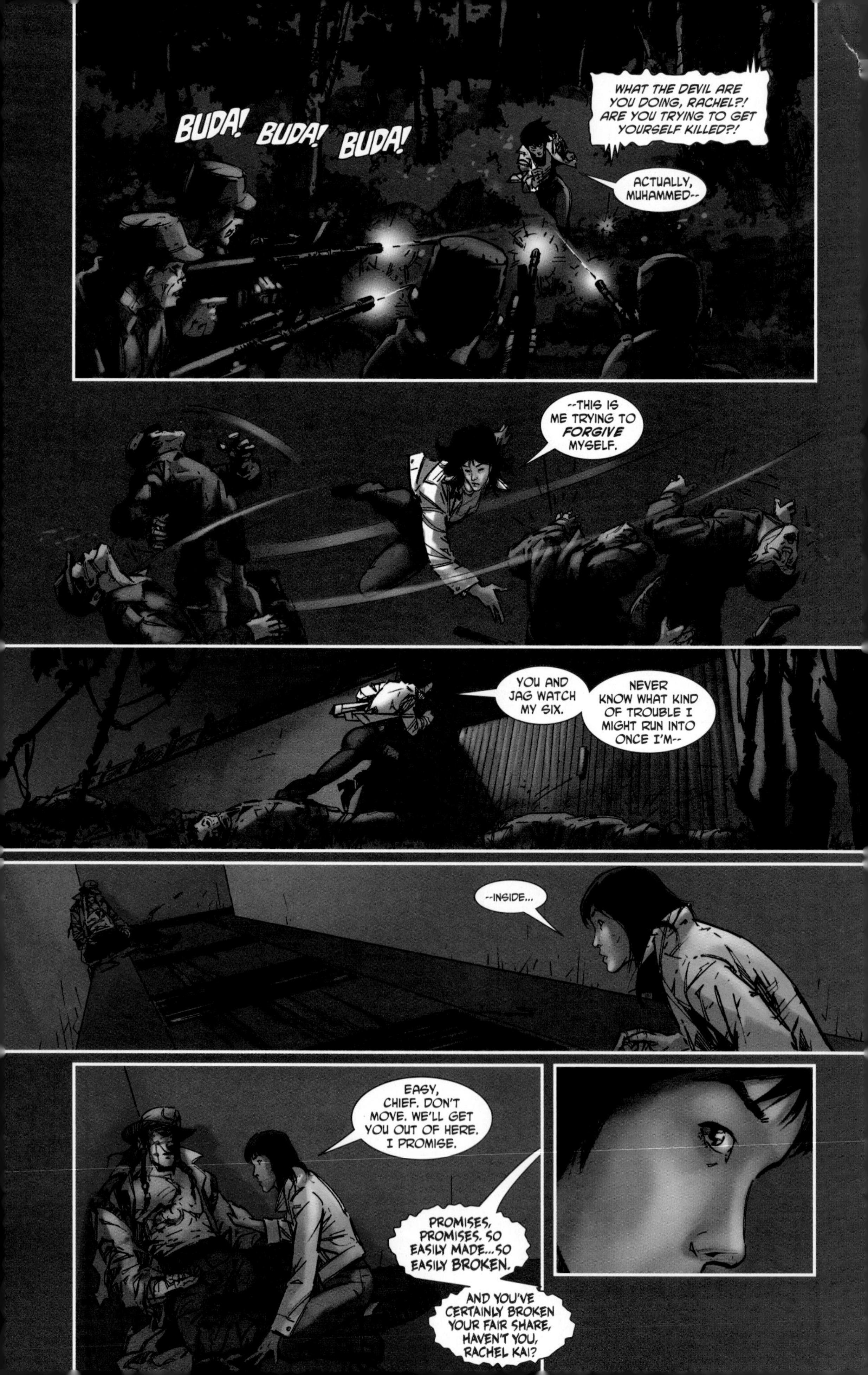

BUDA! BUDA! BUDA!
WHAT THE DEVIL ARE YOU DOING, RACHEL?! ARE YOU TRYING TO GET YOURSELF KILLED?!
ACTUALLY, MUHAMMED--
--THIS IS ME TRYING TO FORGIVE MYSELF.
YOU AND JAG WATCH MY SIX.
NEVER KNOW WHAT KIND OF TROUBLE I MIGHT RUN INTO ONCE I'M--
--INSIDE...
EASY, CHIEF. DON'T MOVE. WE'LL GET YOU OUT OF HERE. I PROMISE.
PROMISES, PROMISES. SO EASILY MADE...SO EASILY BROKEN.
AND YOU'VE CERTAINLY BROKEN YOUR FAIR SHARE, HAVEN'T YOU, RACHEL KAI?

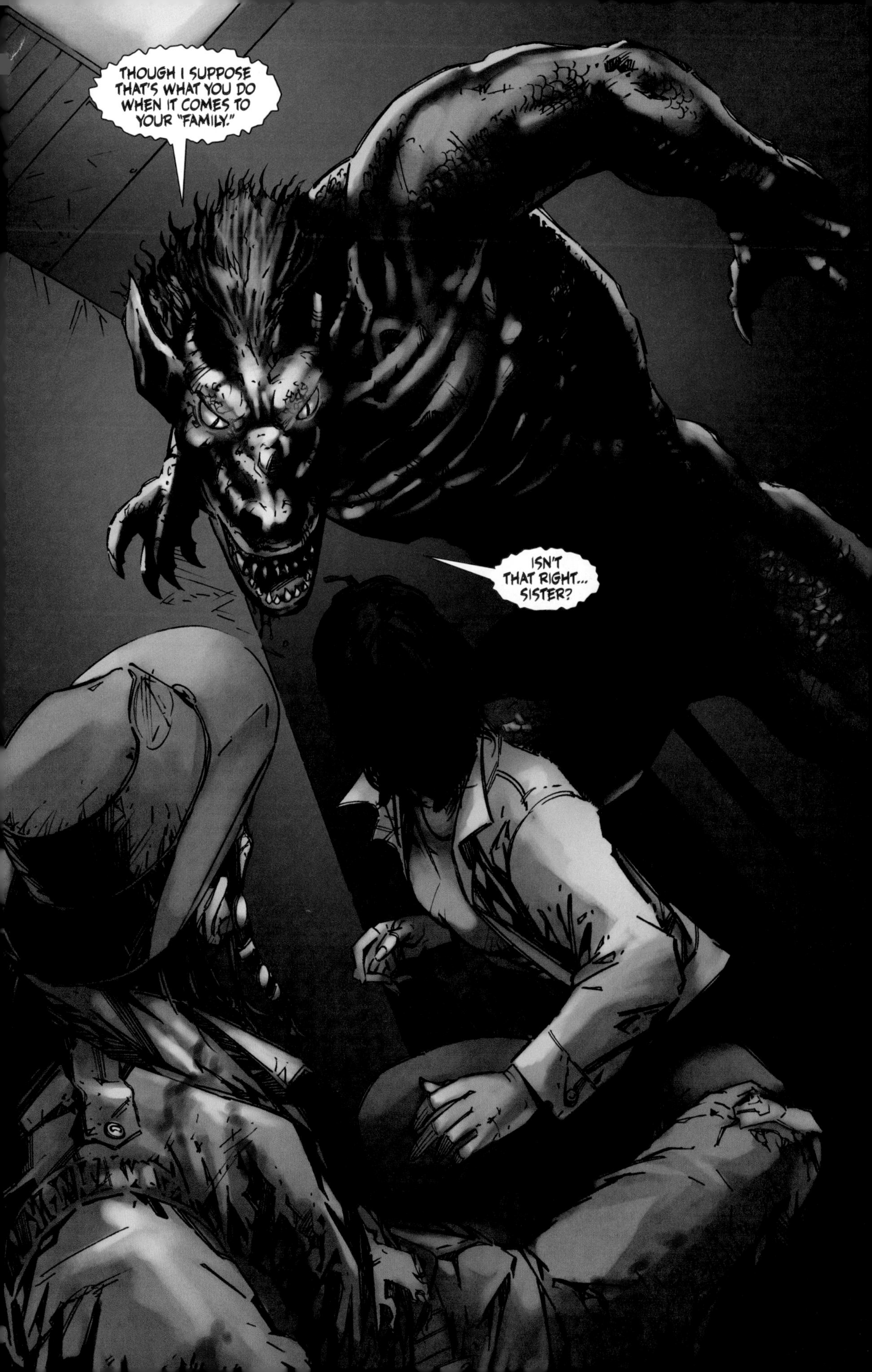
THOUGH I SUPPOSE THAT'S WHAT YOU DO WHEN IT COMES TO YOUR "FAMILY."
ISN'T THAT RIGHT... SISTER?

Thym—

Guanine

uanine   Cytosine

MACK

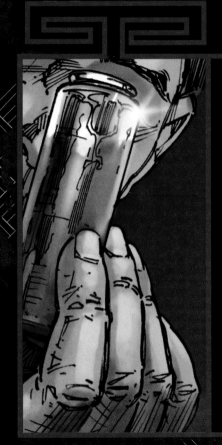

"Sun Tzu 101. Conquer your most powerful opponent first, then turn his power against your enemies."
— Rachel Kai

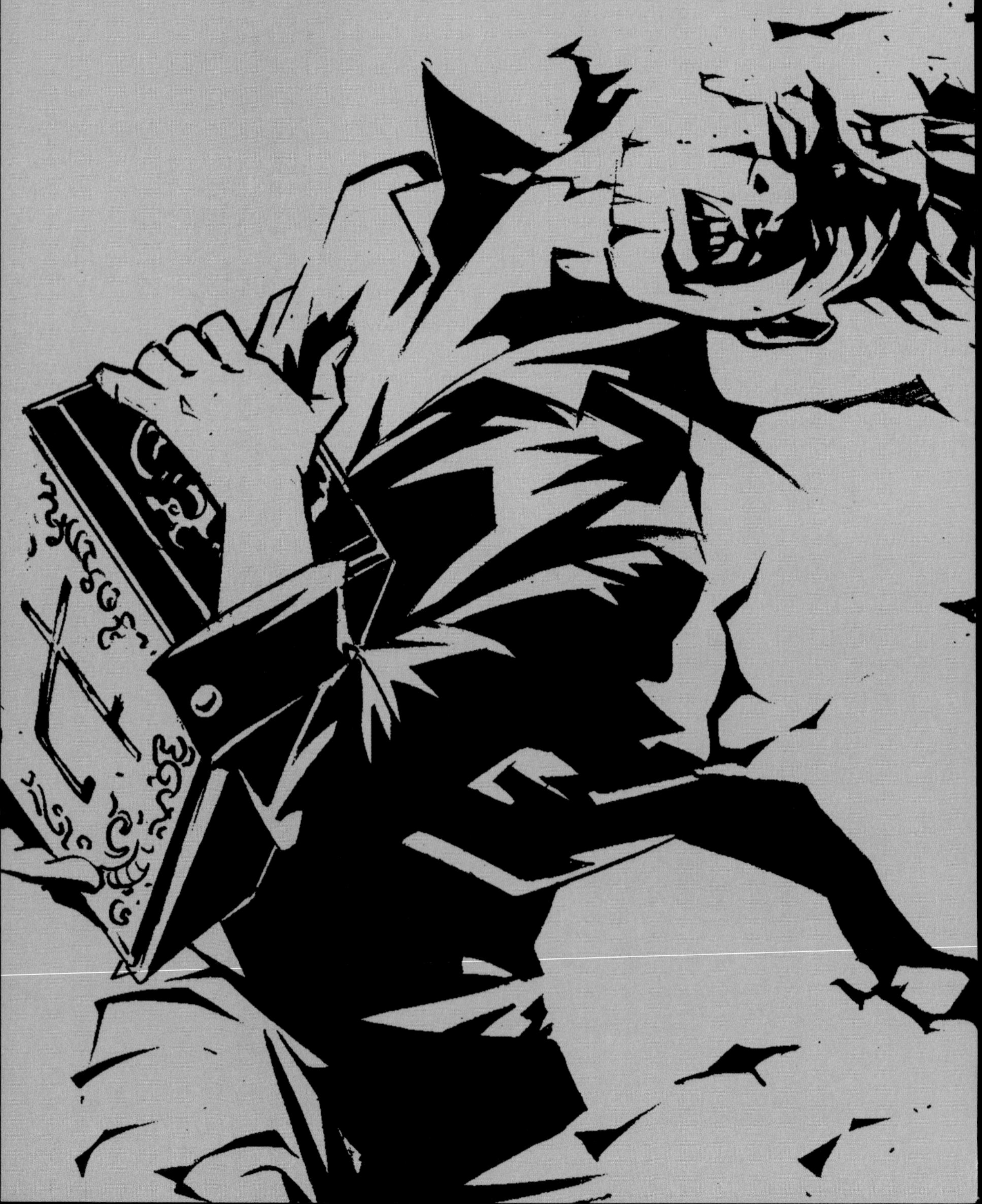

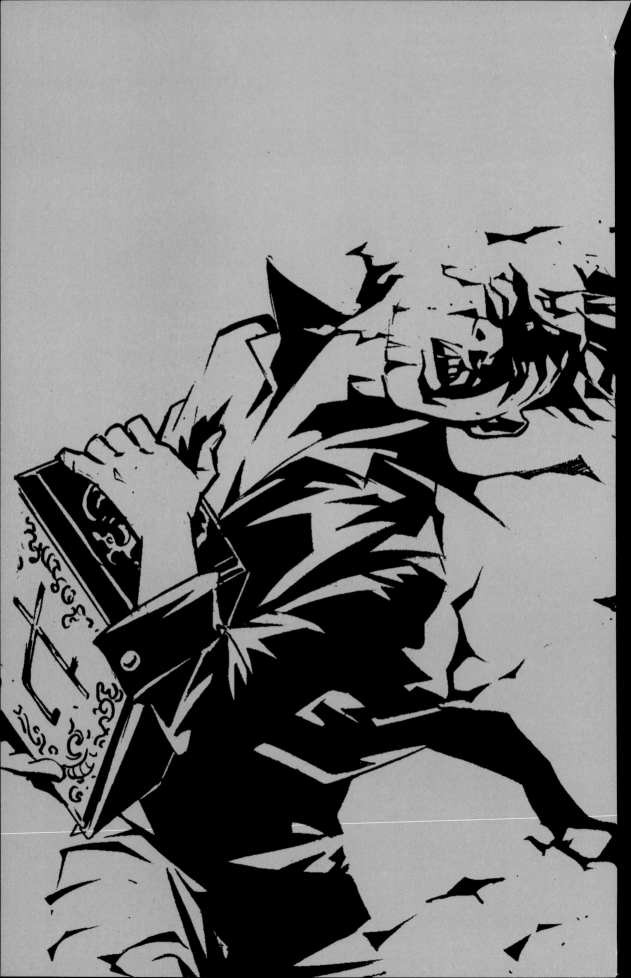

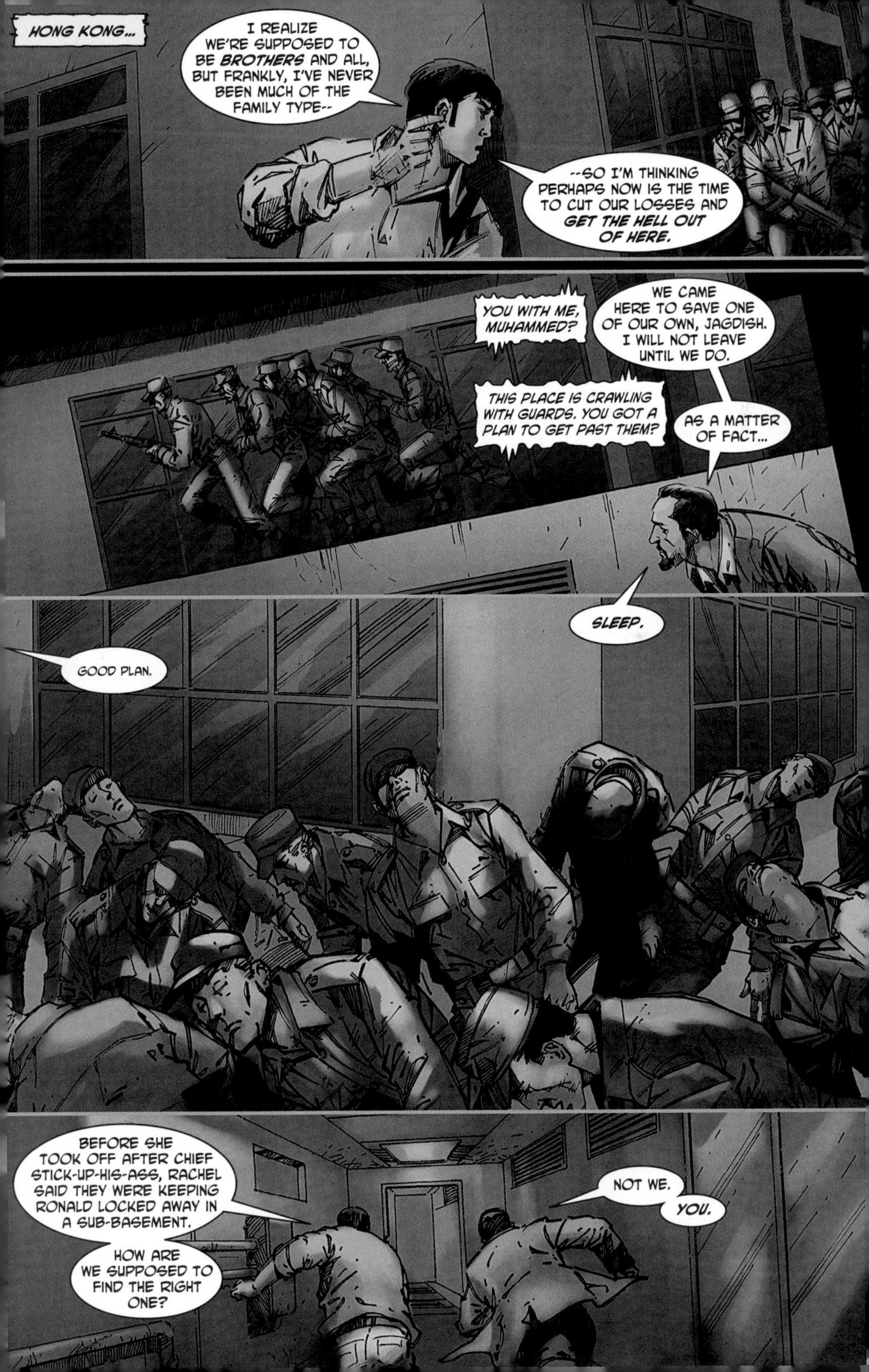
HONG KONG...
I REALIZE WE'RE SUPPOSED TO BE BROTHERS AND ALL, BUT FRANKLY, I'VE NEVER BEEN MUCH OF THE FAMILY TYPE--
--SO I'M THINKING PERHAPS NOW IS THE TIME TO CUT OUR LOSSES AND GET THE HELL OUT OF HERE.
YOU WITH ME, MUHAMMED?
WE CAME HERE TO SAVE ONE OF OUR OWN, JAGDISH. I WILL NOT LEAVE UNTIL WE DO.
THIS PLACE IS CRAWLING WITH GUARDS. YOU GOT A PLAN TO GET PAST THEM?
AS A MATTER OF FACT...
SLEEP.
GOOD PLAN.
BEFORE SHE TOOK OFF AFTER CHIEF STICK-UP-HIS-ASS, RACHEL SAID THEY WERE KEEPING RONALD LOCKED AWAY IN A SUB-BASEMENT.
HOW ARE WE SUPPOSED TO FIND THE RIGHT ONE?
NOT WE. YOU.

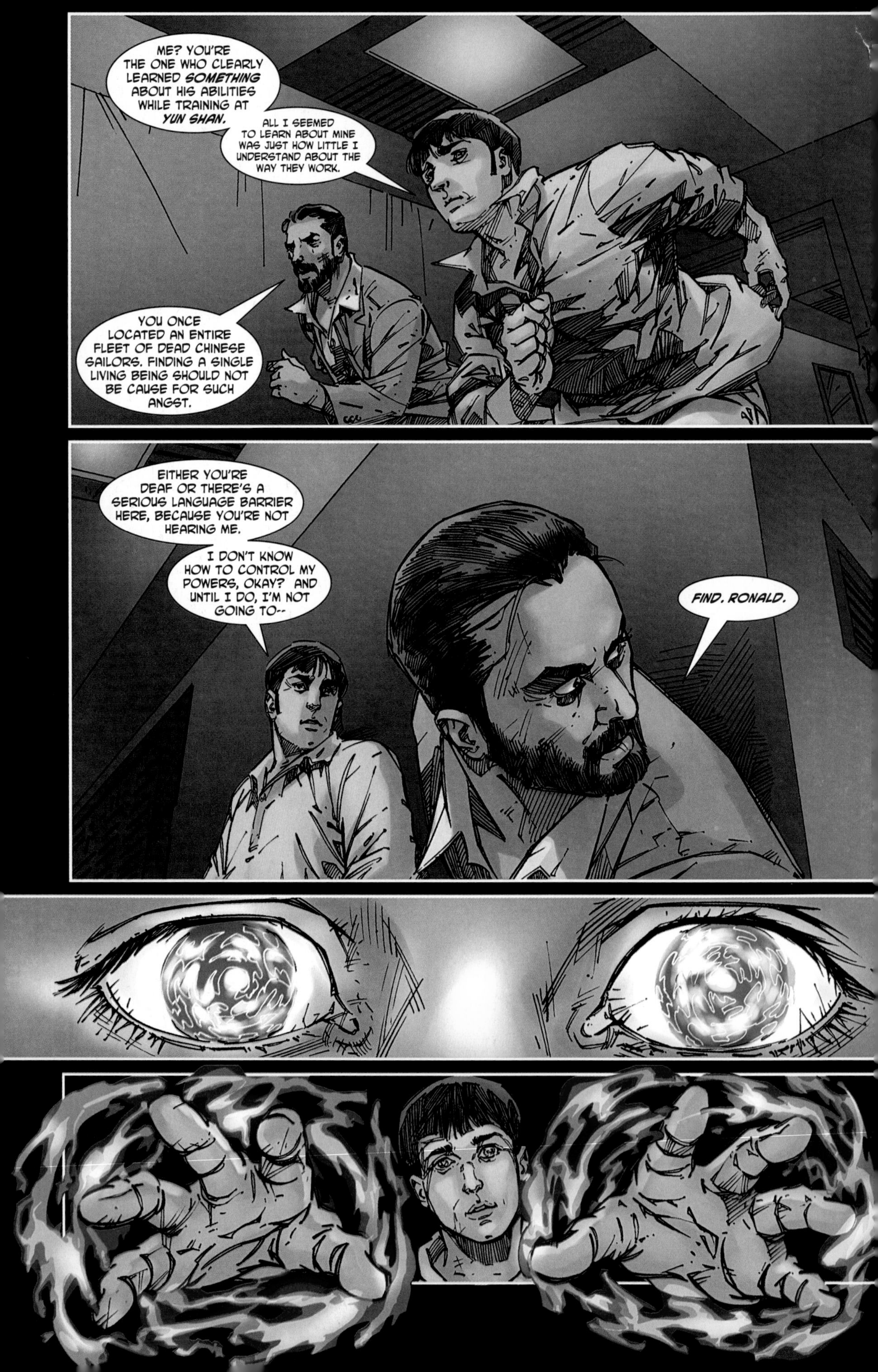
ME? YOU'RE THE ONE WHO CLEARLY LEARNED SOMETHING ABOUT HIS ABILITIES WHILE TRAINING AT YUN SHAN.
ALL I SEEMED TO LEARN ABOUT MINE WAS JUST HOW LITTLE I UNDERSTAND ABOUT THE WAY THEY WORK.
YOU ONCE LOCATED AN ENTIRE FLEET OF DEAD CHINESE SAILORS. FINDING A SINGLE LIVING BEING SHOULD NOT BE CAUSE FOR SUCH ANGST.
EITHER YOU'RE DEAF OR THERE'S A SERIOUS LANGUAGE BARRIER HERE, BECAUSE YOU'RE NOT HEARING ME.
I DON'T KNOW HOW TO CONTROL MY POWERS, OKAY? AND UNTIL I DO, I'M NOT GOING TO--
FIND. RONALD.

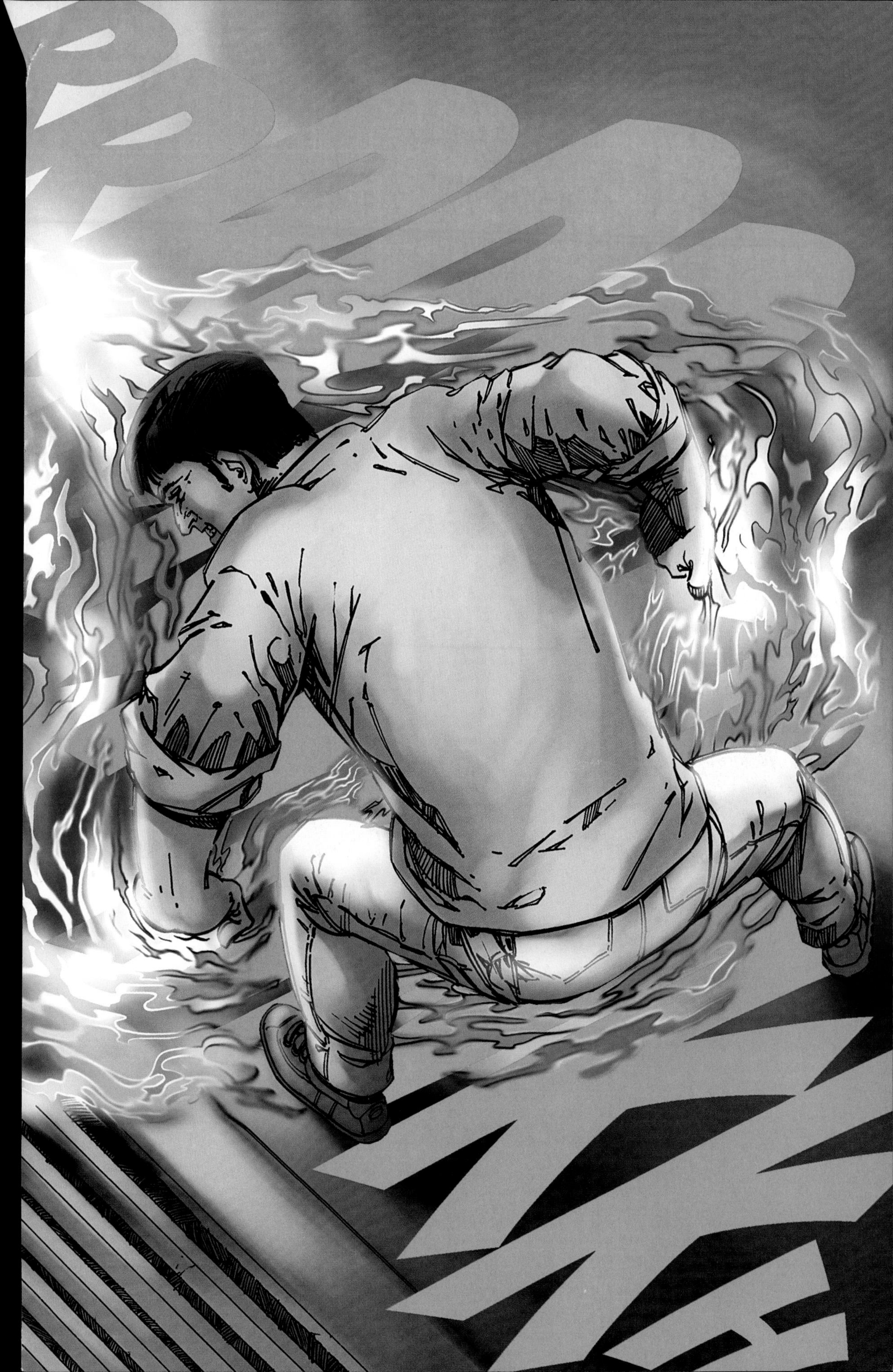

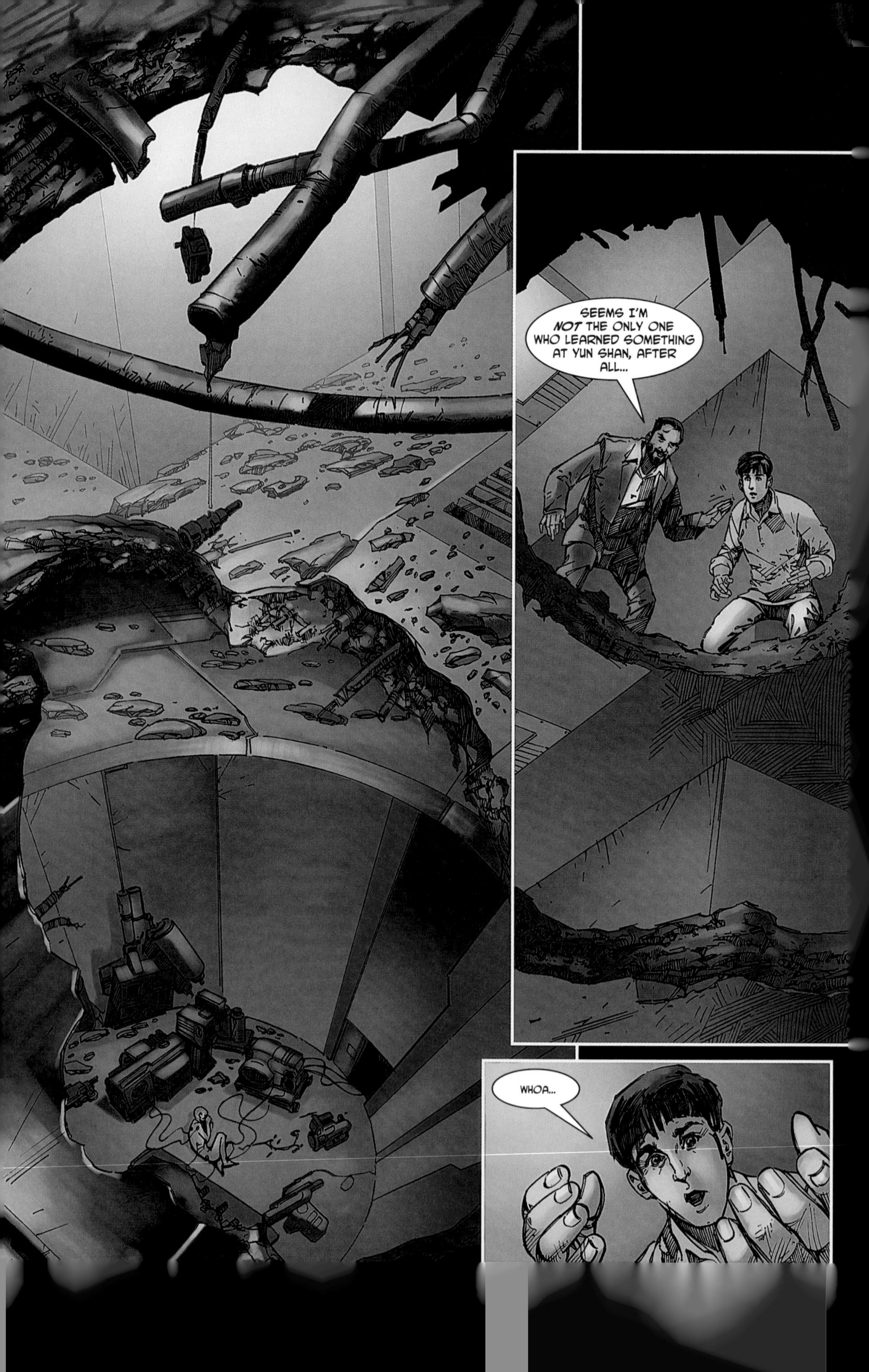
SEEMS I'M *NOT* THE ONLY ONE WHO LEARNED SOMETHING AT YUN SHAN, AFTER ALL...
WHOA...

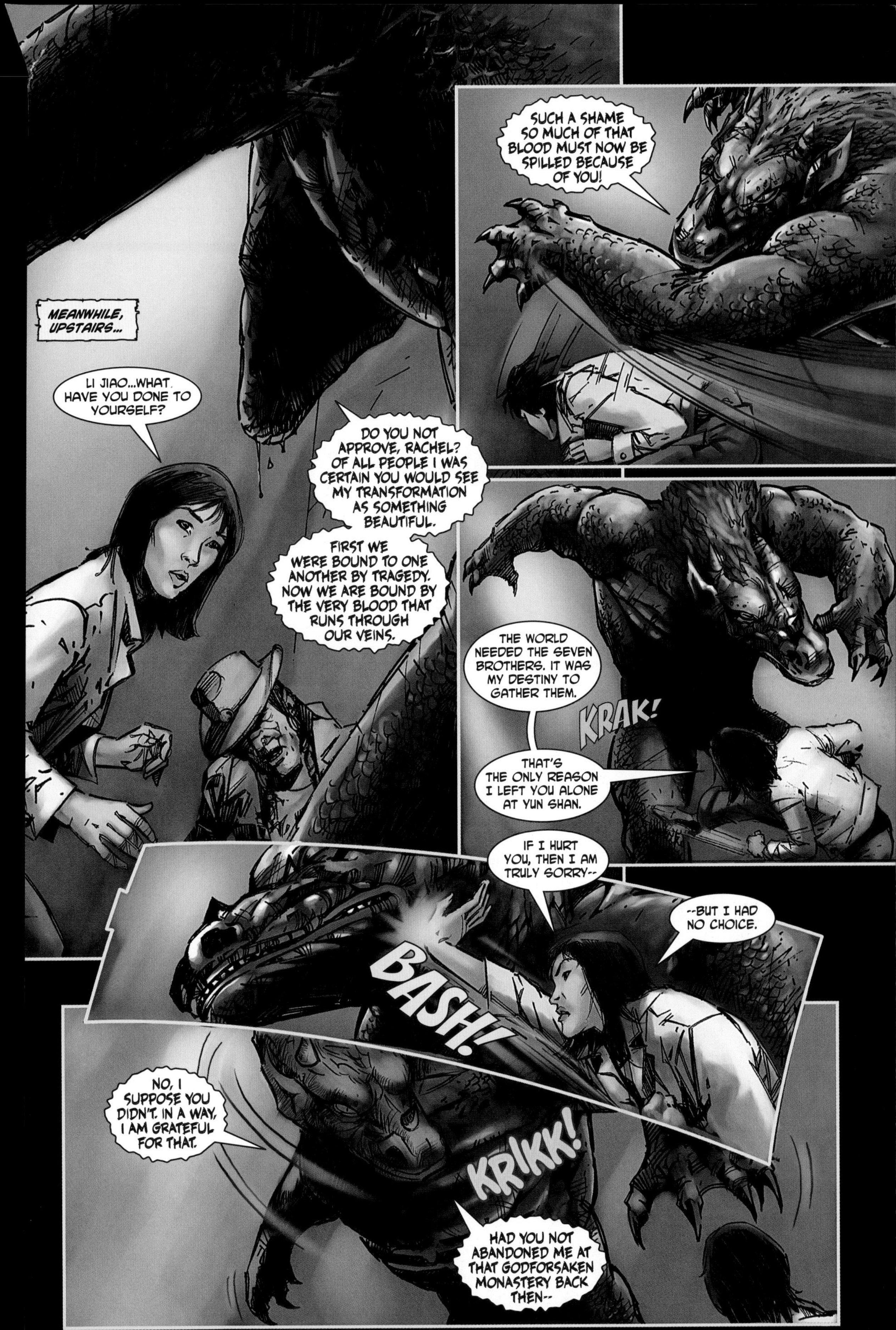
MEANWHILE, UPSTAIRS...
LI JIAO...WHAT HAVE YOU DONE TO YOURSELF?
DO YOU NOT APPROVE, RACHEL? OF ALL PEOPLE I WAS CERTAIN YOU WOULD SEE MY TRANSFORMATION AS SOMETHING BEAUTIFUL.
FIRST WE WERE BOUND TO ONE ANOTHER BY TRAGEDY. NOW WE ARE BOUND BY THE VERY BLOOD THAT RUNS THROUGH OUR VEINS.
SUCH A SHAME SO MUCH OF THAT BLOOD MUST NOW BE SPILLED BECAUSE OF YOU!
THE WORLD NEEDED THE SEVEN BROTHERS. IT WAS MY DESTINY TO GATHER THEM.
KRAK!
THAT'S THE ONLY REASON I LEFT YOU ALONE AT YUN SHAN.
IF I HURT YOU, THEN I AM TRULY SORRY--
--BUT I HAD NO CHOICE.
BASH!
NO, I SUPPOSE YOU DIDN'T. IN A WAY, I AM GRATEFUL FOR THAT.
KRIKK!
HAD YOU NOT ABANDONED ME AT THAT GODFORSAKEN MONASTERY BACK THEN--

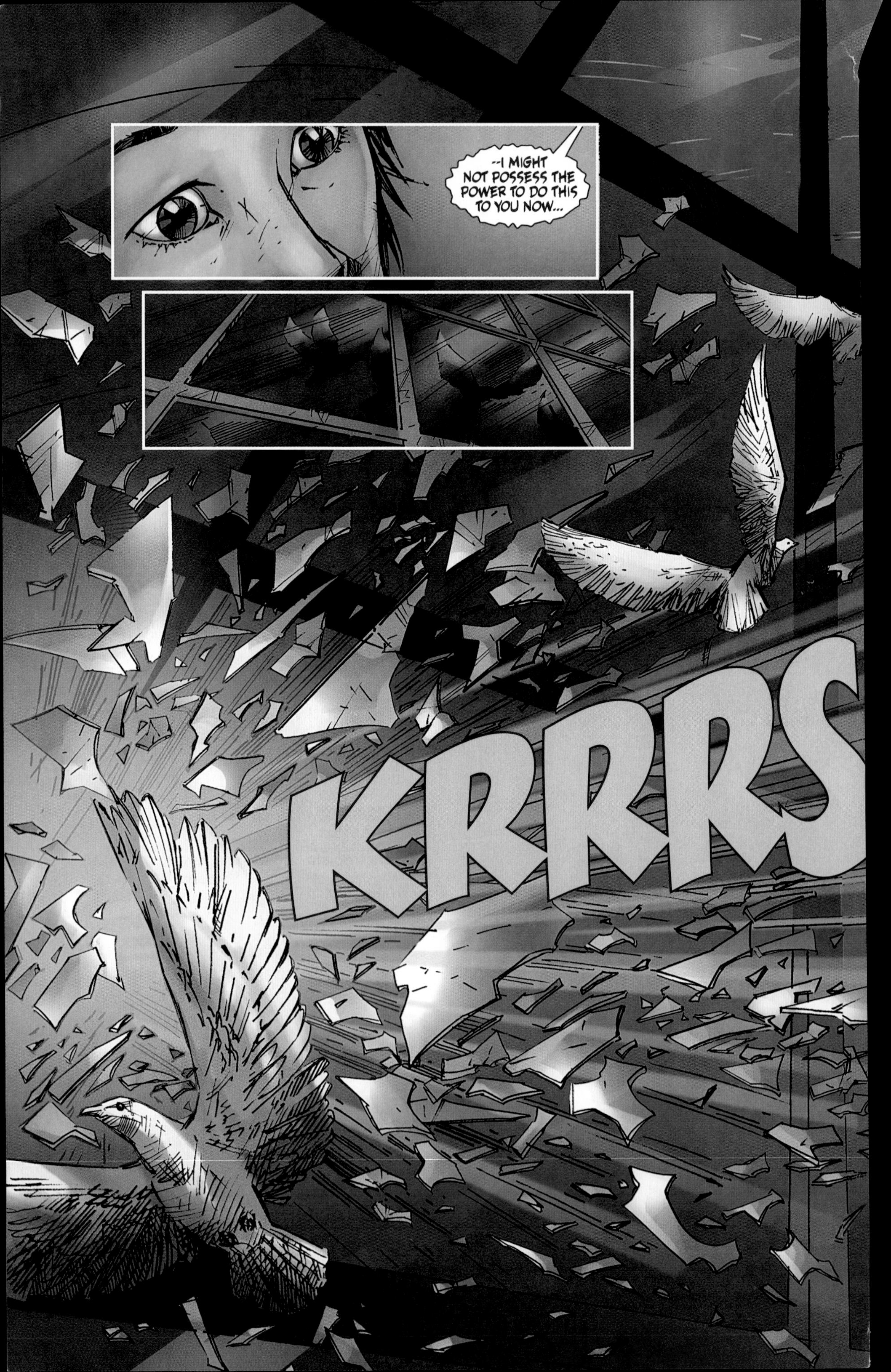
--I MIGHT NOT POSSESS THE POWER TO DO THIS TO YOU NOW...
KRRRS

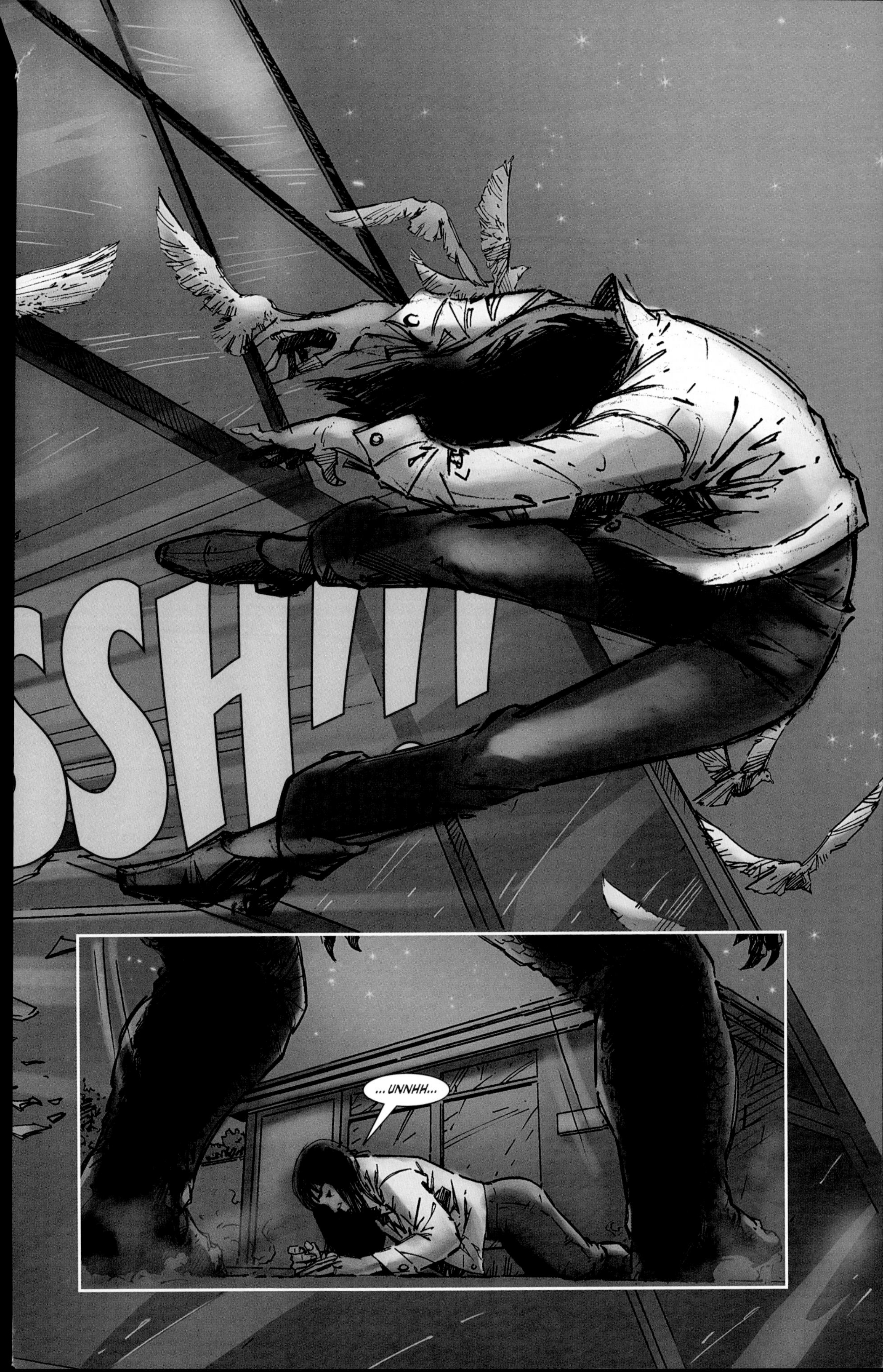
...UNNHH...

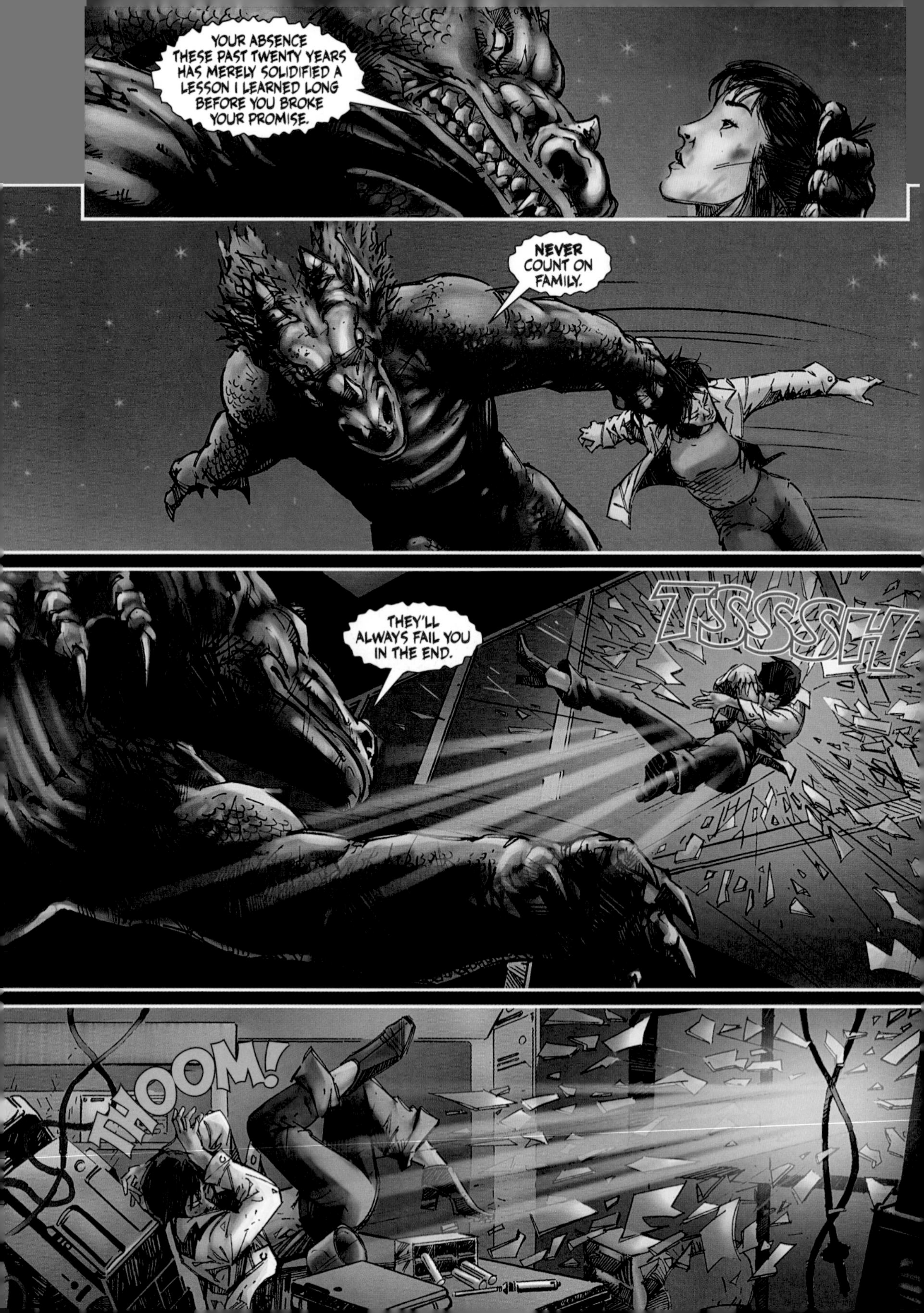
YOUR ABSENCE THESE PAST TWENTY YEARS HAS MERELY SOLIDIFIED A LESSON I LEARNED LONG BEFORE YOU BROKE YOUR PROMISE.
NEVER COUNT ON FAMILY.
THEY'LL ALWAYS FAIL YOU IN THE END.
TSSSSH
THOOM!

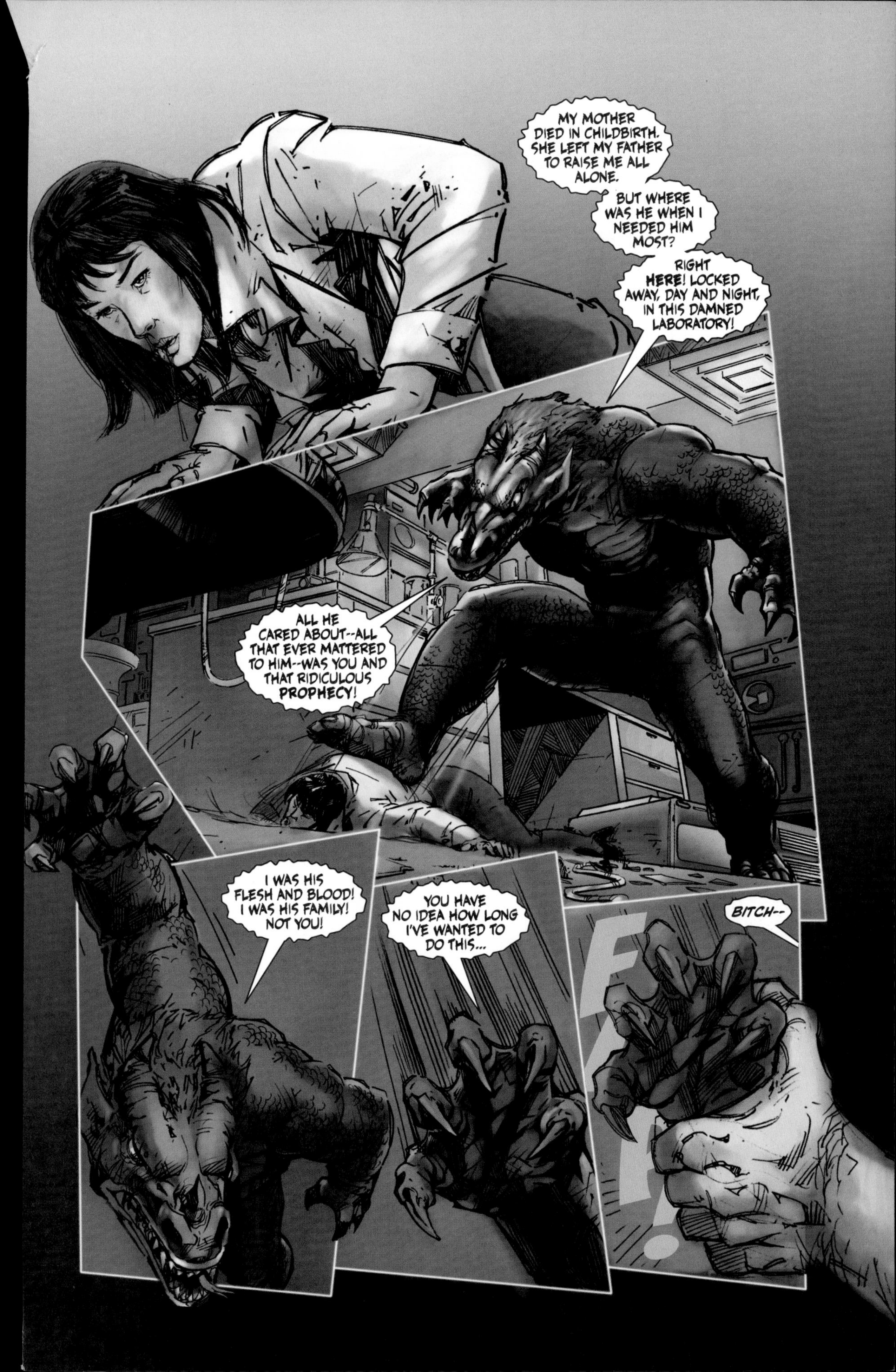
MY MOTHER DIED IN CHILDBIRTH. SHE LEFT MY FATHER TO RAISE ME ALL ALONE.
BUT WHERE WAS HE WHEN I NEEDED HIM MOST?
RIGHT HERE! LOCKED AWAY, DAY AND NIGHT, IN THIS DAMNED LABORATORY!
ALL HE CARED ABOUT--ALL THAT EVER MATTERED TO HIM--WAS YOU AND THAT RIDICULOUS PROPHECY!
I WAS HIS FLESH AND BLOOD! I WAS HIS FAMILY! NOT YOU!
YOU HAVE NO IDEA HOW LONG I'VE WANTED TO DO THIS...
BITCH--

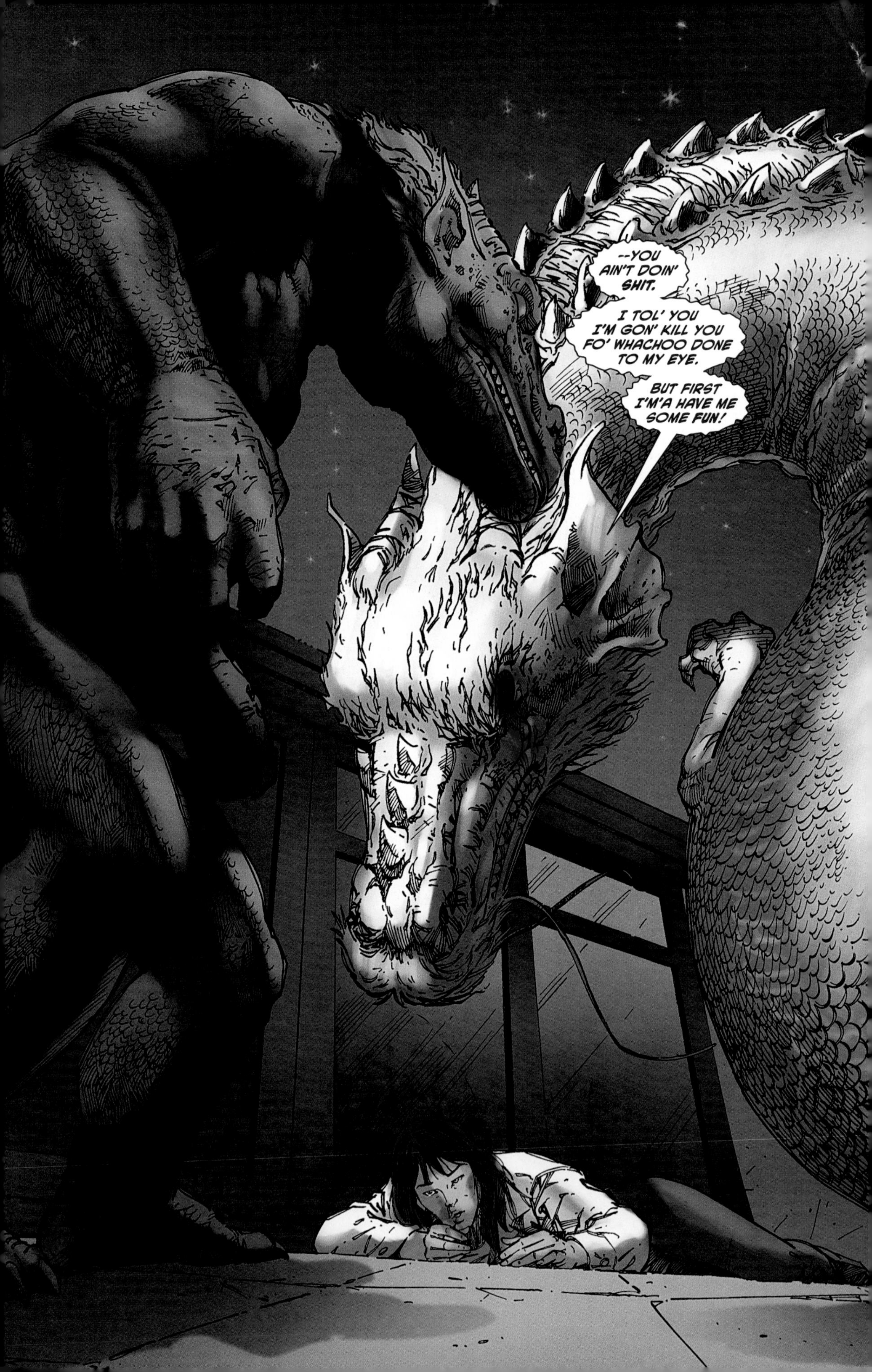
--YOU AIN'T DOIN' SHIT.
I TOL' YOU I'M GON' KILL YOU FO' WHACHOO DONE TO MY EYE.
BUT FIRST I'M'A HAVE ME SOME FUN!

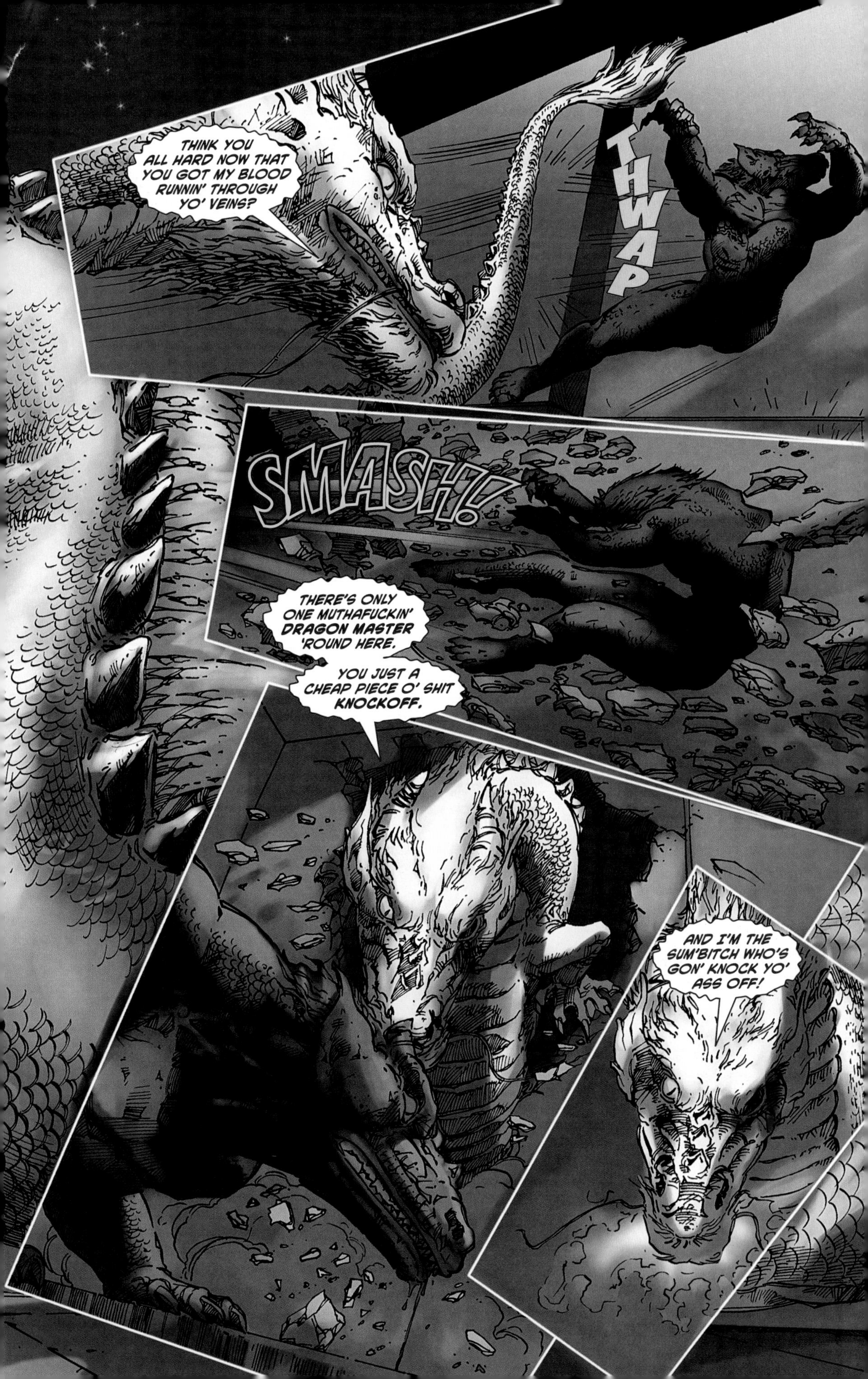
THINK YOU ALL HARD NOW THAT YOU GOT MY BLOOD RUNNIN' THROUGH YO' VEINS?
THWAP
SMASH!
THERE'S ONLY ONE MUTHAFUCKIN' DRAGON MASTER 'ROUND HERE.
YOU JUST A CHEAP PIECE O' SHIT KNOCKOFF.
AND I'M THE SUM'BITCH WHO'S GON' KNOCK YO' ASS OFF!

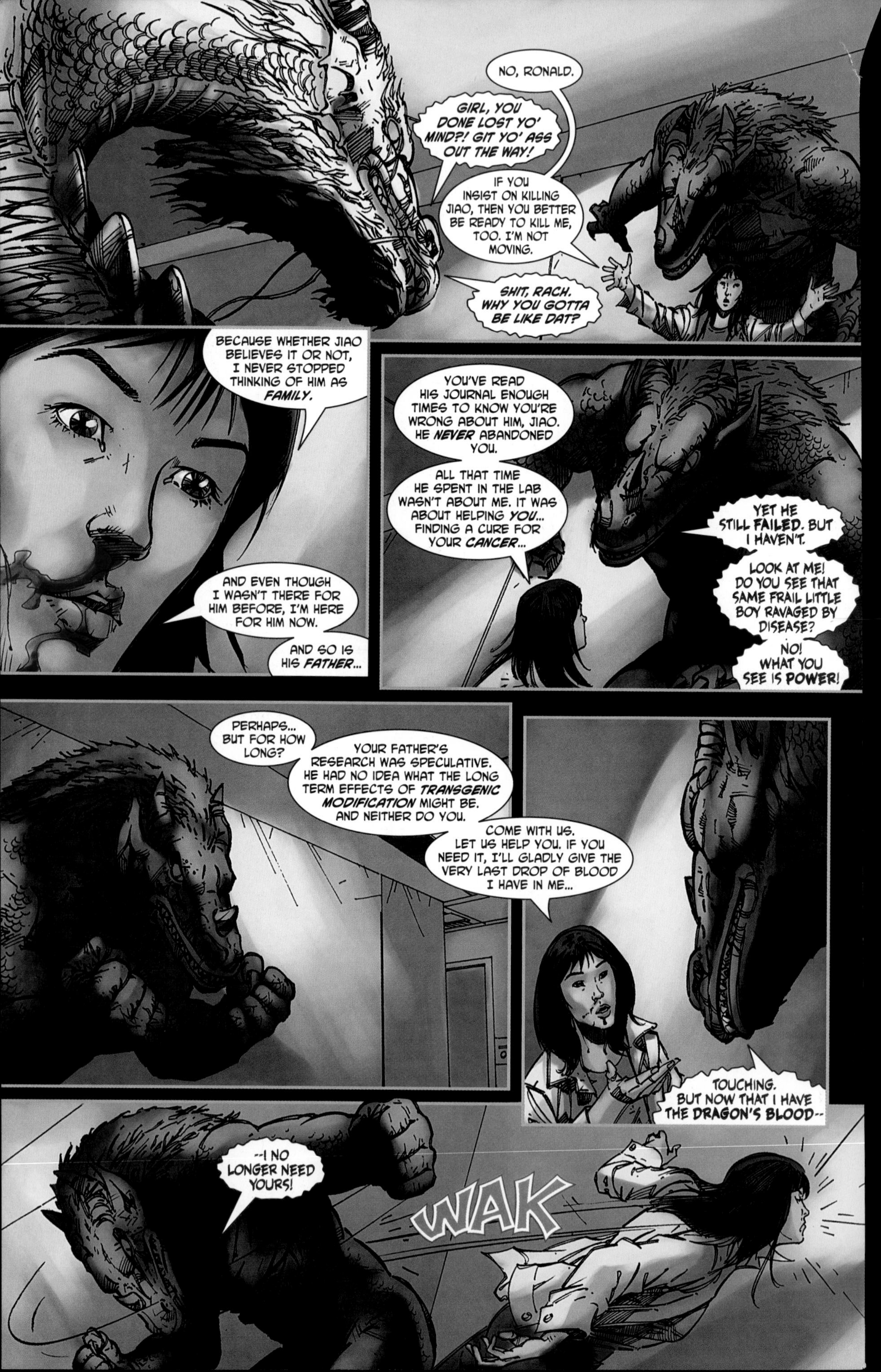

NO, RONALD.
GIRL, YOU DONE LOST YO' MIND?! GIT YO' ASS OUT THE WAY!
IF YOU INSIST ON KILLING JIAO, THEN YOU BETTER BE READY TO KILL ME, TOO. I'M NOT MOVING.
SHIT, RACH. WHY YOU GOTTA BE LIKE DAT?
BECAUSE WHETHER JIAO BELIEVES IT OR NOT, I NEVER STOPPED THINKING OF HIM AS FAMILY.
AND EVEN THOUGH I WASN'T THERE FOR HIM BEFORE, I'M HERE FOR HIM NOW.
AND SO IS HIS FATHER...
YOU'VE READ HIS JOURNAL ENOUGH TIMES TO KNOW YOU'RE WRONG ABOUT HIM, JIAO. HE NEVER ABANDONED YOU.
ALL THAT TIME HE SPENT IN THE LAB WASN'T ABOUT ME. IT WAS ABOUT HELPING YOU... FINDING A CURE FOR YOUR CANCER...
YET HE STILL FAILED. BUT I HAVEN'T.
LOOK AT ME! DO YOU SEE THAT SAME FRAIL LITTLE BOY RAVAGED BY DISEASE?
NO! WHAT YOU SEE IS POWER!
PERHAPS... BUT FOR HOW LONG?
YOUR FATHER'S RESEARCH WAS SPECULATIVE. HE HAD NO IDEA WHAT THE LONG TERM EFFECTS OF TRANSGENIC MODIFICATION MIGHT BE. AND NEITHER DO YOU.
COME WITH US. LET US HELP YOU. IF YOU NEED IT, I'LL GLADLY GIVE THE VERY LAST DROP OF BLOOD I HAVE IN ME...
TOUCHING. BUT NOW THAT I HAVE THE DRAGON'S BLOOD--
--I NO LONGER NEED YOURS!
WAK

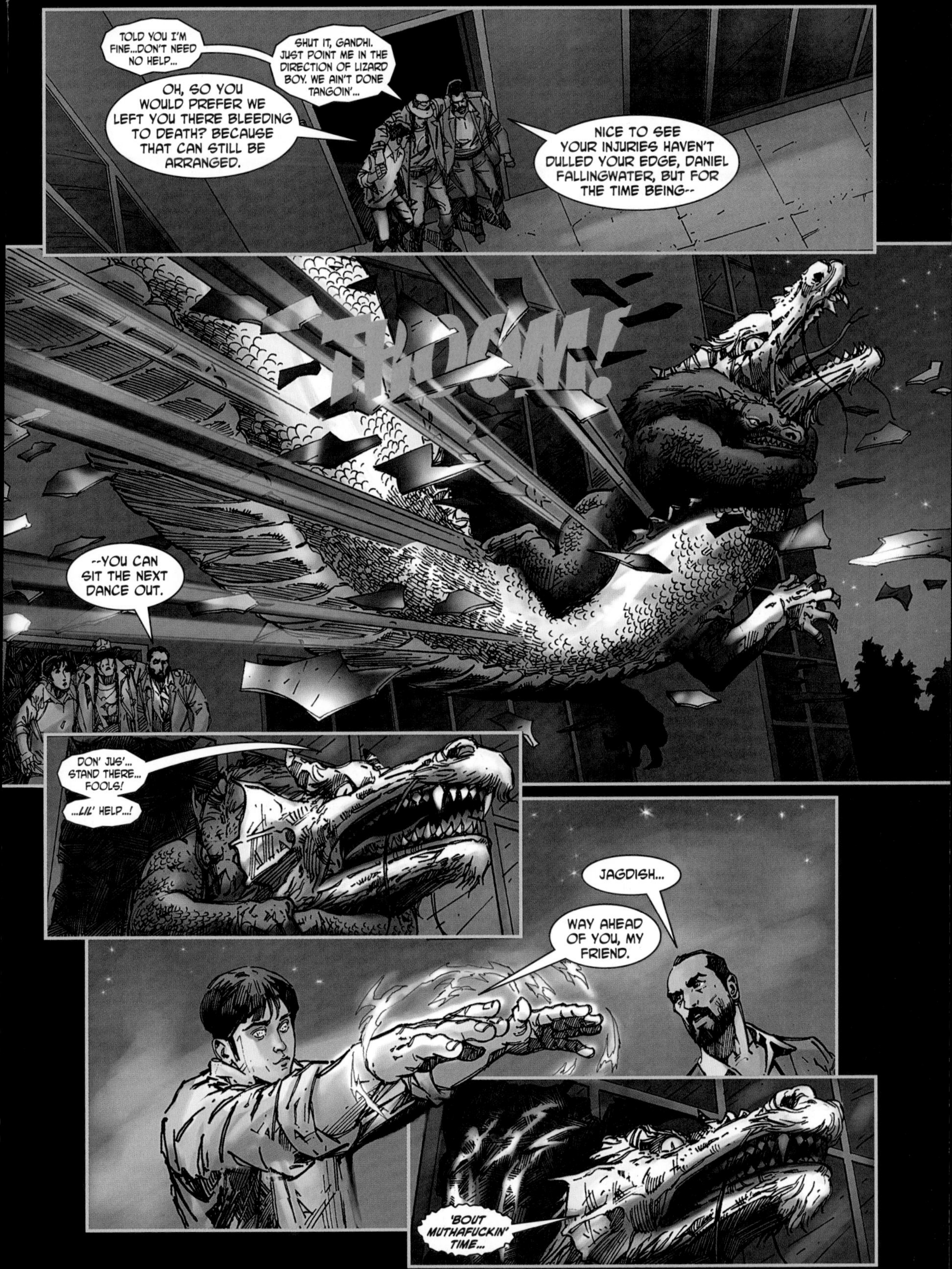
TOLD YOU I'M FINE...DON'T NEED NO HELP...
SHUT IT, GANDHI. JUST POINT ME IN THE DIRECTION OF LIZARD BOY. WE AIN'T DONE TANGOIN'...
OH, SO YOU WOULD PREFER WE LEFT YOU THERE BLEEDING TO DEATH? BECAUSE THAT CAN STILL BE ARRANGED.
NICE TO SEE YOUR INJURIES HAVEN'T DULLED YOUR EDGE, DANIEL FALLINGWATER, BUT FOR THE TIME BEING--
THOOM!
--YOU CAN SIT THE NEXT DANCE OUT.
DON' JUS'... STAND THERE... FOOLS!
...LIL' HELP...!
JAGDISH...
WAY AHEAD OF YOU, MY FRIEND.
'BOUT MUTHAFUCKIN' TIME...

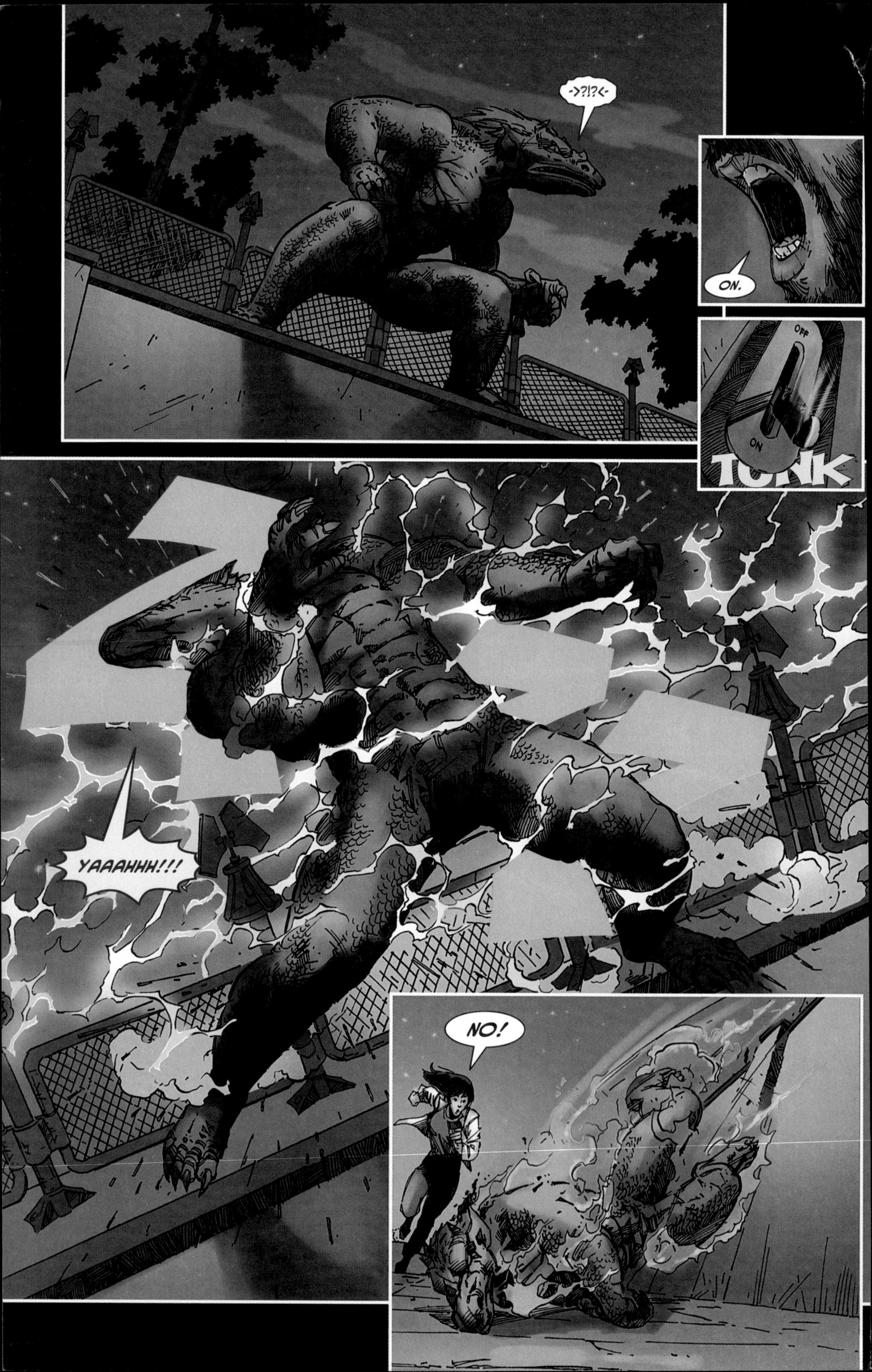

->?!?<-
ON.
OFF
ON
TUNK
YAAAHHH!!!
NO!

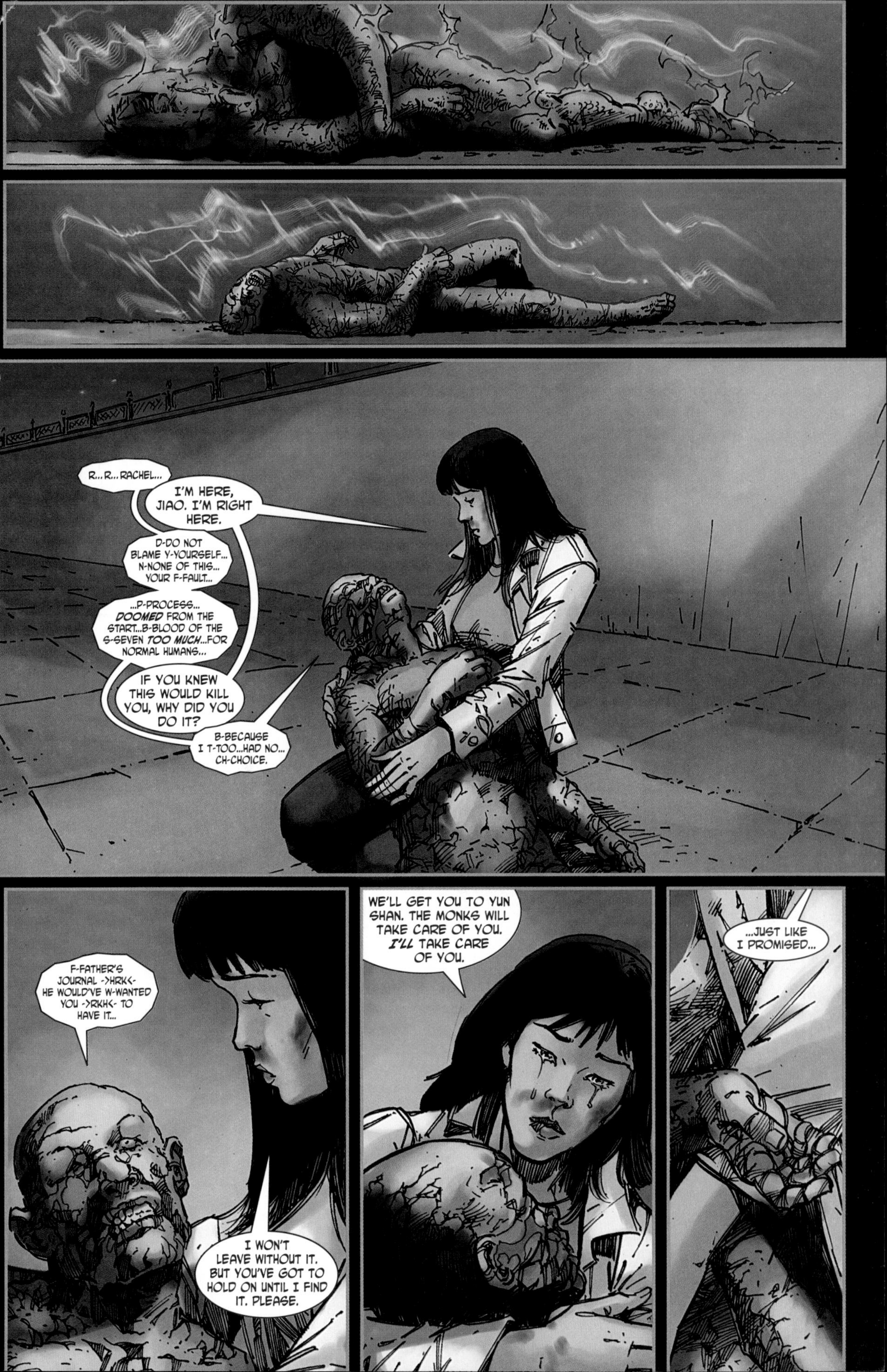
R... R... RACHEL...
I'M HERE, JIAO. I'M RIGHT HERE.
D-DO NOT BLAME Y-YOURSELF... N-NONE OF THIS... YOUR F-FAULT...
...P-PROCESS... DOOMED FROM THE START...B-BLOOD OF THE S-SEVEN TOO MUCH...FOR NORMAL HUMANS...
IF YOU KNEW THIS WOULD KILL YOU, WHY DID YOU DO IT?
B-BECAUSE I T-TOO...HAD NO... CH-CHOICE.
F-FATHER'S JOURNAL ->HRK<- HE WOULD'VE W-WANTED YOU ->RKH<- TO HAVE IT...
I WON'T LEAVE WITHOUT IT. BUT YOU'VE GOT TO HOLD ON UNTIL I FIND IT. PLEASE.
WE'LL GET YOU TO YUN SHAN. THE MONKS WILL TAKE CARE OF YOU. I'LL TAKE CARE OF YOU.
...JUST LIKE I PROMISED...

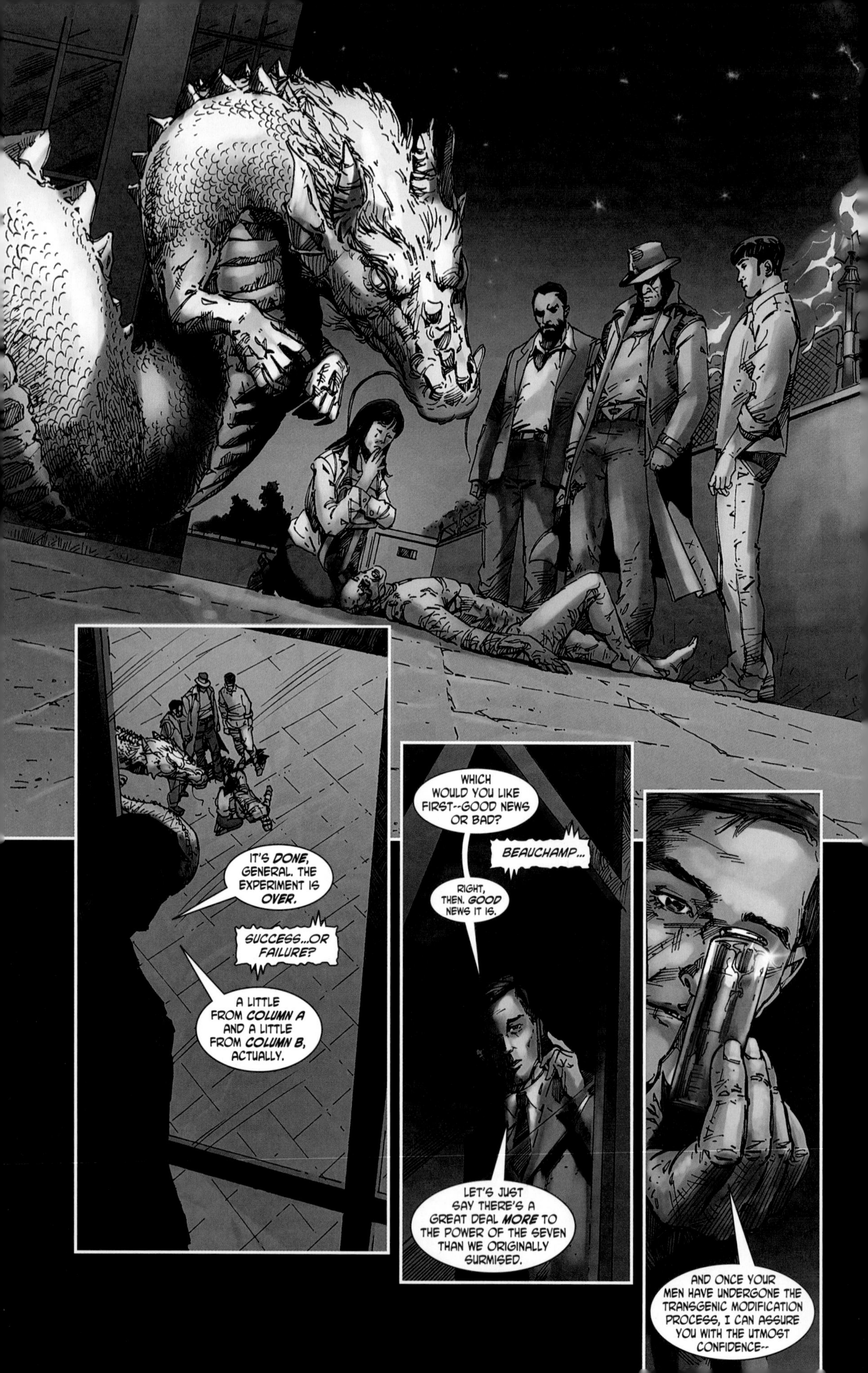
IT'S DONE, GENERAL. THE EXPERIMENT IS OVER.
SUCCESS...OR FAILURE?
A LITTLE FROM COLUMN A AND A LITTLE FROM COLUMN B, ACTUALLY.
WHICH WOULD YOU LIKE FIRST--GOOD NEWS OR BAD?
BEAUCHAMP...
RIGHT, THEN. GOOD NEWS IT IS.
LET'S JUST SAY THERE'S A GREAT DEAL MORE TO THE POWER OF THE SEVEN THAN WE ORIGINALLY SURMISED.
AND ONCE YOUR MEN HAVE UNDERGONE THE TRANSGENIC MODIFICATION PROCESS, I CAN ASSURE YOU WITH THE UTMOST CONFIDENCE--

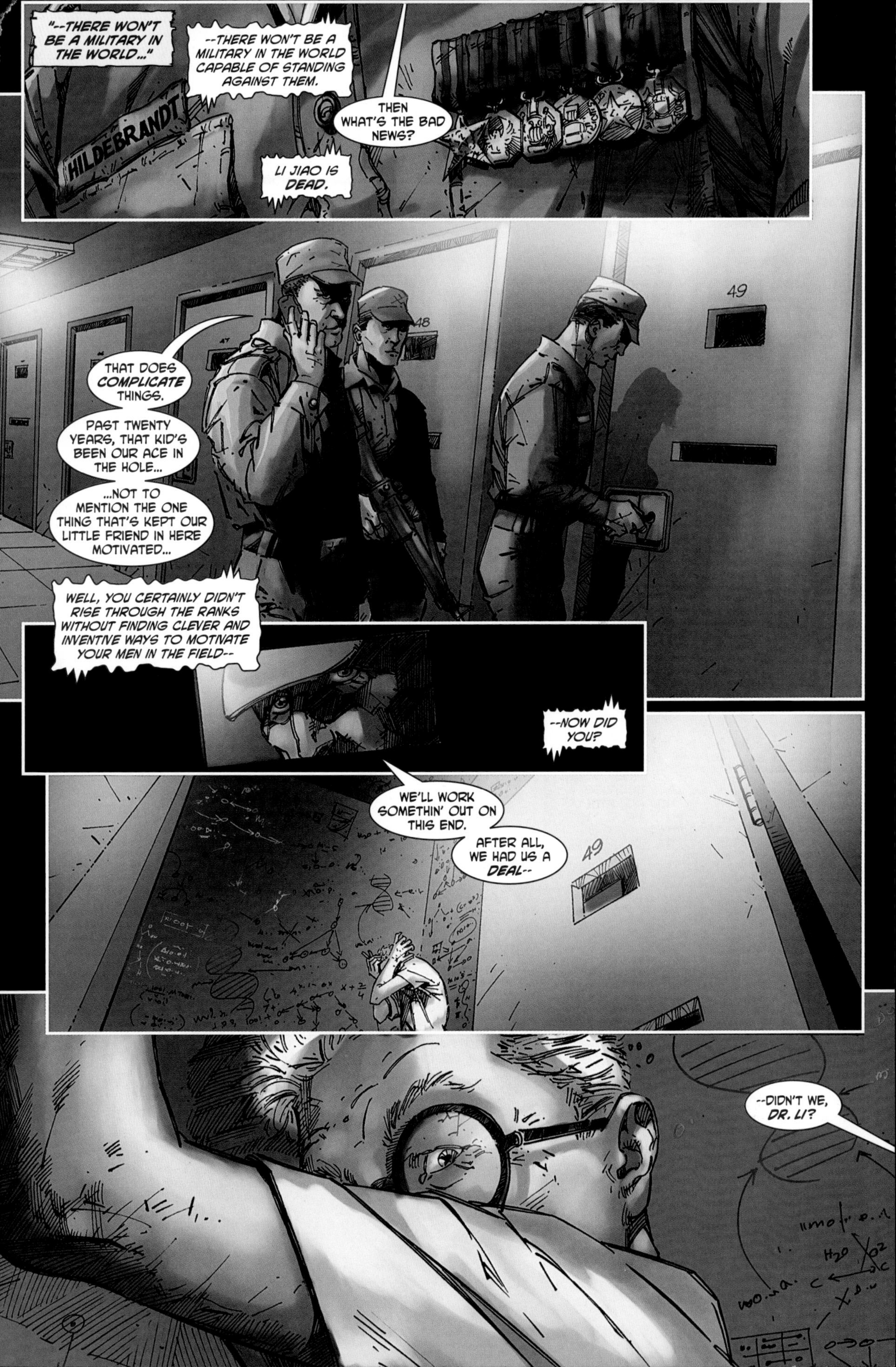
"--THERE WON'T BE A MILITARY IN THE WORLD..."
--THERE WON'T BE A MILITARY IN THE WORLD CAPABLE OF STANDING AGAINST THEM.
HILDEBRANDT
THEN WHAT'S THE BAD NEWS?
LI JIAO IS *DEAD.*
49
THAT DOES *COMPLICATE* THINGS.
PAST TWENTY YEARS, THAT KID'S BEEN OUR ACE IN THE HOLE...
...NOT TO MENTION THE ONE THING THAT'S KEPT OUR LITTLE FRIEND IN HERE MOTIVATED...
WELL, YOU CERTAINLY DIDN'T RISE THROUGH THE RANKS WITHOUT FINDING CLEVER AND INVENTIVE WAYS TO MOTIVATE YOUR MEN IN THE FIELD--
--NOW DID YOU?
WE'LL WORK SOMETHIN' OUT ON THIS END.
AFTER ALL, WE HAD US A *DEAL--*
49
--DIDN'T WE, *DR. LI?*

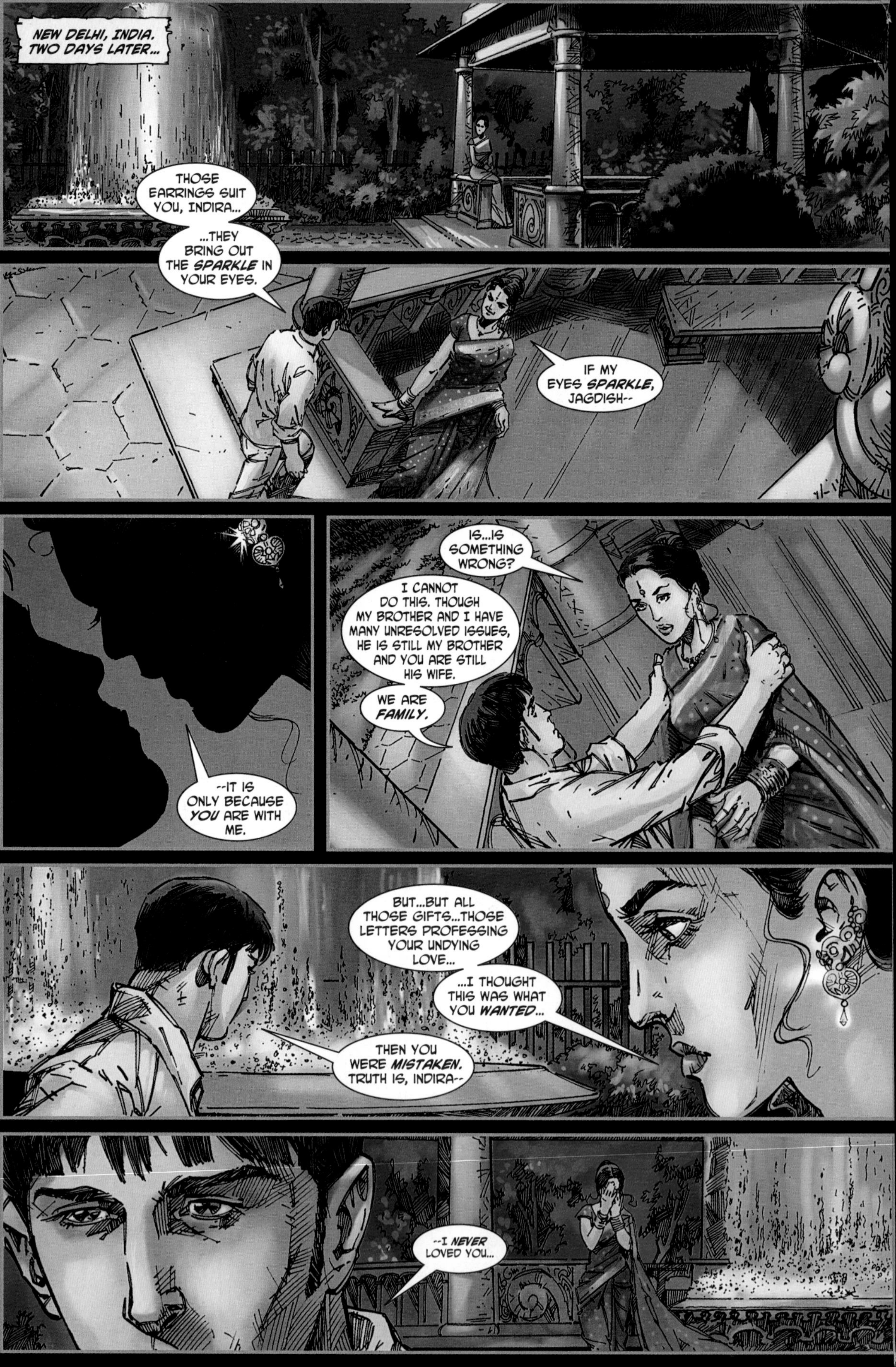
NEW DELHI, INDIA. TWO DAYS LATER...
THOSE EARRINGS SUIT YOU, INDIRA...
...THEY BRING OUT THE SPARKLE IN YOUR EYES.
IF MY EYES SPARKLE, JAGDISH--
--IT IS ONLY BECAUSE YOU ARE WITH ME.
IS...IS SOMETHING WRONG?
I CANNOT DO THIS. THOUGH MY BROTHER AND I HAVE MANY UNRESOLVED ISSUES, HE IS STILL MY BROTHER AND YOU ARE STILL HIS WIFE.
WE ARE FAMILY.
BUT...BUT ALL THOSE GIFTS...THOSE LETTERS PROFESSING YOUR UNDYING LOVE...
...I THOUGHT THIS WAS WHAT YOU WANTED...
THEN YOU WERE MISTAKEN. TRUTH IS, INDIRA--
--I NEVER LOVED YOU...

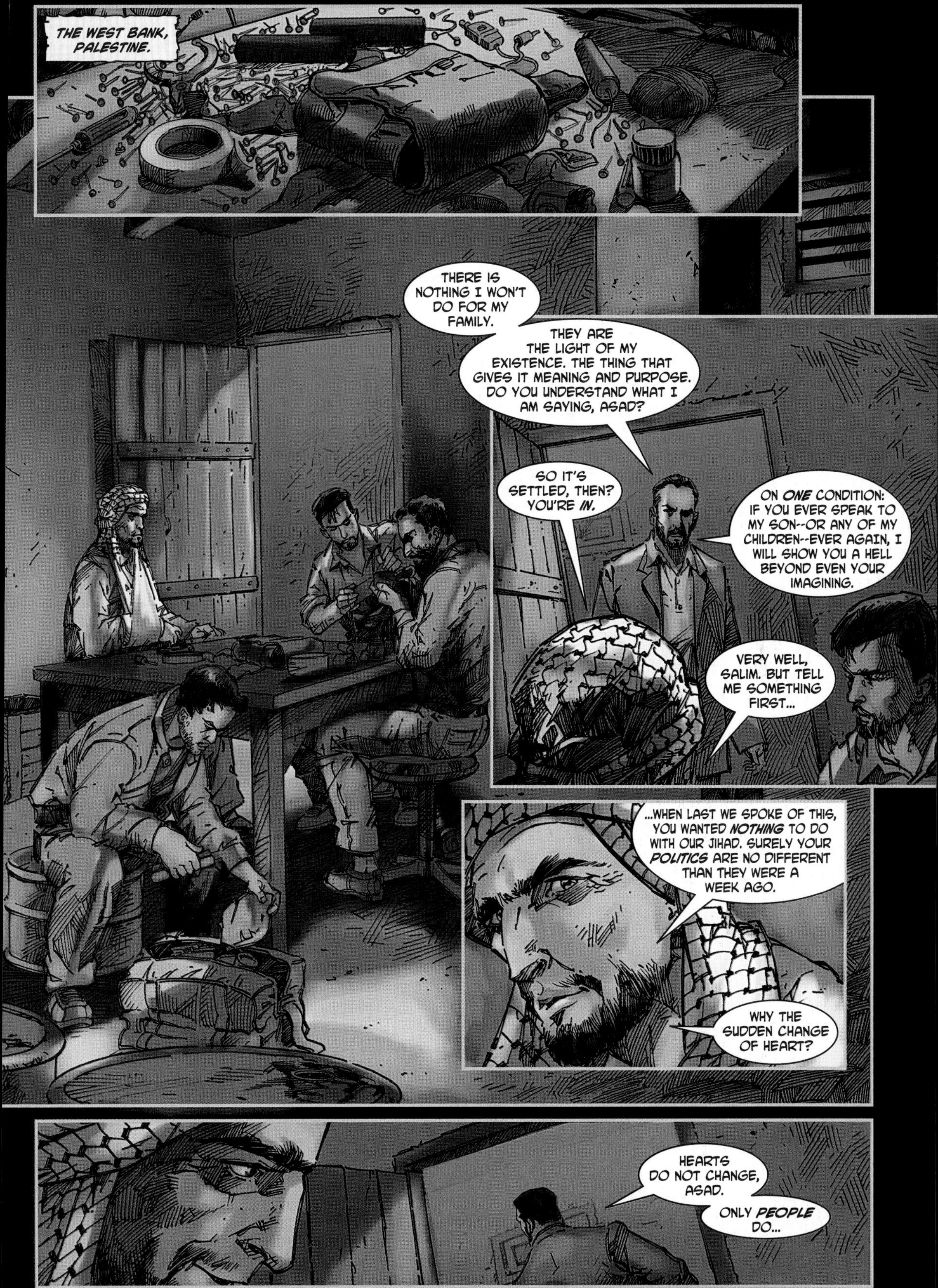
THE WEST BANK, PALESTINE.
THERE IS NOTHING I WON'T DO FOR MY FAMILY.
THEY ARE THE LIGHT OF MY EXISTENCE. THE THING THAT GIVES IT MEANING AND PURPOSE. DO YOU UNDERSTAND WHAT I AM SAYING, ASAD?
SO IT'S SETTLED, THEN? YOU'RE *IN.*
ON *ONE* CONDITION: IF YOU EVER SPEAK TO MY SON--OR ANY OF MY CHILDREN--EVER AGAIN, I WILL SHOW YOU A HELL BEYOND EVEN YOUR IMAGINING.
VERY WELL, SALIM. BUT TELL ME SOMETHING FIRST...
...WHEN LAST WE SPOKE OF THIS, YOU WANTED *NOTHING* TO DO WITH OUR JIHAD. SURELY YOUR *POLITICS* ARE NO DIFFERENT THAN THEY WERE A WEEK AGO.
WHY THE SUDDEN CHANGE OF HEART?
HEARTS DO NOT CHANGE, ASAD.
ONLY *PEOPLE* DO...

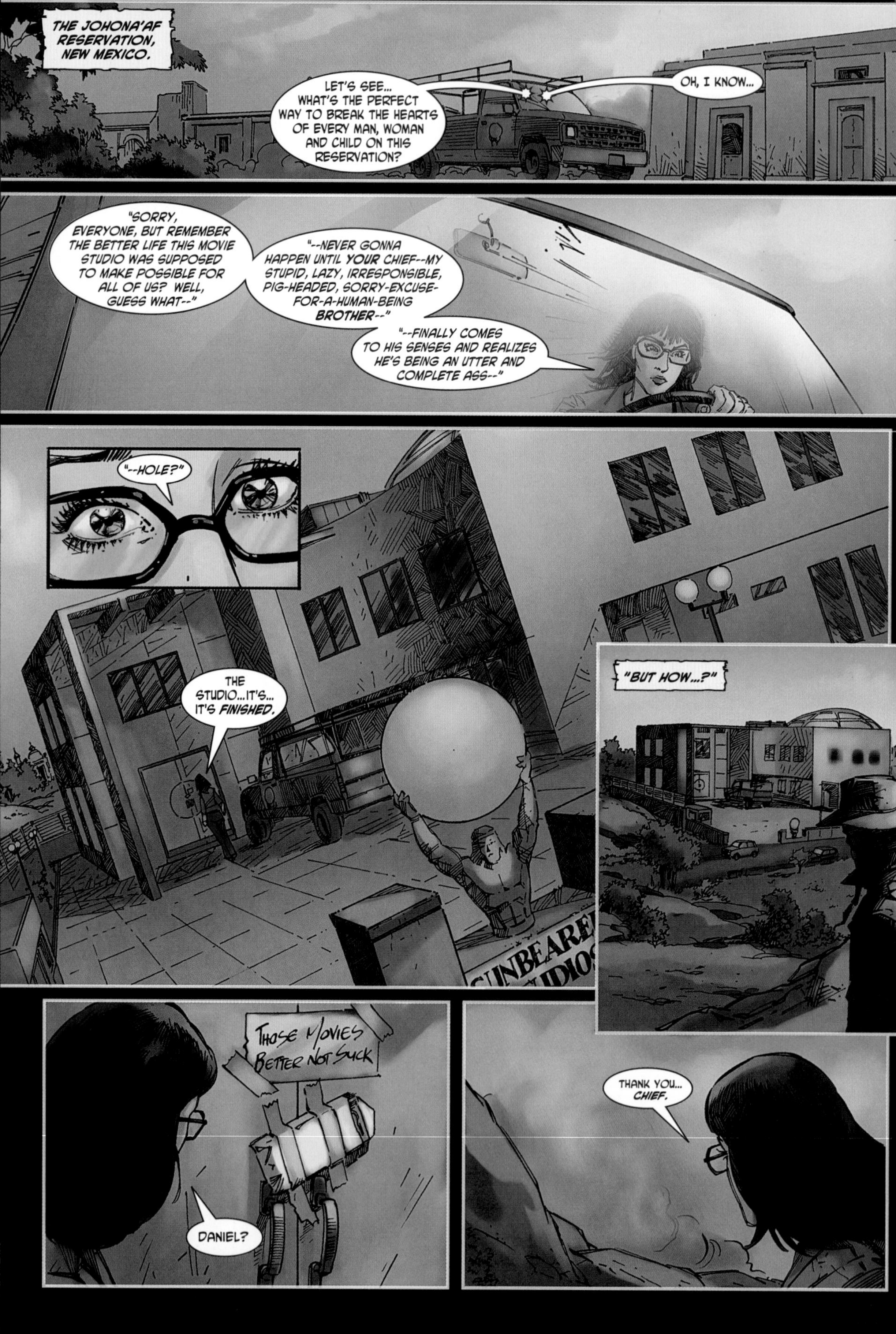
THE JOHONA'AF RESERVATION, NEW MEXICO.
LET'S SEE... WHAT'S THE PERFECT WAY TO BREAK THE HEARTS OF EVERY MAN, WOMAN AND CHILD ON THIS RESERVATION?
OH, I KNOW...
"SORRY, EVERYONE, BUT REMEMBER THE BETTER LIFE THIS MOVIE STUDIO WAS SUPPOSED TO MAKE POSSIBLE FOR ALL OF US? WELL, GUESS WHAT--"
"--NEVER GONNA HAPPEN UNTIL YOUR CHIEF--MY STUPID, LAZY, IRRESPONSIBLE, PIG-HEADED, SORRY-EXCUSE-FOR-A-HUMAN-BEING BROTHER--"
"--FINALLY COMES TO HIS SENSES AND REALIZES HE'S BEING AN UTTER AND COMPLETE ASS--"
"--HOLE?"
THE STUDIO...IT'S... IT'S FINISHED.
SUNBEARE
UDIOS
"BUT HOW...?"
THOSE MOVIES BETTER NOT SUCK
DANIEL?
THANK YOU... CHIEF.

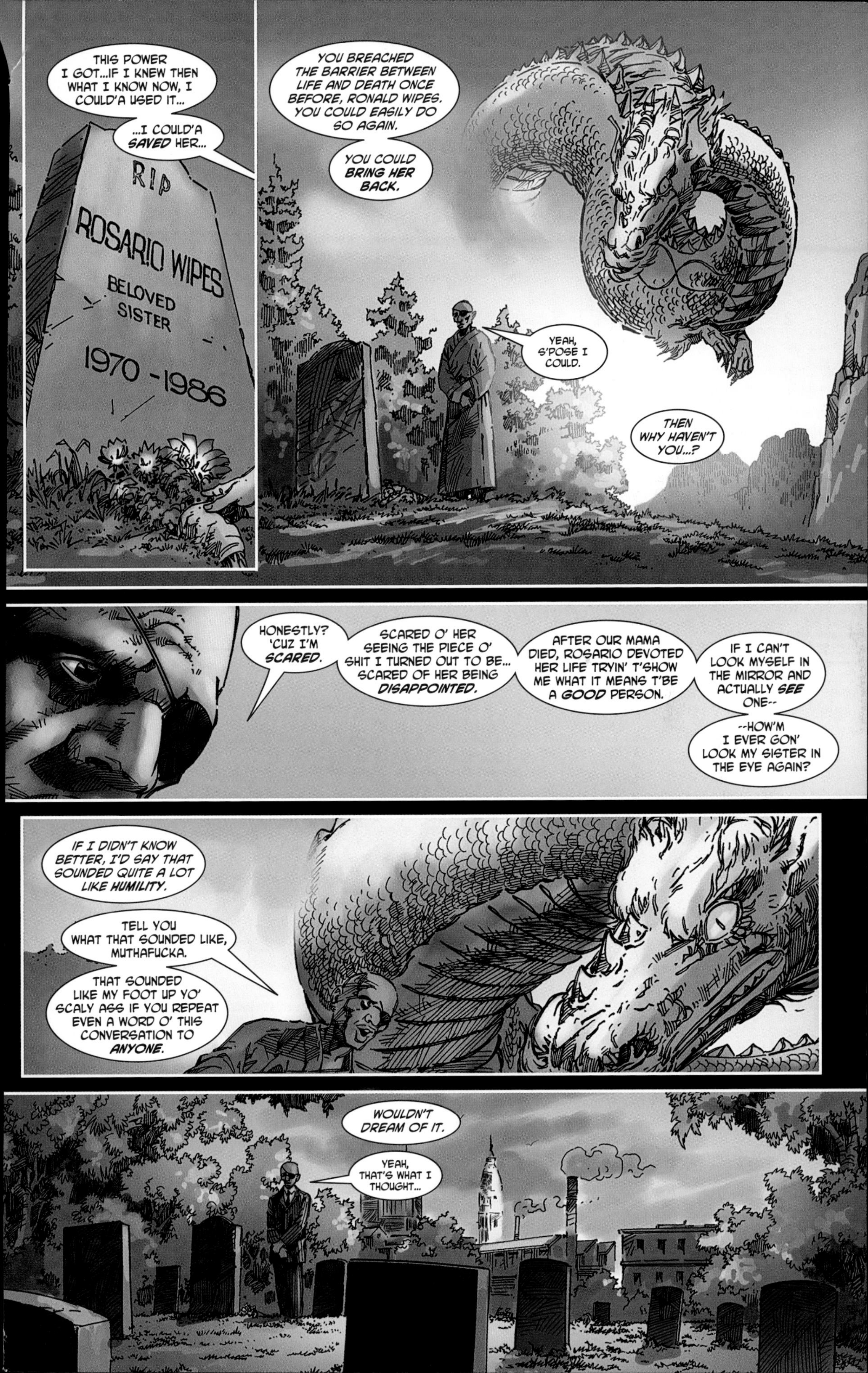
THIS POWER I GOT...IF I KNEW THEN WHAT I KNOW NOW, I COULD'A USED IT...
...I COULD'A SAVED HER...
RIP ROSARIO WIPES BELOVED SISTER 1970 - 1986
YOU BREACHED THE BARRIER BETWEEN LIFE AND DEATH ONCE BEFORE, RONALD WIPES. YOU COULD EASILY DO SO AGAIN.
YOU COULD BRING HER BACK.
YEAH, S'POSE I COULD.
THEN WHY HAVEN'T YOU...?
HONESTLY? 'CUZ I'M SCARED.
SCARED O' HER SEEING THE PIECE O' SHIT I TURNED OUT TO BE... SCARED OF HER BEING DISAPPOINTED.
AFTER OUR MAMA DIED, ROSARIO DEVOTED HER LIFE TRYIN' T'SHOW ME WHAT IT MEANS T'BE A GOOD PERSON.
IF I CAN'T LOOK MYSELF IN THE MIRROR AND ACTUALLY SEE ONE--
--HOW'M I EVER GON' LOOK MY SISTER IN THE EYE AGAIN?
IF I DIDN'T KNOW BETTER, I'D SAY THAT SOUNDED QUITE A LOT LIKE HUMILITY.
TELL YOU WHAT THAT SOUNDED LIKE, MUTHAFUCKA.
THAT SOUNDED LIKE MY FOOT UP YO' SCALY ASS IF YOU REPEAT EVEN A WORD O' THIS CONVERSATION TO ANYONE.
WOULDN'T DREAM OF IT.
YEAH, THAT'S WHAT I THOUGHT...

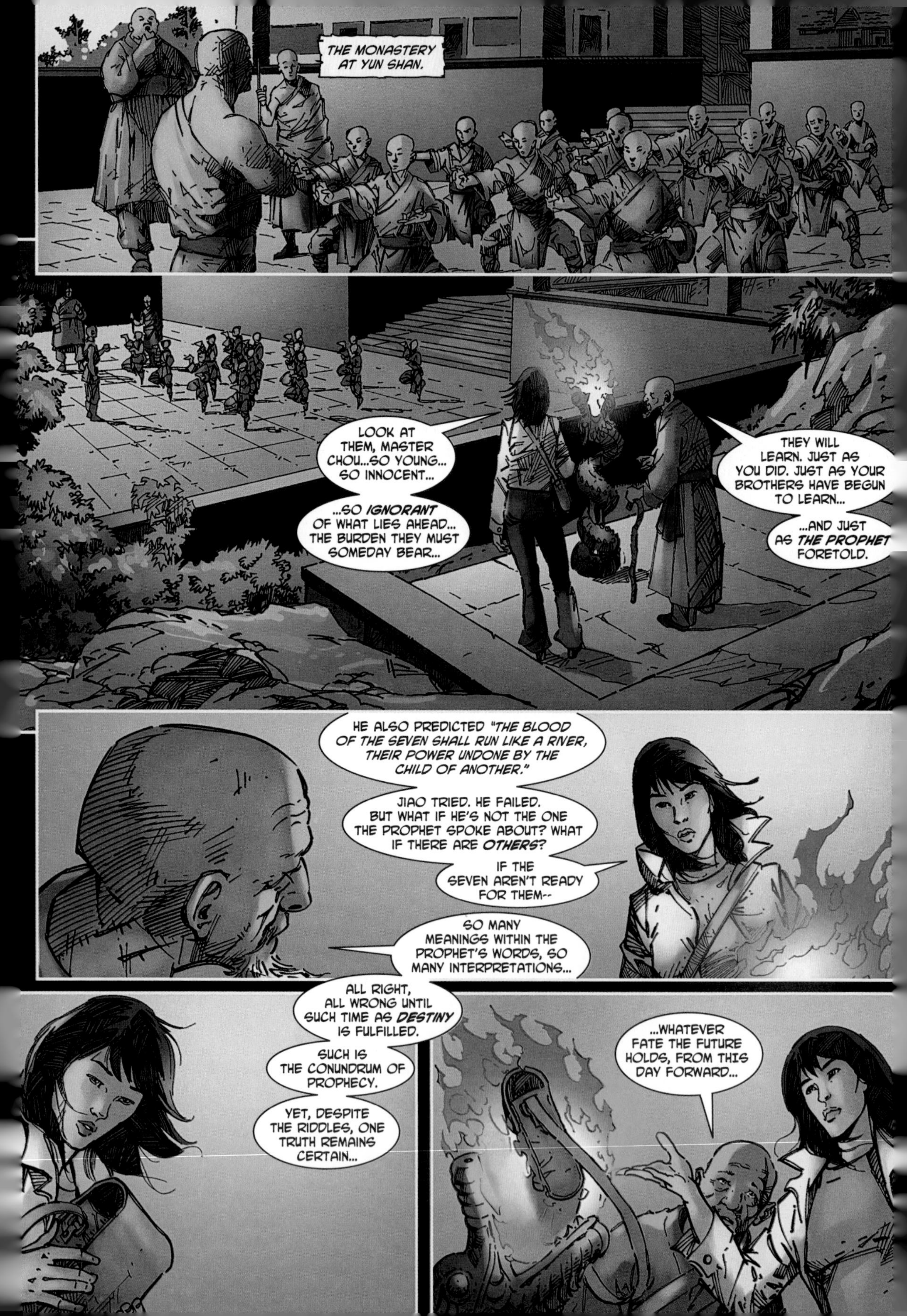
THE MONASTERY AT YUN SHAN.
LOOK AT THEM, MASTER CHOU...SO YOUNG... SO INNOCENT...
...SO IGNORANT OF WHAT LIES AHEAD... THE BURDEN THEY MUST SOMEDAY BEAR...
THEY WILL LEARN. JUST AS YOU DID. JUST AS YOUR BROTHERS HAVE BEGUN TO LEARN...
...AND JUST AS THE PROPHET FORETOLD.
HE ALSO PREDICTED "THE BLOOD OF THE SEVEN SHALL RUN LIKE A RIVER, THEIR POWER UNDONE BY THE CHILD OF ANOTHER."
JIAO TRIED. HE FAILED. BUT WHAT IF HE'S NOT THE ONE THE PROPHET SPOKE ABOUT? WHAT IF THERE ARE OTHERS?
IF THE SEVEN AREN'T READY FOR THEM--
SO MANY MEANINGS WITHIN THE PROPHET'S WORDS, SO MANY INTERPRETATIONS...
ALL RIGHT, ALL WRONG UNTIL SUCH TIME AS DESTINY IS FULFILLED.
SUCH IS THE CONUNDRUM OF PROPHECY.
YET, DESPITE THE RIDDLES, ONE TRUTH REMAINS CERTAIN...
...WHATEVER FATE THE FUTURE HOLDS, FROM THIS DAY FORWARD...

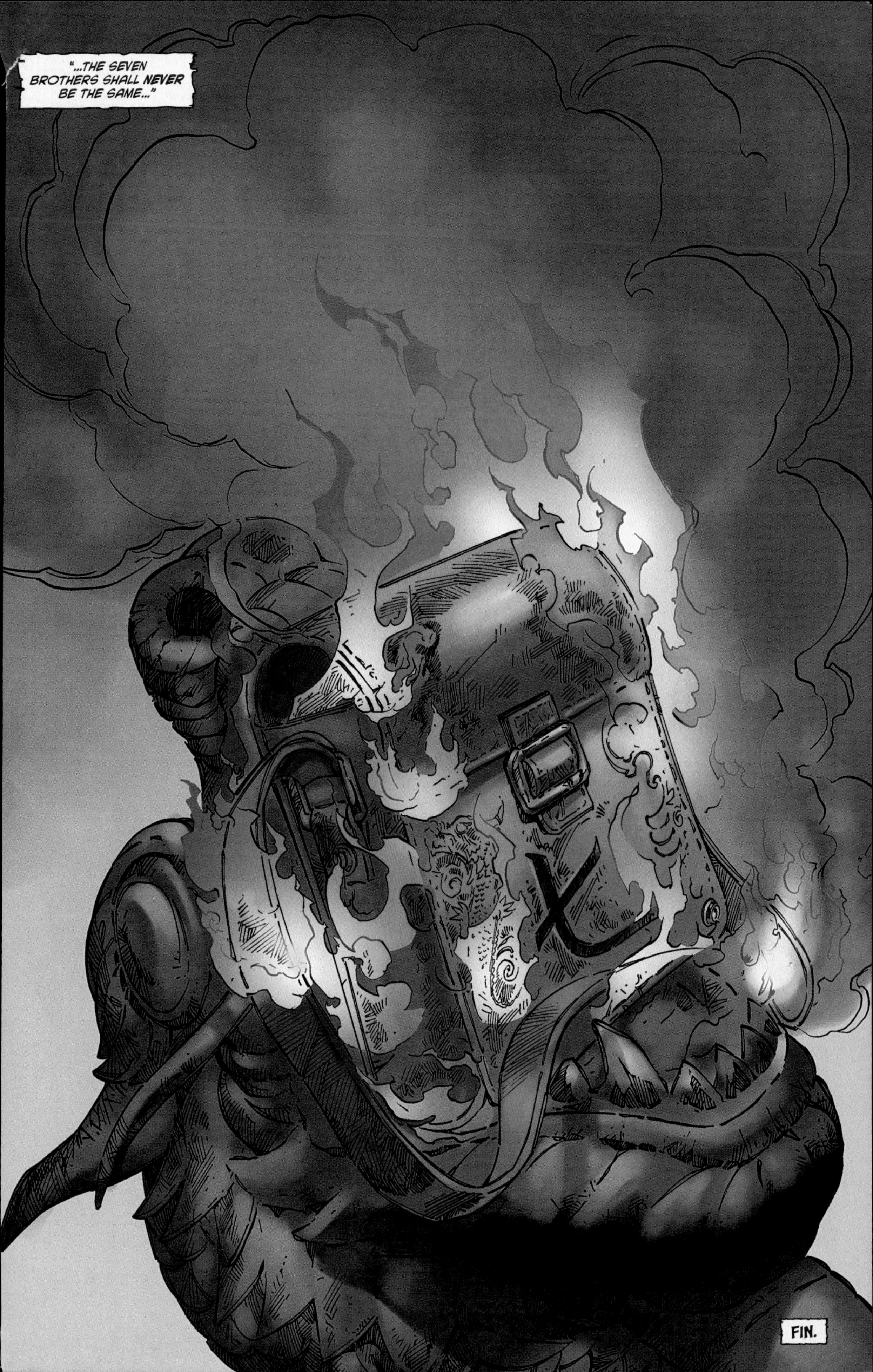
"...THE SEVEN BROTHERS SHALL NEVER BE THE SAME..."
FIN.

WE ARE FAMILY...

...And so ends the second exciting arc of JOHN WOO'S SEVEN BROTHERS...

Seems like only yesterday when were first asked by our good friend and colleague, Lori Tilkin—a.k.a. Tiger Hill's resident comic book and video game Goddess—if we'd be interested in writing the series and taking the franchise to the next level with a bold, new direction of our own unique design? A question to which we simultaneously replied, "DUH!"

No, that's not what we really said, but it definitely ran through our minds. After all, we're talking about John Woo here! This is the man who redefined a whole generation of storytellers and filmmakers. For those most familiar with his work, we're pretty sure you can recall cinematic confrontations where flurries of red hot bullets are exchanged between men in black coats as blood twirls through the air like some sort of macabre ribbon dance, forever seared into your memories. Oh, and let's not forget those signature white doves. But we digress...

Needless to say, we were pretty geeked and eager to get going. So we dove right in and started spit-balling ideas. And that's when the panic set in...

After re-reading the first arc, written by the incomparable Garth Ennis, we knew there were going to be some challenges. Not just because we were following Garth freakin' Ennis, but because the book is called JOHN WOO'S *SEVEN* BROTHERS. Not two. Not three. Not four. Not even five. *SEVEN*. That's a lot of damn siblings! Sure, it's possible to juggle that many characters in a five-chapter arc. Everyone gets a line here, some action there, just enough to remind the readers who they are and what their shtick is. But at the end of the day, it's only surface. You don't really get to dig deep enough to really explore them. Before you know it, it's the next character's turn to strut their stuff. Ultimately, we decided to do a little fancy math and subtract a couple of characters from the equation. This bought us some room to focus on the characters that remained. But which ones...?

Well, there was no doubt in our minds the first person would be Rachel Kai. While technically not a "brother" of the Seven, Rachel is certainly the linchpin that holds them all together. And since very little was revealed about Rachel in the first arc, there was an air of mystery about her we felt we could mine. Some of the questions nagging at the back of our minds included: *How old was she, really? How did she learn how to kick such ungodly ass? Why did she assemble the brothers in the first place? And what was her real motive? Were her intentions truly noble, or was there some Machiavellian master plan behind it all?* And, most importantly, *does she have a sister?* Once we began answering them, everything else fell into place.

Now, that isn't to say that all our ideas for Rachel saw print in this arc. One such idea that ended up on the cutting room floor was the revelation that Rachel was terminally ill and that Dr. Li's journal contained clues about her fate. But alas, due to page constraints and us falling more in love with how Rachel played into the greater mythology of the Seven Brothers, we decided against it.

The next character whose surface we felt hid something deeper was ex-wannabe pimp, Mr. Ronald Wipes. What made Ronald so interesting was his own self-delusion. Here's a guy who acted like he was the shit all the time—and that was even before he knew he was the host of a mighty dragon spirit. Any armchair psychologist would say that Ronald's bravado was merely a mask hiding some deep-seated weakness. But what could that weakness possibly be? Well, seeing as how this arc was all about family, we decided that the truth about Ronald Wipes—the reason why he feels so compelled to act like a badass—is that somehow, someway, he failed his family as a child. And, as we've just seen, this failure will likely haunt him for a very long time...

But Ronald wasn't the only brother whose as-yet-unseen personal life proved fertile soil for the growth of their character. In the first arc, it was suggested that perhaps Jagdish had feelings for his sister-in-law and no compunctions about acting on them should the opportunity present itself. What if it did? What does that say about his view of family? And "Chief" Daniel Fallingwater... Was he truly a leader to his tribe, or was he merely Chief in name alone? And finally, Muhammed... the man who would do anything to protect his wife and kids. Or would he? If the only way to save his family meant having to sacrifice his own beliefs, could he still do it?

By the time you read this, the answers to these questions—and many more—will have already been revealed inside these pages. But fear not, for revelations a'plenty await down the road about the brothers whose seeds we've yet to harvest... Truths about Robert Akimbe, Baz Hooker and Gabriel Castillo... Secrets so shocking that Master Chou's proclamation that *"the Seven Brothers will never be the same again"* may turn out to be the greatest understatement of our time.

We sincerely hope you'll stick around to see what comes next.

You won't be disappointed...

B.R. & D.H.
Somewhere in Los Angeles
2008

ART EVOLUTION

SEE HOW SELECT SCENES FROM SEVEN BROTHERS EVOLVED FROM PANEL DESCRIPTION TO LAYOUT TO PENCILS TO FINAL COLORS.

ISSUE 1: PAGE ONE

.1: EXT. CHINESE COUNTRY VILLAGE - NIGHT: THE LOCALS DUCK AND COVER AS AN UNMARKED MILITARY JEEP PURSUES A DAIHATSU VAN (ALL VEHICLES FROM CIRCA THE MID '80S) THROUGH THE HEART OF THEIR SMALL, MIDDLE-OF-NOWHERE TOWN. MERCS LEAN OUT BOTH SIDES OF THE JEEP, LIBERALLY UNLOADING THEIR SEMI-AUTOMATIC RIFLES TRYING TO TAKE DOWN THE VAN.

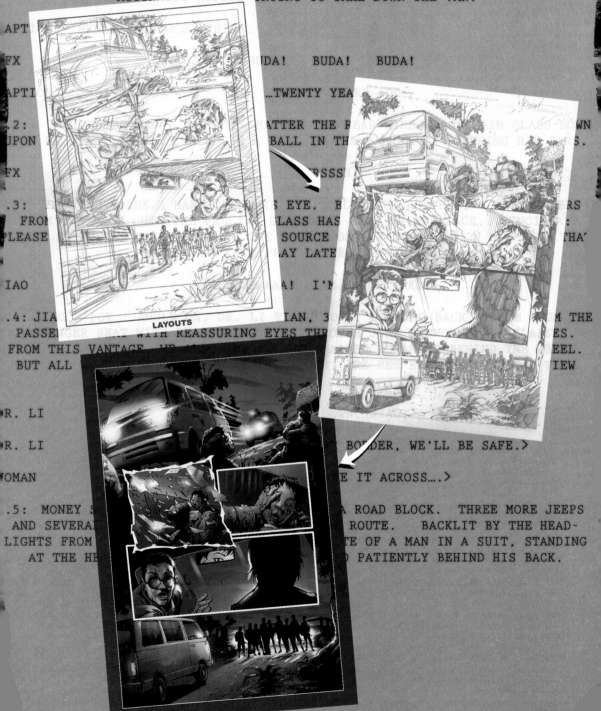

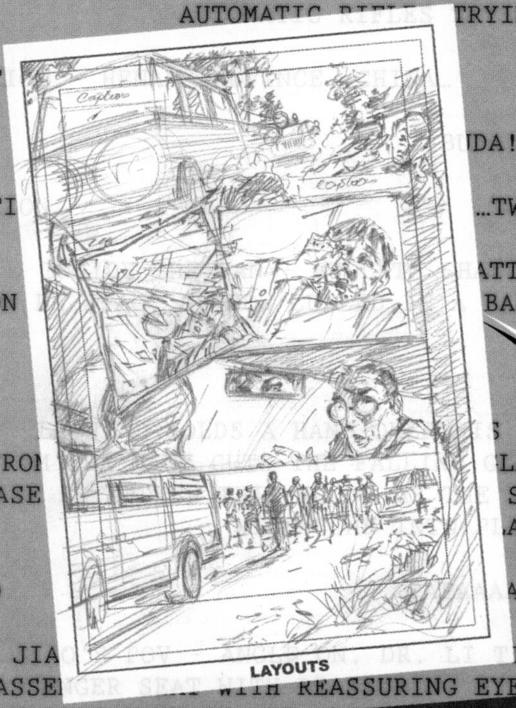
LAYOUTS

APTI

FX BUDA! BUDA! BUDA!

APTI …TWENTY YEA

.2: HATTER THE REAR ... GLASS DOWN UPON ... BALL IN THE ... HIS EARS.

FX RSSSH

.3: ... EYE. ... RS FROM ... GLASS HAS ... PLEASE ... SOURCE ... THAT ... PLAY LATER

IAO AA! I'M

.4: JIA ... DR. LI TIAN, 3 ... BACK ... THE PASSENGER SEAT WITH REASSURING EYES THRO ... SES. FROM THIS VANTAGE ... HEEL. BUT ALL ... VIEW

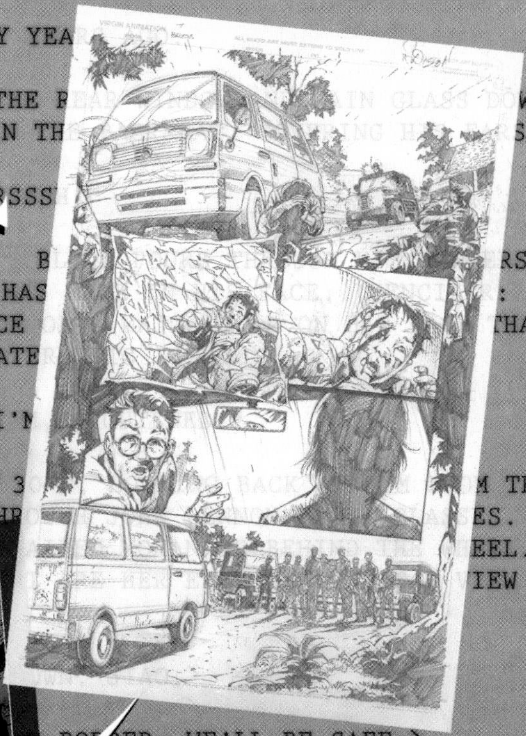

R. LI

R. LI BORDER, WE'LL BE SAFE.>

OMAN E IT ACROSS….>

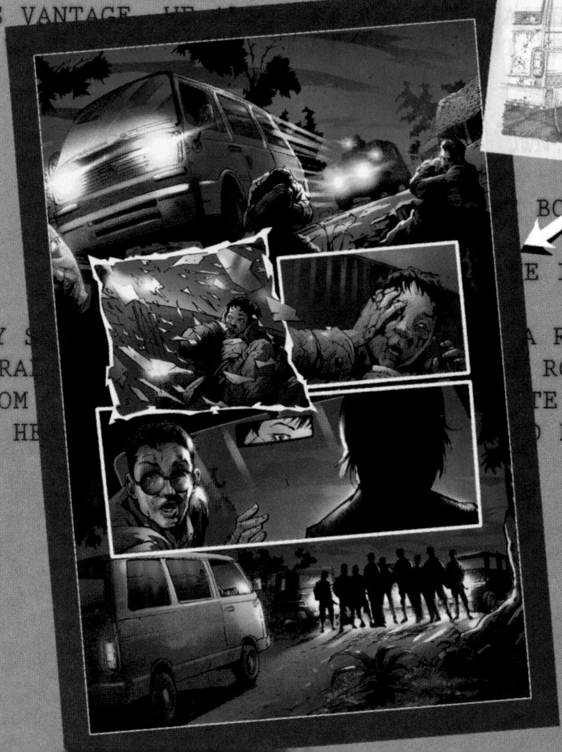

.5: MONEY S ... A ROAD BLOCK. THREE MORE JEEPS AND SEVERA ... ROUTE. BACKLIT BY THE HEAD-LIGHTS FROM ... E OF A MAN IN A SUIT, STANDING AT THE HE ... PATIENTLY BEHIND HIS BACK.

ISSUE 2: PAGE ELEVEN

11.1: MEDIUM CLOSE ON DANIEL, A SNARL ON HIS FACE AS HE MOVES AT SUPER-SONIC SPEED AT THE HEAD OF THE DUST CLOUD.

SFX RRRRRMMMMMBBBLLLE

11.2: DANIEL'S "SUPERSONIC" POV ON THE CO... FAST. (EDISON/COLORIST: LET'S HAVE SOME FUN ... DANIEL'S EYES. TRY TO BLUR OUT THE EDGES ... SHOW HE PERCEIVES REALITY BENDING AROUN... SPEED...)

SFX RRRRRMMMMM...

11.3: CLOSE JAGDISH'S HAND REACHING OUT ... RE-ALITY TO GRAB DANIEL BY ...

SFX

11.4: ...EL, UTTERLY CONFUSED ... ...LF BARRELING TOWARD...

SFX —HHHZZZZHM!

DANIEL HUH?!?

11.5: ... FOR "CRICHTON HOUSE APARTMENTS" WHERE "CRI... OVER WIT... THAT CU... WE'RE IN ... CA-TI... USE TH... N ...PANEL 2

DANI... WHE...

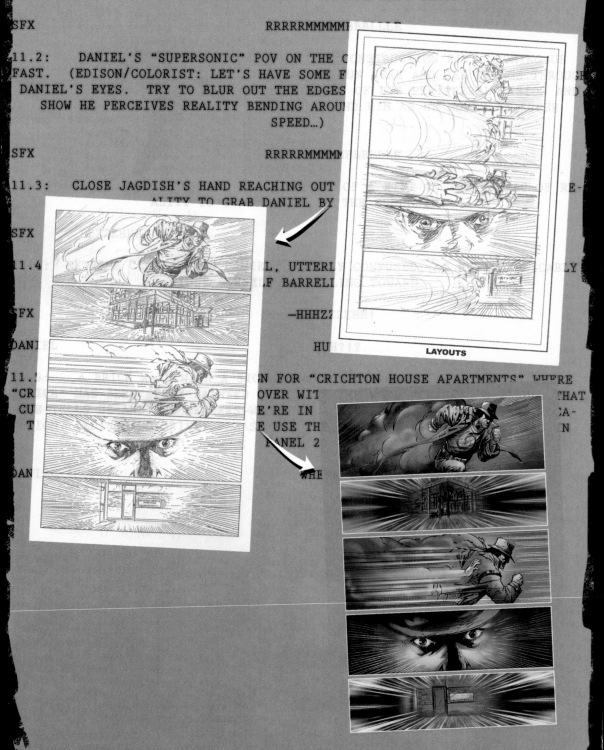

LAYOUTS

ISSUE 5: PAGE 21

21.1: CLOSE ON A TOMBSTONE WITH THE CARVED INSCRIPTION "ROSARIO WIPES, BELOVED SISTER, 1970-1986" AS RONALD'S HAND REACHES INTO FRAME AND LAYS A BOUQUET OF FLOWERS IN FRONT OF IT.

1_RONALD (O.P.) THIS POWER I GOT… IF I KNEW THEN WHAT I KNOW NOW, I COULD'A USED IT…

2_RONALD (O.P.) …I COULD'A SAVED HER…

21.2: WIDER TO REVEAL… EXT. CELESTIAL GARDEN (FROM ISSUE 1)—DAWN: HIS LEFT EYE COVERED WITH AN EYE PATCH, RONALD (IN ROBES AGAIN) STANDS BEFORE HIS SISTER'S GRAVE. HIS DRAGON SELF … BESIDE HIM, BATHED IN THE LIGHT OF THE RISING SUN.

LAYOUTS

3_DRAGON YOU BREACHED THE BARRIER BETWEEN … BEFORE, RONALD WIPES. YOU COULD EAS…

4_DRAGON YOU COULD BRIN…

5_RONALD YEAH, S'PO…

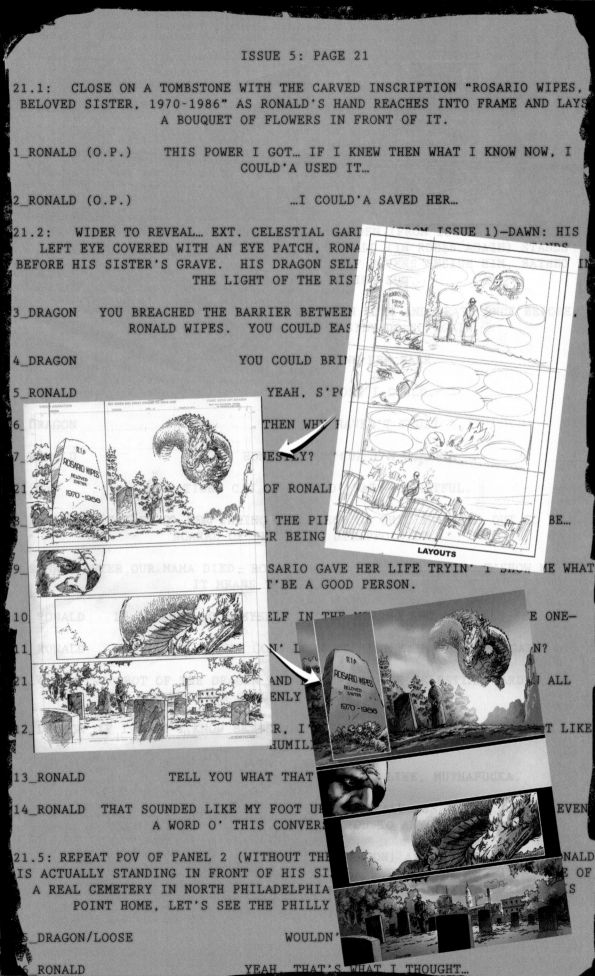

RIP
ROSARIO WIPES
BELOVED SISTER
1970-1986

6_DRAGON THEN WH…

7_… …ESTLY? …

21… … OF RONALD…

8_… … THE PI… … BE…
… ER BEING …

9_… … ROSARIO GAVE HER LIFE TRYIN' T'SHOW ME WHAT IT MEANS T'BE A GOOD PERSON.

10_… …ELF IN THE … …E ONE—

11_… … N?

21… … AND … ALL … DENLY …

RIP
ROSARIO WIPES
BELOVED SISTER
1970-1986

12_… … R, I'… …T LIKE … HUMILI…

13_RONALD TELL YOU WHAT THAT …

14_RONALD THAT SOUNDED LIKE MY FOOT U… …EVEN A WORD O' THIS CONVERS…

21.5: REPEAT POV OF PANEL 2 (WITHOUT THE … …ONALD IS ACTUALLY STANDING IN FRONT OF HIS SI… …E OF A REAL CEMETERY IN NORTH PHILADELPHIA … …S POINT HOME, LET'S SEE THE PHILLY …

…5_DRAGON/LOOSE WOULDN'…

…6_RONALD YEAH, THAT'S WHAT I THOUGHT…

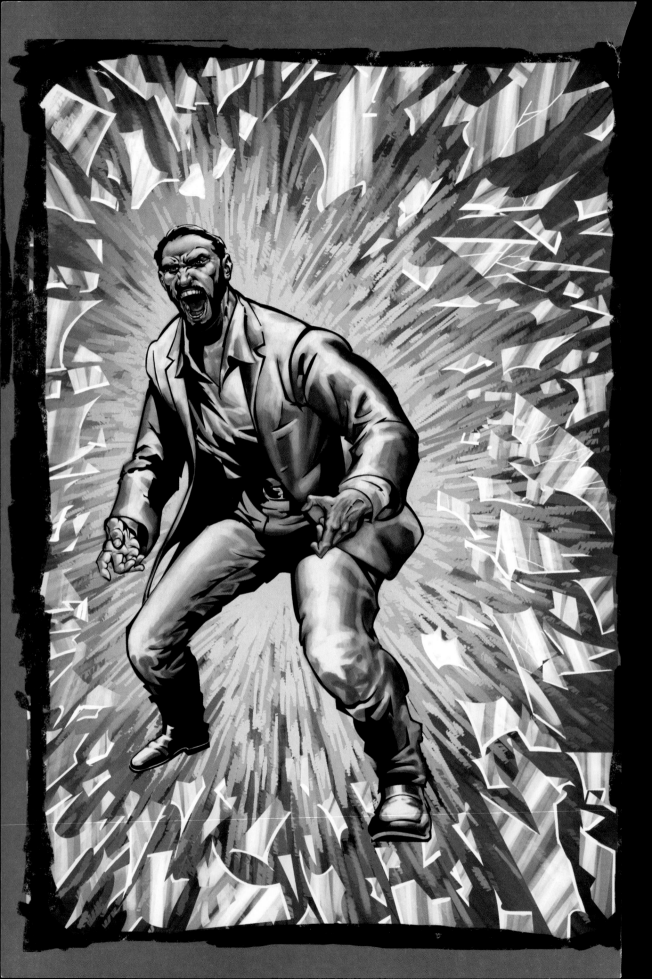

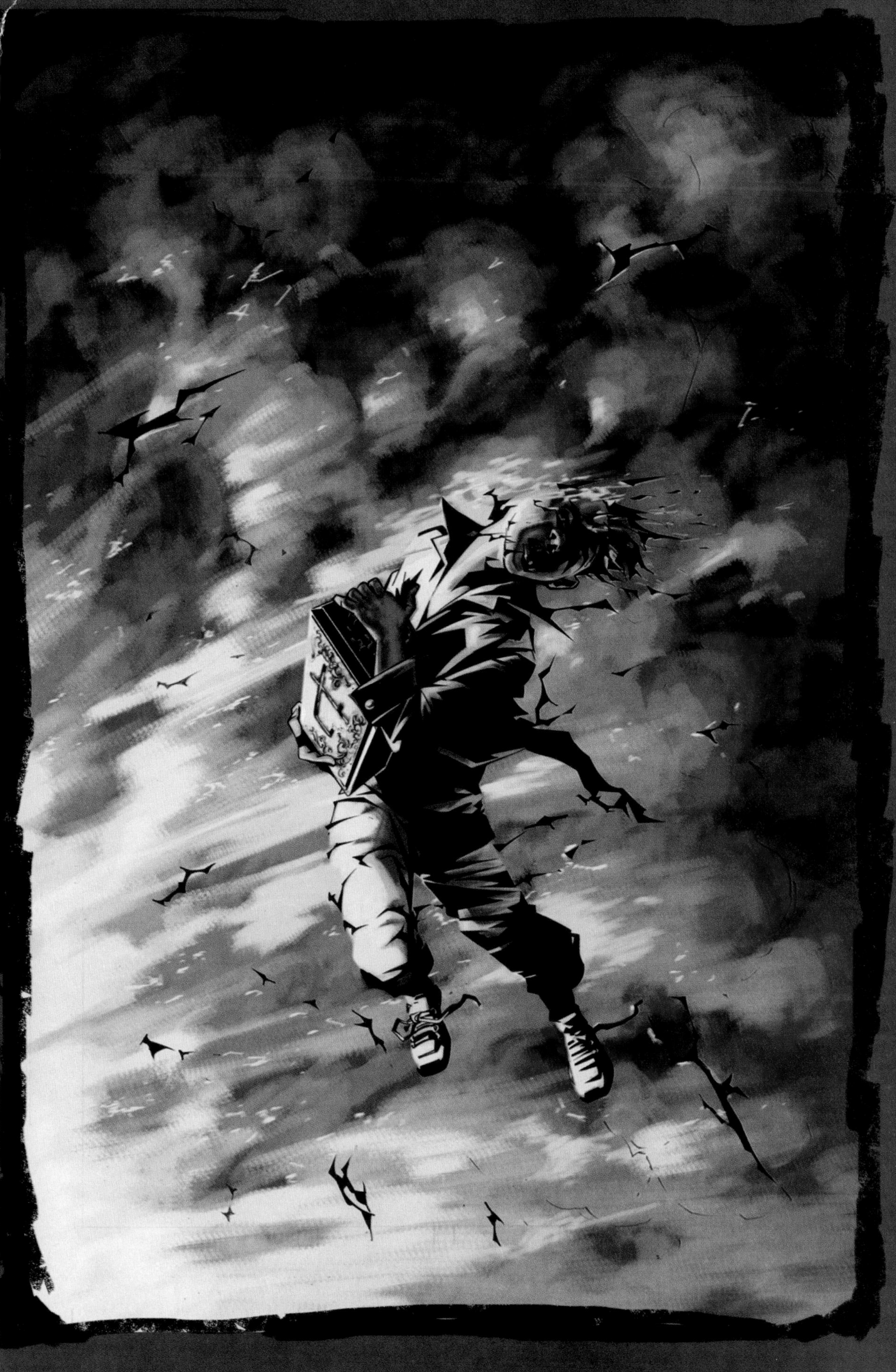

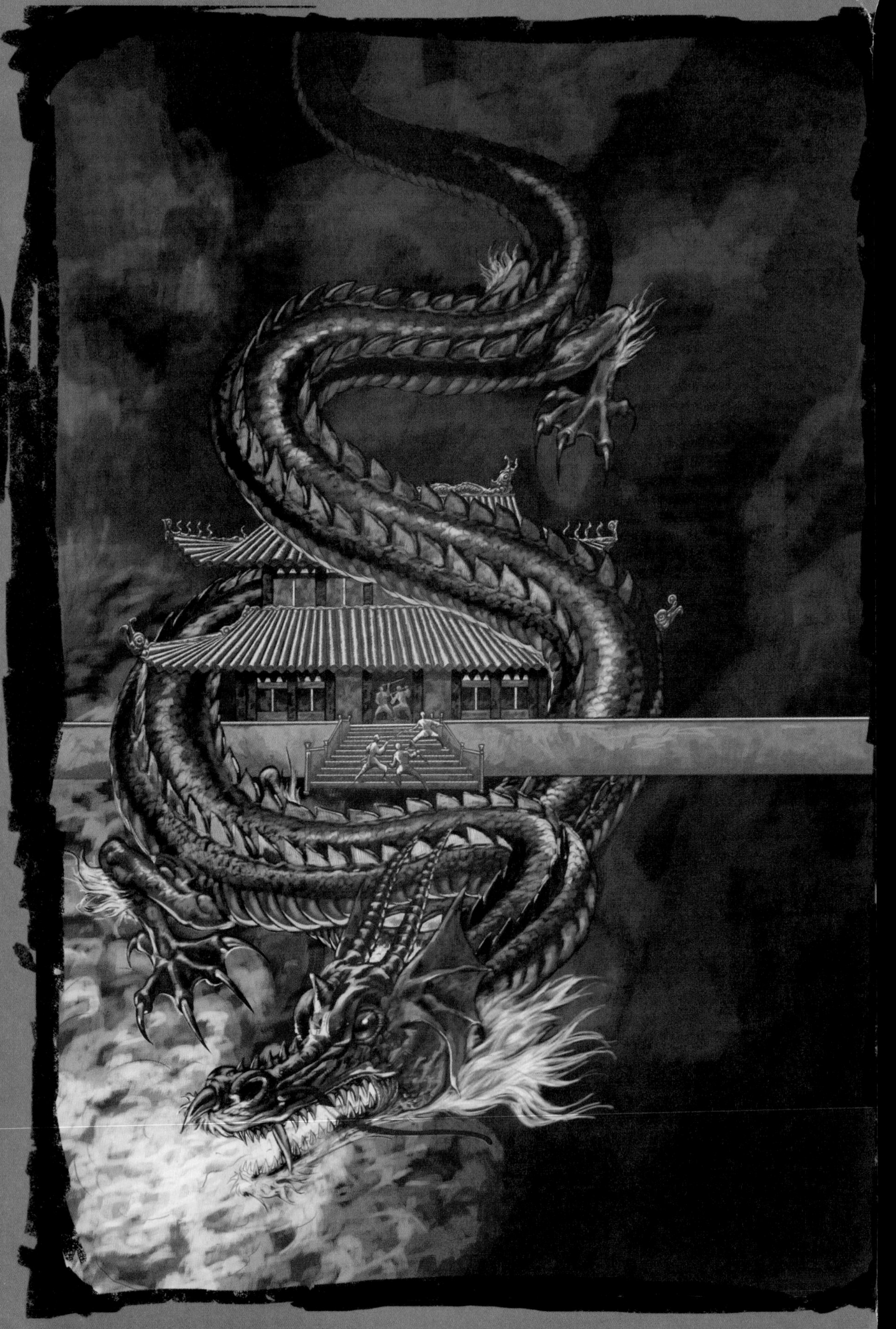

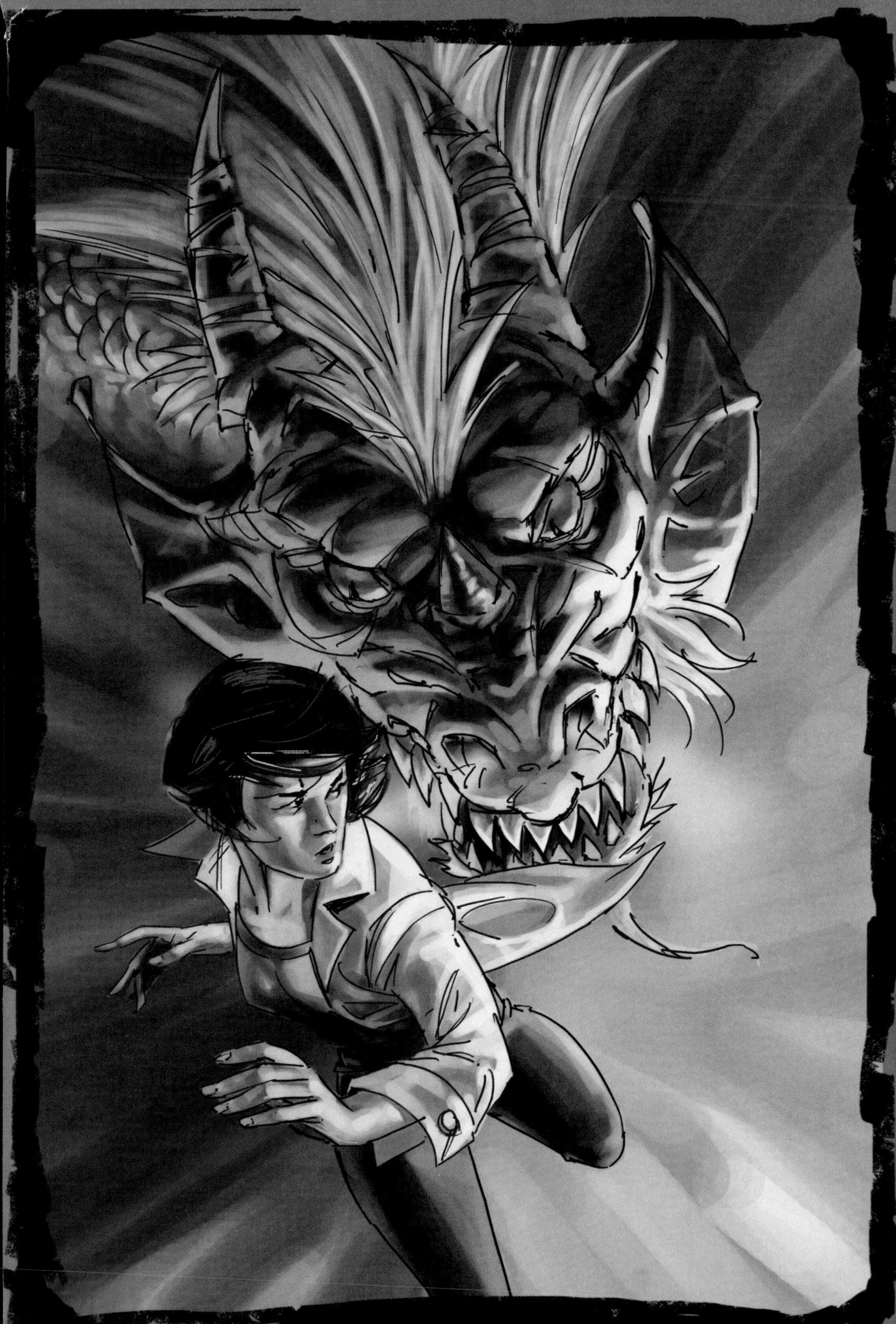

VIRGIN COMICS
COLLECTED EDITIONS

ON SALE NOW!

VIRGIN COMICS TRADE PAPERBACKS
DEVI

DEVI VOL.1

VIRGIN COMICS TRADE PAPERBACKS
SHEKHAR KAPUR'S
DEVI

DEVI VOL.2

DEVI

DEVI VOL.3

DAVE STEWART'S
WALK IN

WALK IN

JOHN WOO'S
7 BROTHERS
ALSO AVAILABLE IN LIMITED EDITION HARDCOVER

SEVEN BROTHERS VOL.1

JOHN WOO'S
7 BROTHERS

SEVEN BROTHERS VOL.2

VIRGIN COMICS TRADE PAPERBACKS
SNAKE WOMAN

SNAKE WOMAN VOL.1

SNAKE WOMAN

SNAKE WOMAN VOL.2

GUY RITCHIE'S
GAME KEEPER
ALSO AVAILABLE IN LIMITED EDITION HARDCOVER

GAMEKEEPER VOL.1

DEEPAK CHOPRA PRESENTS
india authentic
SHIVA

INDIA AUTHENTIC VOL.1

RaMayaN

RAMAYAN 3392 A.D. VOL.1

WESTON CAGE & NICOLAS CAGE'S
VOODOO CHILD

VOODOO CHILD

sādhu

THE SADHU VOL.1